ASSET PROTECTION
Concepts and Strategies for Protecting Your Wealth

ASSET PROTECTION

Concepts and Strategies for Protecting Your Wealth

JAY D. ADKISSON
CHRISTOPHER M. RISER

McGraw-Hill

New York Chicago San Francisco Lisbon London Madrid
Mexico City Milan New Delhi San Juan Seoul
Singapore Sydney Toronto

6 7 8 9 0   DOC/DOC   0 9 8 7 6

ISBN 0-07-143216-7

This publication is designed to provide accurate and authoritative information in regard to the subject matter covered. It is sold with the understanding that the publisher is not engaged in rendering legal, accounting or other professional service. If legal advice or other expert assistance is required, the services of a competent professional person should be sought.
> —*From a Declaration of Principles Jointly Adopted by a Committee of the American Bar Association and a Committed of Publishers and Associations.*

 This book is printed on recycled, acid-free paper containing a minimum of 50% recycled de-inked paper.

McGraw-Hill books are available at special discounts to use as premiums and sales promotions, or for use in corporate training programs. For more information, please write to the Director of Special Sales, McGraw-Hill Professional, Two Penn Plaza, New York, NY 10011-2298. Or contact your local bookstore.

Library of Congress Cataloging-in-Publication Data

Adkisson, Jay D.
    Asset protection : concepts and strategies for protecting your wealth / by Jay D. Adkisson and Christopher M. Riser.
      p. cm.
    ISBN 0-07-143216-7 (hardcover : alk. paper)
    1. Executions (Law)—United States—Popular works.   2. Debtor and creditor—United States—Popular works.   3. Finance, Personal—United States—Popular works.   I. Riser, Christopher M.   II. Title.
KF9025.Z9A93   2004
346.7307'7—dc22   2003028278

CONTENTS

PREFACE

$\mathbf{A}$s a defined professional practice area, asset protection planning is still quite new. As such, there are widely varying theories among practitioners about how to address even the most common situations. With little or no settled case law that deals with many planning strategies, one theory may seem as good as another until the theory is tested in the crucible of the courtroom. With the current unsettled state of affairs in the field of asset protection planning, anyone who advocates a particular theory might seem a genius or a fool, depending on how others in the field view that theory.

Although there may be no case law on a particular subject, an attorney who has been in a courtroom and has stood before a judge in a contentious case will have a sense for how a judge might view a particular strategy. One of the principal purposes of this book is to offer our impressions of how courts are likely to treat particular asset protection strategies, regardless of the technical legal theory behind the strategies.

Jay's litigation experience in chasing debtors and defending creditors in a number of savings and loan cases in the late 1980s and early 1990s serves him well in this regard. So does his experience in a series of high-profile technology export cases in the 1990s in which he breached many exotic international structures established as barriers against his clients' collection efforts. During the course of this litigation, several of the adverse parties sued Jay, along with the *Houston Chronicle* and Hearst Publishing, for an astronomical sum in an attempt to attempt to force a universal settlement of his clients' case. While the case against Jay was eventually dismissed, it forced him to consider what he needed to do to protect his own assets.

When asset protection planning became a hot professional practice area in the mid-1990s, Jay had actually litigated many of the issues about which other planners were only theorizing. He established one of the first asset protection information Web sites, which debunks many of the popular asset protection techniques and theories, including the widely held theory that U.S. judges would be powerless against U.S. persons who had set up foreign asset protection trusts in exotic locales. In the late 1990s Chris turned to Jay and other creative thinkers in the asset protection field as his mentors when he began to shift the focus of his estate planning and tax practice to asset protection planning. Tens of thousands of pages of research and tens of thousands of offshore travel miles later, Chris was convinced that Jay and these few others had it right.

As members of the American Bar Association's Asset Protection Planning Committee, as professional education seminar speakers, and as the authors of many journal articles and this book, we have tried to present a balanced view of asset protection planning rather than simply repeating the marketing hype that has made a growing number of self-proclaimed asset protection experts wealthy. The simple truth is that asset protection planning is like any other form of legal planning. There is no bulletproof theory, no impenetrable legal fortress. For asset protection planning to work for you, you must be able to look a judge in the eye and honestly proclaim confidence in the abilities of your planner, who analyzed the information you provided, and gave you sound professional advice that you followed in the course of perfectly legitimate personal, financial, and business planning. This is hard to do, for example, if another of your planner's clients was laughed out of court and into jail last year, or if your planner was indicted in the meantime for assisting others in tax evasion or money laundering. Good asset protection planning requires the best and most reputable attorneys who have the training and experience required to put it all together. These attorneys will welcome difficult questions and will even welcome suggestions. We hope that this book will do its small part to convince planners and clients to abandon strategies that have outlasted their useful lives. More so, we hope that this book encourages planners and clients alike to continue to develop asset protection planning as a practice area like any other, and within the rules.

ACKNOWLEDGMENTS

First, thanks go to Jay's father, Ron Adkisson, who researched the process of publication, contacted publishers, initially courted McGraw-Hill, pushed us to write when we were busy with our practices, and edited our early drafts. Without Ron, this book would not have seen the light of day. Thanks also to Alex Fugairon for her editing of the early drafts, and to John Barrick for his meticulous work in creating the book's illustrations. Thanks to our good friend Arnold Cornez, author of "The Offshore Money Book", for his encouragements and advice. Special thanks to Joe Petrucelli for his last-minute help with the material on Employee Stock Ownership Plans. And of course thanks to Karen and Betsy for their patience and understanding in living with two chronic overworkers. Finally, we are very grateful to have Stephen Isaacs of McGraw-Hill as our editor, and we thank him for leading two first-time authors through the book writing and publishing process.

Introduction

Consider the case of Stephen J. Lawrence, a derivatives trader who went bust in the stock market crash of October 1987. Not only was Lawrence's firm wiped out, but his own personal finances were jeopardized by a margin call from Bear Stearns. After several years of trying to settle the controversy privately, Bear Stearns commenced arbitration proceedings to recover the money it claimed Lawrence owed on the margin call.

The case was a purely civil dispute over a debt. If Lawrence had lost the arbitration, the worst result would have been that he would have owed money to Bear Stearns. But with just a little smart planning by Lawrence, Bear Stearns likely would not have recovered the full amount owed. Lawrence could have bought an expensive home in Florida and moved there. Florida's generous homestead exemption would have protected the home and equity from Bear Stearns's collection efforts. Indeed, over the years, Florida's homestead exemption has protected the property of debtors who have committed sins much worse than the failure to meet a margin call.

As extensive and foolproof as it is, the homestead exemption was not the only means of asset protection available to Lawrence. The laws of many states also protect life insurance, annuities, and retirement plans. Although not foolproof, these financial products might have protected Lawrence's assets as well, and they are completely legal means of doing so.

THE WRONG TURN

Despite this protection, in early 1991, with the arbitration decision only a few weeks away, Lawrence decided to take more drastic measures. In short, he transferred all of his liquid assets out of the United States—and thus the reach of Bear Stearns—to an offshore asset protection trust. At first, the trust was established according to the law of Jersey, a U.K. protectorate in the English Channel. A month later, apparently not satisfied that the Isle of Jersey was far enough away, Lawrence changed the controlling law to that of Mauritius, a small island nation in the Indian Ocean.

The prevailing asset protection theory of the day dictated that Bear Stearns's attorneys would learn of the offshore trust and simply know that their client would never be able to reach any of the trust assets. Therefore, so the theory went, Bear Stearns either would give up its claim to avoid further litigation expense or would settle for pennies on the dollar.

Lawrence's hunch that the arbitrators would rule against him proved to be well founded. The judgment was announced a few weeks after Lawrence transferred his assets to the far side of the good Earth. Several years of legal wrangling followed as Bear Stearns attempted to reach Lawrence's assets, including those transferred to the offshore trust. In 1997, Lawrence filed for bankruptcy protection, hoping to wipe out the Bear Stearns debt and finally to live a life free from collection attorneys.

Unfortunately, Lawrence and his advisors were terribly wrong in predicting what the federal bankruptcy judge would do. For his too-cute foreign trust maneuvers and evasive answers to questions about the trust and its assets, Lawrence was found in contempt of court and jailed for several years. Furthermore, he was denied a discharge of his debts in bankruptcy. The bottom line is that Lawrence took a purely civil dispute that should have resulted in just a money judgment and, by means of a foreign asset protection trust, converted it into substantial jail time and a judgment that may never go away.

How did Lawrence end up in such dire straits? Had not the attorneys for Bear Stearns seen the detailed analysis by the asset protection gurus in dozens of seminars nationwide declaring that foreign asset protection trusts were "invincible"? Didn't Bear Stearns know that it would be foolish even to attempt to penetrate one? Why was Lawrence not able to thumb his nose at the federal bankruptcy judge, telling him there was nothing he could do about the foreign asset protection trust? Certainly, all these results were what the asset protection advertisements in the airline magazines promised.

The Lawrence case was not the first one where a foreign asset protection trust had failed, and it would not be the worst. A few months earlier, a San Diego couple, Michael and Denyse Anderson, were jailed for refusing to repatriate money from their Cook Islands asset protection trust after being caught by the Federal Trade Commission in a telemarketing scheme. Nevada federal district court judge Lloyd George imprisoned the Andersons for six months for contempt of court. During this time, a number of asset protection experts opined that Judge George's action quickly would be overturned. Instead, the U.S. Court of Appeals for the Ninth Circuit enthusiastically endorsed the finding of contempt and subsequent jailing of the Andersons as an appropriate way to coerce debtors to turn over assets from offshore trusts.

In later cases, it became routine for courts to employ "Anderson relief" against debtors with offshore trusts. Some debtors languished in jail for years, refusing to turn over offshore trust assets, while other debtors immediately agreed to turn over trust assets after only a few nights in jail. Some debtors were threatened with bankruptcy fraud in relation to their offshore trusts. As creditors became more aggressive, the debtors' asset protection planners were sued under civil conspiracy and similar theories for participating in this type of planning.

The Anderson and Lawrence cases exploded the myth of in-your-face asset protection—the prevailing mode of asset protection planning in the 1990s. The failure of the foreign asset protection trust to live up to the expectations promised in legal publications and in expensive seminars called into question the entire concept of asset protection planning to mitigate the risk of future judgments. Many clients realized that they had been misled by the promises of the offshore trust gurus. They began to look for sound planning techniques that were effective and that would not land them in jail.

By 2002, the two professional journals devoted to asset protection planning, the *Asset Protection Journal* and the *Journal of Asset*

Protection, both of which had commenced publication in the middle of the offshore trust boom, had ceased publication. Stephen Lawrence still sat in jail, thanks to his Mauritius trust, and had been joined by at least a half-dozen other defendants who also had shared unrealistic hopes for their own offshore planning. Nevertheless, the marketing of asset protection planning shifted into high gear. Planners continued to pitch offshore trusts and other dubious schemes in spite of their shortcomings and despite sharp criticism from judges and legal academics.

Where had asset protection gone wrong?

ASSET PROTECTION DEFINED

For literally centuries before the offshore trust boom, debtors had been having considerable successes against creditors by using more conventional tactics to shield assets. Litigation and bankruptcy attorneys legitimately and successfully had been protecting their clients' vast wealth for years by using state and federal exemptions, corporations and partnerships, equity stripping, cross-collateralization, and other creative debt-financing techniques. What offshore trusts brought was not proven methodology but rather the marketing "sizzle" of using exotic locales. Asset protection was suddenly thought of as a "new" practice area, when in fact it is anything but.

From the time the second caveman borrowed an axe from the first caveman and then didn't give it back, creditors have been pursuing debtors. The touchstone case relating to asset protection is Twyne's Case, an English case heard in 1601 by Lord Coke, who for the first time listed the "badges of fraud" still used by the courts of every U.S. jurisdiction to test transfers as fraudulent. (For more on badges of fraud, see Chapter 6.) For better or worse, the federal government adopted a liberal bankruptcy policy that allowed debtors to wipe their slates clean of debt, while maintaining some assets. All states adopted statutes that protected to one degree or another certain core assets such as a person's home or interests in a life insurance policy. The effect of these protections unfortunately encouraged debtors to game the system to protect as much wealth as the statutes would allow. Debtor planning, by whatever name, has been a field of legal planning ever since.

What was "new" about asset protection was the concept of a specific practice area to be marketed to affluent clients to quell their fears about lurking "predator plaintiffs" and soon-to-be ex-spouses divesting them of their worldly wealth. Yet, as a matter of legal academics, there is no body of law identifiable as the law of asset protection. Look in a statute book or law digest and there will be no section or chapter entitled "Asset Protection." Court cases rarely refer to asset protection except with regard to the marketing materials of promoters caught overtly assisting their clients in hiding assets. So what is asset protection?

In practice, asset protection is risk management planning that is designed to discourage a potential lawsuit before it begins or to promote a settlement most favorable to the client. The risk being managed is the legal risk that the client may lose wealth in a lawsuit. The purpose of this book is to discuss the tools that are appropriate for doing just this, and to discuss other means that are not appropriate.

ASSET PROTECTION PLANNING

Asset protection planning is about creating a plausible story to tell to a judge or jury, which has as its end result that assets are protected. Yes, there are statutes, codes, regulations, and notices, but all of these are applied in the context of specific facts. The whole of English common law is a collection of stories embodied in the factual recitations of the opinions recorded in the law reporters. When an attorney makes her opening statement, lays out the evidence, and makes her closing argument, she is telling the story of that case. When the judge summarizes the case in the opinion, he is retelling that story. Litigation is competitive storytelling based on provable facts.

The importance of a good story is emphasized throughout this book as being a crucial component of asset protection. Having a good story is the basis of prelitigation planning. If a reader finishes this book having learned nothing else, he should come away knowing that the documents of an asset protection plan should lay out the facts so that if the plan is challenged, a good story can be recited truthfully.

Asset protection planning is like writing a script for a grand play. Good planning makes for a happy ending. The story must be one that puts the client on the high road, so that when the judge or jury rules in the client's favor, it will be because it was the only logical and fair conclusion to the story. For asset protection is fundamentally prelitigation planning. An asset protection plan is one that is intended to be seen, and seen favorably, by whatever judge or jury that must evaluate it at a later time. Paradoxically, the story will never be about asset protection. Although there are significant exceptions, such as statutory exemptions and spendthrift trusts (see Chapters 9 and 12, respectively), the law generally frowns upon asset protection. No one has an inherent right to protect his assets from creditors, other than as state law or federal bankruptcy law provides—and state law and federal bankruptcy law provide only limited exemptions for debtors. Short of throwing debtors out on the street to live with relatives or at the homeless shelter (which some states allow), or the raiding of a debtor's pension (which, starting with the Enron debacle, many people think should be allowed, at least as to wrongdoing corporate chieftains), the law offers little protection for the average debtor. Indeed, recent proposals to change the bankruptcy laws would substantially limit homestead and other state law exemptions.

Judges are also generally hesitant to allow debtors to shield themselves against the judgment that their courts have produced. Very simply, judges want to see their judgments enforced, and they are aware that debtors will attempt to game the system in their favor. Thus, exemptions from collection actions typically are construed narrowly. Many judges, too, have revealed both aversion to expanding theories in favor of debtors and outright zeal in deflating theories that would thwart their own powers to see their judgments enforced.

So, much of asset protection takes advantage of legal loopholes in the same way that many tax shelters attempt to take advantage of the tax code: by exploiting the unintended effects of statutes and court rulings intended to do something else. For example, contemporary asset protection may involve taking advantage of *charging order protection*, as we shall see in Chapter 19. This protection prevents a creditor of an owner of particular types of business interests from reaching the assets of the business and from gaining voting control over the business interest. Rather, the creditor can only get a court order charging the debtor's interest with the debt, meaning that the creditor will receive any distributions made in respect of the debtor's interest. If the person in charge of making such distributions never makes one, the creditor may be out of luck. Originally, this protection arose to protect non-debtor partners from the debts of other partners of a business enterprise. The fact that charging order protection can be used proactively is perhaps an unforeseen consequence, but it is precisely the type of unintended consequence that planners look for and attempt to take advantage of in asset protection planning.

KEEPING AHEAD OF CREDITORS

Asset protection is also a race where wily debtors play the role of the hares and plodding creditors play that of the tortoises. Debtors are almost always several steps ahead of the creditors for several reasons. First, debtors are trying new strategies to protect assets, and the creditors must identify those strategies. Second, creditors must devise tactics to attempt to defeat the debtors' strategies. Third, creditors must persuade either the courts or legislatures that the debtors' strategies are fundamentally contrary to public policy and that these strategies should be forbidden. Asset protection is thus a continuing struggle for those who are innovative to keep ahead of those who are tenacious.

From the debtor's asset protection standpoint, identifying effective strategies is an ever-moving target. What might protect assets today may be practically useless tomorrow. It is very difficult to perform an "asset freeze" that will be respected by the courts unless significant time has passed. Even if significant time has passed, a court or legislative change can negate an asset protection strategy. This is very different from tax or estate planning, where the applicable law is the law in effect on the date that a particular transaction occurred. The IRS or state taxing authority cannot change the law retroactively, but an expansive procreditor interpretation by a judge can retroactively change the law in the asset protection context. Thus, the plan and the structures created thereby must be very flexible to take into account changes in the laws, and planners must periodically revisit plans to ensure that their strategies still make sense for their clients under current law.

Because the legal landscape across which creditors chase debtors is ever changing, an asset protection strategy will fall into one of three general categories. The first category, *Efficacy Known*, includes those strategies that are readily identifiable and either do or do not work according to established law. For instance, we know that if a debtor sells his assets for a dollar to his brother the night before a judgment creditor is to question him about his assets, with the idea that he will disclaim ownership of the assets, and then buy them back the very next day for the same one dollar price, then that transfer will probably be set aside and undone. On the other hand, in some states with favorable homestead exemptions, a debtor can invest cash that would be otherwise available to her creditors into her home and the law will protect the home and that increased equity from her creditors.

The second category, *Efficacy Challenged*, comprises those strategies identified as asset protection strategies (typically in the marketing materials of asset protection promoters), but about which the law is not yet settled. Often, strategies in this category work initially. However, creditors' attorneys will try one innovative theory after another to defeat them. Eventually, a body of law develops that will either defeat or affirm the strategy in particular circumstances.

There is no perfect strategy that will protect all assets all the time. Even homestead exemptions, often considered the strongest debtor's bastion, are subject to exceptions. You cannot rob a bank in Alabama, for example, drive across the border, and buy a home in Florida with the money and expect that it will be protected. In recent years, Congress has contemplated substantial changes to the bankruptcy code that would substantially limit the state homestead protections previously believed to be sacrosanct. Because no strategy will be allowed that protects debtors from all comers in all circumstances, there will never be a perfect strategy. While seminar speakers often speak of "bulletproof" asset protection strategies, these strategies are yet to be seen in real life. Good asset protection planners employ known strategies that creditors have not yet defeated and strategies that have not been identified.

The third category, the *Innovative Frontier*, includes new and unique strategies that have not been identified as asset protection strategies, and which have not been the subject of studied attempts to pierce. Strategies falling into this third category may be overlooked altogether by a creditor in a particular case. However, even if a creditor did suspect an innovative strategy was emplaced for asset protection, she would not have the benefit of prior cases or experience in breaking through the strategy.

In asset protection planning, the phrase "new is good" is axiomatic because new strategies likely have not been identified yet as asset protection strategies. Thus, strategies in the third category tend to be more much effective than strategies in the second category, with the downside that any third category strategy that becomes popular eventually falls into the second category. Asset protection planning must be flexible enough that when everyone starts using a particular strategy—and they will—the planning can be modified to become innovative once again.

The best asset protection strategies employ a combination of tools from all categories, particularly proven tools in the first category, and innovative tools in the third category. Certainly, risky tools from the second category should be avoided. This is the area where most poor planning in the name of asset protection is conducted, often with regrettable results for the client.

Asset protection is incredibly dynamic. No treatment of the subject can be comprehensive, for the simple reason that the best asset protection planners are creating new strategies and techniques each year. Furthermore, changes in the law can come quickly and can invalidate even tried-and-proven strategies on a large scale.

The purpose of this book is not to reveal strategies or tools that work today and will work for decades to come, or even through the next year. Instead, the purpose is to take a thoughtful and practical look at how asset protection planning is approached and how strategies are developed, both broadly and in specific situations.

Similarly, the purpose of this book is not to analyze in detail the tax treatment of certain asset protection strategies. Because the tax laws change and evolve much more quickly than debtor-creditor law, the best that can be done herein is to give a general idea what the tax impact may be and to suggest that independent research will be required by the planner at the time of implementation.

Regrettably, a bad asset protection strategy dies hard and is defended long after its useful life (if it ever had one) has expired.

This is often so because the reputations of the promoters of bad strategies are at stake. The dead horse continues to be beaten, although it lies dead on the track. Asset protection strategies often are founded purely on theory. Thus, the theory is promoted along with the strategy itself, and a promoter stakes his professional reputation—whether he realizes it or not—on the particular theory that backs the strategy he is selling. When the theory is crushed in court, legislated away, or otherwise expires, the promoter's reputation may go with it. Planners do not like to admit to their hard-earned clients that they were wrong. The promoter thus has a substantial self-interest in continuing to promote the theory and to deny the defects or the demise of his pet theory to the detriment of his clients and the clients of other planners who have hitched their wagons to that promoter. Demonstrably bad theories continue to be promoted long after they have gone up in smoke in the crucible of the courtroom. Another purpose of this book is to expose the tried-and-failed asset protection theories, to analyze why they failed, and to analyze why they were promoted even after they had been proven as failures.

AVOIDING THE LANDMINES

We have seen many asset protection promoters come and go over the years. The offshore planning boom on the late 1990s brought forth a slew of books by Jerome Schneider, extolling the virtues of offshore secrecy and privacy and the benefits of private banks formed in tiny Pacific islands, and heavy Internet marketing by Marc Harris, whose Panama-based Harris Organization promised discount-priced offshore foundations and mutual funds. For several years, these and other promoters dominated the asset protection landscape, offering asset protection and "tax reduction" to the masses on a cheap and totally confidential basis—at least for a while.

Within a few years after his appearance on the offshore scene, Marc Harris became a fugitive after some $20 million of his client funds went missing. He was eventually extradited to the United States and convicted of 16 counts of money laundering and conspiracy. Meanwhile, the prolific Schneider agreed to plead guilty to a single count of conspiracy, in exchange for cooperating with the

U.S. Attorney's office in the investigation of his former clients. Even after his plea bargain, however, Schneider's books were readily available to all who wanted a dose of his offshore snake oil.

Prestige and professional licenses may provide little comfort to those seeking quality planning. The Salt Lake City–based law firm of Merrill Scott & Associates, Ltd. generated an enormous client base by advertising their tax reduction and asset protection services in luxury lifestyle magazines. The firm serviced these clients by engaging in aggressive planning involving offshore life insurance and annuity contracts. Unfortunately for their clients, they also controlled the offshore life insurance company and its investments. Millions of dollars of client funds, sent offshore by clients as their "nest eggs," went missing, and the firm and its affiliates were placed into receivership.

Just before these and similar offshore planning gurus began to meet their fates, the IRS had successfully subpoenaed the offshore credit card records of thousands of U.S. citizens and was busy matching those credit card accounts to thousands of undisclosed offshore financial accounts. The task was made much easier by "mutual assistance" treaties that the United States forced on most offshore havens. Thus ended "offshore secrecy and privacy" as an alternative to fundamentally solid planning.

The promotion of asset protection went from shady to shameless. Attorneys crisscrossed the country giving seminars to the masses on family limited partnerships and offshore trusts. At the conclusion of each seminar, many attendees arose to flock to the back of the seminar room where they could not turn over checks fast enough to pay for $2000 kits giving them the blueprints for a bulletproof asset protection plan. Of course, many of the eager buyers who rushed to the back of the room first were paid shills who showed up at every seminar and whose checks would be torn up that night. The few real attendees who were caught up in the herd mentality and actually paid real money for these kits ended up with a simple Nevada partnership or corporate structure that was useless against a moderately sophisticated creditor, or a boilerplate offshore trust offering them protection so long as they were prepared to flee the country to avoid being jailed for contempt of court. The only thing many of these kits accomplished was to generate millions of dollars in needless tax liabilities, when their do-it-yourself purchasers undertook complex business and estate planning maneuvers without understanding the tax ramifications.

At the very bottom of the asset protection food chain, other promoters sold "pure trusts" like hotcakes, promising that these trusts were impenetrable under certain provisions of the U.S. Constitution and vague cases dating back to the 1800s. The promoters falsely claimed that all of America's wealthiest families used such trusts. The promoters also claimed that these trusts obviated the need to pay any income taxes as well. Unfortunately for those who bought these trusts, the IRS did not agree. The IRS launched an initiative aimed at jailing as many promoters and pure trust advocates as possible. So far, the IRS's success rate against those with pure trusts has been 100 percent. This has not kept the promoters from continuing to sell them. Indeed, at times pure trusts have even been sold to the masses through multilevel marketing organizations.

Multilevel marketing of asset protection plans has not been limited to pure trusts. Various groups now sell asset protection distributorships to persons with no legal education or background, who then become "asset protection consultants" and attempt to sell Nevada corporations on a mass basis. Never mind that the only planning credentials of these franchisees is that their check cleared and that they know basically nothing about debtor-creditor law or anything else that one needs to know to be a good asset protection planner, such as what happens in a postjudgment debtor's examination or the tax treatment of complex business arrangements. By the time their plans implode for their customers, the promoters will have sold dozens of franchises and made off with the loot, leaving their surprised franchisees alone to face the messes that were created.

Even among licensed professionals, there simply are no standards for being an asset protection planner. Many estate planning attorneys have hung out an asset protection shingle because it seemed like a way to generate more fees. Even if they have little litigation and collection experience, at least their clients will benefit from the attorney-client privilege and the attorney's ability to research legal issues to avoid the worst problems. Unfortunately, a number of accountants have jumped into asset protection planning under the apparent premise that because they can understand the tax implications of an asset protection strategy, they also understand the legal implications. However, while understanding tax implications is crucial to keeping a client out of trouble with the IRS, it has nothing to do with the efficacy of asset protection planning. Some tremendous asset protection disasters have been caused by accountant planners who thought they understood the nontax law relating to asset protection planning.

Penalties for bad promoters range from none at all (since many of them vanish when their clients get into litigation) to the recent trend of being joined as co-defendants in civil conspiracy actions, thus becoming jointly responsible for the debts of their clients. The real harm is to clients, many of whom could have protected themselves substantially if planning had been conducted in a sensible fashion. Instead, money disappears offshore, clients are prosecuted for tax evasion and bankruptcy fraud, and creditors not only slice through asset protection plans but then chase debtors for additional money for the costs of penetrating the debtors' defective structure. The client's best hope in these cases is to tie up the creditors and hope to tire them out in extended litigation, although extended litigation is often as costly to the debtor as it is to the creditor.

While asset protection planning can be quite creative, it is not done in a vacuum. To the contrary, there are myriad laws relating to fraudulent transfers, bankruptcy, corporations, partnerships, contracts, insurance, taxes, and many other areas that can significantly impact the effectiveness of a plan, if they are not taken into consideration. A major part of asset protection planning is to avoid the numerous landmines that exist for naïve clients and inexperienced planners. A substantial purpose of this book is to identify many of the landmines and to suggest alternative methods of planning.

CHAPTER 2

What Is Asset Protection?

That asset protection means to protect assets from creditors seems a rather self-evident definition. Yet, that takes a very limited view as to what the practice area is all about. Instead, asset protection is better defined as prelitigation planning to deter lawsuits and promote settlements. The primary goal of asset protection is to bring closure to actual or potential litigation with as little disruption to the debtor's business and with as little loss of wealth as possible. Indeed, a much more accurate phrase that describes what asset protection planners do is *wealth preservation*, for the idea is not so much to protect an inanimate object from a creditor as it is to preserve wealth over time against numerous unforeseen circumstances.

WHAT ASSET PROTECTION PLANNING IS ALL ABOUT

Fighting over an asset is not what it is all about; having the greatest amount of wealth remaining after litigation is. Too often people become bogged down in litigation when they could be making money. Even if they win the court battle, they may lose the war because they were not focused on making money, or to put it in homespun terms, they are fighting over a dime when they could be making a dollar. Good asset protection plans will get defendants out of the litigation quickly or isolate the litigation so that it can be managed efficiently, leaving the client to spend her or his valuable time making money.

Asset protection is really part of the larger, nonlegal concept of *risk management*. Risk management is planning that seeks to protect a client from potential future losses and encompasses a wide variety of activities. Planning to prevent financial losses due to market fluctuations is a part of financial risk management. Conducting manufacturing audits to eliminate employee injuries, testing products to reduce safety hazards, and purchasing insurance are also forms of risk management.

Within this larger concept of risk management is the subset of *legal risk management*. The goal of legal risk management is to anticipate and deter future legal problems and to end current legal problems efficiently. Ending lawsuits efficiently usually means by early settlements, so promoting early settlements is a principal goal of asset protection.

FACING THE SLEAZE FACTOR

Many people think of asset protection as a sleazy endeavor. After all, if people would simply pay their debts, there would be no need for asset protection, right? But at its core, asset protection is not about the avoidance of debts. The better asset protection planning focuses on risk management. If the asset protection planner does a good job, the resulting plan will allow the client to avoid risks or, if risks have materialized, the plan will contain and manage those risks and allow the client to settle a dispute quickly.

Nonetheless, asset protection is perceived as sleazy by many people, including judges and juries. So, let's confront the problem: Why is asset protection planning considered sleazy?

First, legitimate creditors can suffer. Asset protection plans generally do not make distinctions between good or just creditors and bad or unjust creditors. Neither do they anticipate that if the protected client does something wrong, he will do the right thing to remedy the situation. Asset protection plans too often are used to shield the ill-gotten gains of criminal or fraudulent activity or to cheat an unsuspecting spouse out of marital assets in a divorce. The morality of asset protection is discussed more fully in Chapter 3.

Second, asset protection planning has a guilt-by-association problem with the often truly sleazy offshore financial services industry. Although the offshore sector has been cleaned up to some extent in the last few years, the impression persists that the industry is riddled with drug traffickers, money launderers, fraudsters, and tax evaders. As the saying goes, "Sunny climes are for shady people." So, if an asset protection plan utilizes an offshore component, such as an offshore financial account or an offshore business entity, in the minds of many, there is the taint of offshore sleaze in the plan.

Third, too many so-called asset protection plans rely on excessive, even obsessive, secrecy. Something bad must be going on, right? Too often, the answer is yes, because many asset protection plans are really offshore tax evasion plans, which rely on the inability of the IRS to discover them. Asset protection planning has been used as a cover for offshore tax evasion so often that many prosecutors automatically associate the two.

Fourth, the heavy marketing of asset protection planning, particularly the in-your-face variety involving offshore trusts, has led to the circulation of outright lies. In reality, a debtor with an offshore trust simply is not going to thumb her nose at a U.S. judge and get away with it, and those who have actually done this have ended up in jail for contempt. Outrageous claims in this regard have sensitized judges to asset protection planning, and they are all too willing to toss an offshore trust settlor-debtor into jail until she coughs up offshore assets. Before choosing an asset protection planner, consider how the planner's marketing materials will look in front of a judge or jury.

Fifth, because the asset protection industry, particularly offshore, historically has been entwined with the tax evasion industry, it has attracted plenty of unscrupulous planners. These planners are perfectly willing to cheat the government out of taxes. It should come as no surprise that many of them are just as willing to cheat legitimate creditors, and often even their own clients.

Our first experience with the offshore industry came in 1988, while we were pursuing an attorney malpractice case against three U.S. tax attorneys who had assisted a client in setting up a chain of Panamanian corporations to evade U.S. taxes. The attorneys neglected to tell the client that they were the owners of the Panamanian bank to which the proceeds were forwarded and also that they had embezzled to satisfy their cocaine habits and other vices. When the offshore tax scheme fell apart and the client needed money to pay back taxes, interest and penalties, there was no money available and the client was forced into bankruptcy. What little of the client's money that was recovered came from the attorneys' malpractice insurance carrier, which then went directly to the IRS.

If you think that asset protection is something you may need but the idea makes you somewhat uneasy, you're on track. The key to asset protection is to avoid the sleaze and to conduct the planning in a respectable fashion.

ASSET PROTECTION AND THE LAW

There is no legal casebook on asset protection. The term doesn't appear in the U.S. Code or in state statutes. It doesn't appear in law digests. There are no law school courses in asset protection. There are no real-world asset protection think tanks. The so-called institutes devoted to asset protection are principally marketing organizations, but their fancy names and fellowships give the false impression that asset protection is studied as if in some vast scientific undertaking.

Each year a number of continuing professional education courses on asset protection are taught to lawyers, accountants, and financial planners. Unfortunately, these courses are rarely taught by persons having any real-world experience in debtor-creditor litigation. Generally, these seminars simply serve as a forum for repeating the marketing claims of others in the field, with little discussion and analysis of the theory or practice methods of actual prelitigation planning.

A search of Martindale-Hubbell's national attorney directory prior to 1990 probably would have yielded no listings for asset protection attorneys among the hundreds of thousands of attorneys listed. Today, the same search will yield several hundred listings for attorneys who allegedly practice in the field. Many are estate planning and tax attorneys with little practical experience who added asset protection planning to their menu of services as a draw for more will and trust sales. Marketing savvy, however, does not equate to hardcore litigation experience, such as actively sparring with creditor's attorneys in a postjudgment asset hearing.

Because tax evasion was often at the heart of what was called asset protection in the 1980s and early 1990s, there is an association of tax law with asset protection, even though tax and prelitigation planning have little to do with one another, except that the use of certain asset protection tools, as with the use of most business tools, have tax ramifications that must be understood. Also, economic substance is an important component of both asset protection planning and tax planning. Even today, large accounting firms disguise questionable tax transactions as asset protection plans to try to impart some nontax substance to dubious arrangements.

Accountants, tax attorneys, and estate planning attorneys provide valuable services to high-net-worth clients. Nevertheless, some well-meaning practitioners are engaging in asset protection planning with no idea of what happens in litigation. This planning usually relies on the latest marketing ploys of competitors or paid mentors. Too often this planning fails at the first signs of trouble. Unfortunately, this planning can put the client in a situation worse than if no planning at all had been done. We have heard planners argue that a civil court would be required to find one way or another on a debtor-creditor issue because the issue was resolved a certain way for tax purposes. Tax treatment of a transaction does not control the civil law treatment. However, the position that a debtor takes in filing tax returns may be an admission against the debtor, resulting in a peculiar evidentiary one-way street that can only benefit creditors.

Furthermore, other than for limited tax-only purposes, there is no accountant-client confidentiality privilege. When an asset protection plan is challenged, the debtor's accountant likely will be the first witness deposed and will have to tell everything he knows, with the threat of contempt of court hanging over him if he holds anything back. If there were discussions about specific asset protection issues, the creditor would be able to inquire about those discussions and introduce them as proof of actual intent to defraud creditors, probably creating a slam-dunk fraudulent transfer challenge. There is no such risk if the client uses an attorney, who may not reveal client confidences unless the planning was blatantly fraudulent or criminal in nature.

It is difficult to understand why an accountant or other nonattorney would want to engage in asset protection planning. If a nonattorney drafts documents for the client that are part of the planning, that is probably the unauthorized practice of law in most states and can subject the nonattorney to sanctions. Furthermore, accountants are likely more exposed to civil conspiracy lawsuits related to asset protection planning than are attorneys. Attorneys traditionally have engaged in prelitigation planning. Accountants do not. The cost of defending a civil conspiracy lawsuit and any resulting judgment is normally not covered by an accountant's professional liability insurance.

The asset protection sector is also overrun with asset protection mills that grind out thousands of family limited partnership documents on the cheap, usually for $2000 or so. For an extra $1000 they will also throw in a foreign asset protection trust. Behind the scenes, these mills are run by typists who spew hundreds of trust documents from their word processors, while the attorney associated with the "planning" is at a restaurant or hotel conference room whipping up the next crowd of customers into a frenzy over the evils of our justice system. Chances are the attorney has never seen the inside of a courtroom except in the legal malpractice cases brought against him. These mills turn out products with glaring errors, such as making the client the general partner of a family limited partnership, probably ensuring that a creditor will reach partnership assets quickly and easily.

These mills circulate marketing materials that say that a trust formed in one jurisdiction or another is totally impenetrable by creditors. Not only is this statement grossly misleading, but it contributes to the negative image of asset protection planning in U.S. courts. Furthermore, it leads to unreasonable expectations for people who want legitimate and workable asset protection plans.

Finally, there are the outright scam asset protection structures using multiple layers of offshore trusts, which are pushed by certain multilevel marketing groups. Many of these groups have ties to fringe militia groups. These plans are all uniformly worthless. The theoretical underpinnings of these plans are akin to thinking that if you attach two extra wings to a jetliner you would be able to fly to the moon. These plans only "work" so long as those involved are willing to flee the United States at the first sign of trouble and move somewhere where extradition to the United States would be difficult. Moreover, the protection offered by these structures usually involves giving up legitimate protections in exchange for some downright crazy documents that no court will recognize (except, of course, the kangaroo court of the local militia group).

ASSET PROTECTION AND LEGAL RISK MANAGEMENT

We have previously noted that asset protection is a subset of risk management. Asset protection is, first, a method of managing legal risks. Second, asset protection provides a backup in case risk management fails to prevent the risk from materializing and there is a resulting money judgment. This is why asset protection is considered hard planning. It is the last line of defense when everything else has gone wrong. It is not meant to protect a client in easy cases where she is likely to win or where her insurance company will handle it. Asset protection planning is meant for the worst-case scenario. Most clients will never have this worst-case scenario where the asset protection plan is challenged. However, if no plan is in place, the worst-case scenario can be disastrously worse than if proper planning had occurred.

Among legitimate practitioners, asset protection requires expertise in several areas of law and practice. Good asset protection plans are multidisciplined. Rarely does any one person have all the necessary skills to provide the most comprehensive asset protection planning. Nor it is likely that one person could keep up with important changes in all of the areas of law that require competence for good asset protection planning. The most comprehensive and well-structured plans are created by teams of multidisciplined planners.

In the order of importance, the areas of law important in good asset protection planning are civil procedure, commercial law, business entity law, bankruptcy law, tax law, and trust and estate law.

Civil procedure comprises pretrial procedure, conflicts of laws between jurisdictions, evidence, privileges, trial practice, judgments, and remedies. The essence of asset protection is predicting what judges and juries will do when faced with a particular set of circumstances. No one can make these predictions unless he has been in a few trials, sat through some debtor's exams, thwarted prejudgment attachment of assets, and the like. Unfortunately, too many asset protection planners have little training and little or no practical experience in litigation. The creation of asset protection plans without consultations with a planner with some litigation background is foolhardy. If someone has no firm idea what sort of questions a creditor or hostile judge may ask, how can they engage in planning in anticipation of giving the correct answers?

The field of commercial law includes debtor-creditor law, contracts, and the Uniform Commercial Code (UCC). Good asset protection plans are created using transactions that make economic sense and that can be rationally explained to a judge or jury. It makes for a good story. The UCC and commercial law will almost always govern business transactions between entities, as well as the security interests created in those transactions. A planner needs to understand the various types of obligations and remedies that may arise from specific commercial transactions. An understanding of debtor-creditor law, particularly fraudulent transfer law, is critical. A planner who purports to put together asset protection plans who has anything less than a thorough knowledge of the fraudulent transfer law is a fraud.

A comprehensive knowledge of business entity law, including the formation, operation, governance, and defense of corporations, partnerships, limited liability companies (LLCs), and other business entities, is crucial. Boilerplate documents will not suffice for a good asset protection plan. Solid planning requires well-crafted entity documentation.

Bankruptcy will usually not be an issue if an asset protection plan works well, because the debtor will not have to resort to bankruptcy and the creditor will realize the futility of forcing the debtor into involuntary bankruptcy. Nonetheless, bankruptcy is always a possibility, and the planner must be aware of the interplay between the asset protection plan and bankruptcy law. Some planners, however, actually send their clients rushing headlong into bankruptcy, foreign trusts in hand, assuring them that their debts will be wiped out. These planners forget that bankruptcy judges have tremendous powers and the threat of bankruptcy fraud is very real.

As we have mentioned, asset protection as a marketing term originally surfaced when tax evasion plans involving offshore tax havens needed a less sinister moniker. Eventually, however, the offshore tax havens saw the value of adding debtor-friendly asset protection laws to their statute books. Many asset protection plans have at least some offshore component, and planners should be knowledgeable about certain offshore laws as well as international banking and the transfer of funds internationally.

Asset protection plans should be created in coordination with or should be reviewed by a competent tax professional. As a simple economic matter, negative tax consequences need to be avoided to the fullest extent possible. Conversely, if legitimate tax planning opportunities arise in the asset protection planning process, they should be explored and exploited. Many asset protection plans are income tax neutral, meaning that they have no net effect on the amount of income tax the client will pay. However, although such a plan ultimately has no effect on the client's tax situation, it often requires a significant level of tax skill to achieve that neutrality and to avoid creating a tax problem. Too often, asset protection plans are created without regard for tax consequences. The result can be that the client pays more in taxes, penalties, and interest than he saved in court from the asset protection plan. Plans based on secrecy, bearer shares, nominees, and the like are particularly susceptible to this problem.

If possible, asset protection planning should be integrated with estate planning, which also fundamentally involves the protection of wealth over time. So long as the client remains sufficiently solvent and if there are no foreseeable problems on the horizon, an integrated estate and asset protection plan can work well. However, contrary to the claims of the vast majority of asset protection plans marketed, trusts and family and charitable giving are often the worst possible asset protection tools. Gifting may be the boon of estate planners because of the tax laws, but it is the bane of asset protection planners because of the fraudulent transfer laws. Gifts are set aside rather easily under the fraudulent transfer laws for a number of years after they are made.

ASSET PROTECTION AND INSURANCE

The relationship between asset protection and insurance is rarely discussed and is generally poorly understood. Some asset protection planners advise their clients to get rid of their insurance coverage altogether. The rationale is that the existence of an insurance policy creates a target for plaintiffs' attorneys. The money saved by eliminating insurance coverage can be utilized, of course, to pay the planner's fees in setting up the expensive asset protection plan that will render insurance coverage unnecessary.

Of course, this advice is ridiculous and dangerous. The insured person has little or no financial stake in whether an insurance company pays a plaintiff's claim other than the possibility of future premium increases. This advice also does not recognize that plaintiffs' attorneys focus closely on reaching settlements with insurance companies and moving on to the next case, instead of wasting money and, more importantly, time that could be applied to getting their next big insurance settlement. Similarly, the business owner's or professional person's main motivation should be to get rid of a lawsuit and get back to making money, and not to spend years dodging creditors.

Insurance then, is an incredibly useful and often relatively inexpensive asset protection tool. It is specifically designed to transfer the risk of loss away from the insured person and to the insurance company. To the extent that it makes economic sense to cover a particular risk and insurance is available, insurance always should be the primary risk management method and asset protection should play only a secondary role.

Persons at risk of being sued should purchase as much insurance coverage as is economically practical, and the asset protection planning for that person should be closely integrated with that coverage. The goal is to create a scenario where a plaintiff and his attorney are very likely to accept the limits of the insurance coverage in settlement of a claim, even if the plaintiff's potential recovery is greater than the insurance coverage limits. When insurance coverage is available to meet a plaintiff's claim, the plaintiff's attention becomes focused on the insurance company, because it has the proverbial deep pockets. Where an insurance company is on the hook for at least a portion of the liability to a creditor, every attempt should be made to transfer the onus of nonpayment to the insurance company and away from the defendant. At the very least, every business should have a general liability insurance policy, and every household should have umbrella coverage in addition to homeowner and auto liability policies.

So far, we have defined asset protection and also identified the expertise required to properly develop a sound asset protection plan. We have also discussed the interplay of insurance and asset protection planning. The next question to consider is whether asset protection planning is proper in a particular situation. To answer that question, we must now examine the morality of asset protection planning.

Issues of Morality in Asset Protection

Issues of morality are very personal. They are often best left for individuals to decide for themselves, except in cases where others may be harmed. For example, adults in our society are free to decide whether drinking alcohol is right or wrong. However, drunk drivers are harmful to others; therefore, drunk driving is prohibited by the legislatures.

Does asset protection harm creditors? Is it simply a matter of timing or does asset protection planning harm future unknown creditors as well, even when no claims are on the horizon? Various bodies of law help to define when asset protection is improper, but as with many areas of law, there are no clear lines between what is permissible and what is not. Is asset protection planning defensible simply because it is allowed under the law? On the other hand, if a particular course of action is not allowed or reversible under the law, is that course of action always wrong in asset protection planning?

The most difficult question in asset protection planning is deceptively simple: Is it right? This is not merely an abstract moral question. As a practical matter, the answer to this question can be the critical factor in a given case. The moral implications of an asset protection plan in a particular circumstance may determine whether or not the plan works.

Judges and juries are influenced to some extent by moral considerations beyond the confines of the law when determining whether to allow a particular asset protection structure to protect assets from a particular creditor. One must heed, in the vernacular of trial lawyers, "the cornfield equities."

Being technically right under the law does not guarantee victory in the courtroom. Our judicial system has a built-in flexibility that allows judges to deviate from the strict rule of law to avoid unjust results—unjust, that is, in the mind of a particular judge. For example, the badges of fraud test seems to validate the concept of result-oriented decisions by judges in fraudulent transfer cases. Good asset protection planning attempts to create favorable circumstances in advance so that a future creditor-unfriendly result is not seen as unjust or just a typical deadbeat scheme. In fact, the best planning would result in the creditor's failure to reach a debtor's assets being perceived as a just result.

The importance of morality and its effect on the results of asset protection planning has been overlooked in the professional literature, where the question of how to protect particular assets eclipses the larger and more important question of whether those assets should be protected at all. Nevertheless, these issues are intertwined. A good asset protection plan may fail if the client is in the wrong, and a bad asset protection plan may succeed if the client is in the right.

We have created a number of scenarios in this chapter as examples of the moral issues involved in asset protection planning. Each scenario may elicit a gut reaction of sympathy or antipathy much like the reaction a judge or jury may have toward a debtor and, by association, the debtor's planner.

ASSET PROTECTION AND COMMERCIAL RELATIONSHIPS

Consider issues of contractual liability. Break a contract, you're liable. That concept is simple, and every judge and jury can relate to it. In theory, a contractual obligation should never catch you off guard; if you did not want to be responsible for your side of the bargain, then you never should have entered into the contract. On the other hand, if someone contracts with your company but wanted you also to be personally liable under the contract, he should get a personal guarantee and not complain if the company itself proves not to have the financial strength to perform.

If only modern financial relationships were so simple! Consider a typical case of a businessperson (Businessperson) whose company borrows money from the bank (Bank) for the express purpose of making widgets.

Let's start with the easiest case: What if Businessperson does not spend the money on widgets, as he represented to Bank, but instead blows the money on a new yacht? Because it would be entirely unfair for Businessperson to benefit personally from the loan that was made for express business purposes, Businessperson clearly is wrong. So, no one should be surprised when a judge goes out of her way to accommodate arguments that Bank should be able to reach Businessperson's assets to repay the loan.

Next, let's say that Businessperson truly intends to repay Bank but instead of investing in widget manufacturing equipment, he uses the money to speculate in the commodities market. Businessperson's speculation fails and he cannot repay the loan. In this case, Businessperson did use the money for business purposes, even if not as intended by Bank. It is a closer call whether Businessperson's personal assets should be tapped to repay Bank. While a court probably would agree with Bank's arguments for reaching Businessperson's assets, there is some doubt as to what a judge might do, and that doubt would militate toward settlement.

What if Businessperson makes widgets as planned but comes upon an unexpected decline in the demand for widgets and the business fails? Here, Businessperson has utilized the funds for the intended purpose but, through no personal fault, the business is unable to repay Bank. No moral reason exists why Businessperson should be forced to pay Bank from his personal assets. After all, Bank took a calculated economic risk when it made the loan. An asset protection plan in this circumstance should stand up.

Let's take this a step further. Prior to giving the loan, Bank assures Businessperson that if the business needs more money, Bank will make additional loans. Relying on this, Businessperson takes the loan. Later, at a critical point for his new business, Businessperson requests that Bank make the additional loans as Bank had earlier promised. Bank declines to do so, and the business fails.

In a lender liability case like this, Bank may have a claim on the original loan, but it would be unfair if Bank could collect against Businessperson's personal assets. A judge probably would give Businessperson wide sway in protecting his assets against Bank's claims.

Similarly, assume that Bank decides that the business is valuable, and wants to acquire the business. Bank manipulates the widget market to cause a short-term decline in the price of widgets, forcing the business to fail. Bank takes over the business and sues Businessperson for repayment of the loan.

Here, Bank is clearly in the wrong, and the just result is that Businessperson should be able to protect his wealth from Bank's claims. Indeed, if anything, Bank should be paying Businessperson, and a judge would likely view any asset protection planning done by Businessperson to be totally proper in these circumstances.

ASSET PROTECTION AND FIDUCIARIES

Consider another set of facts: A stockbroker (Stockbroker) persuades an investor (Investor) to purchase a particular investment, but the investment doesn't pay off as Investor had hoped. Investor sues Stockbroker and wins a judgment. This scenario plays out every day in our financial markets.

First, assume that Stockbroker created a Ponzi scheme with no economic substance where the investment "gains" of existing investors are paid from the principal of new investors who are brought into the scheme. Stockbroker tells Investor that the investment is legitimate but Investor loses everything when the scheme collapses.

This is outright fraud. If Stockbroker takes money from the scheme and places it into an asset protection structure, it should surprise no one if a judge employs extreme remedies to try to claw the money back to compensate the victims of the scheme.

Next, assume that Stockbroker persuades Investor to invest in a penny stock. Stockbroker knows the company has no real operations but Stockbroker gets enough new investors to pump the stock price up. After the price goes up, Stockbroker dumps her own stock in the company, netting a huge profit. However, this selling drives the price of the stock back down and the other investors, including Investor, suffer big losses.

This scenario is not much better than the first. Again, it would be unjust if Stockbroker were able to protect her ill-gotten gains in an asset protection plan. No one should be upset if a judge employs extreme remedies to get money back for duped investors.

Consider, however, a situation in which Stockbroker, in good faith, analyzes the value of Widget Company and determines it to be worth $100 per share. Widget Company is presently trading at $50 per share. Stockbroker tells her clients that they stand to make $50 per share. Stockbroker moves all of her clients, including Investor, into Widget Company, but through no fault of the Stockbroker, Widget Company stock falls from $50 per share to $10 per share, causing Investor to lose 80 percent of his investment.

In this situation, no element of fraud exists. Stockbroker was simply trying to maximize investment returns for her clients. Still, Investor lost a lot of money and no one should be surprised if Investor sued and won a judgment against Stockbroker. But should Stockbroker be required to satisfy Investor's losses out of her own pocket? The answer probably depends on other factors, such as whether Stockbroker advised Investor of the market risk in such transactions or whether Investor was a sophisticated investor or a pensioner counting on those funds for retirement income.

Next consider the situation in which Stockbroker analyzes the value of Widget Company to be worth $100 per share. Widget Company is presently trading at $50 per share. Stockbroker tells her clients that they stand to make $50 per share. She moves all of her clients, including Investor, into Widget Company, and the stock peaks at $98 per share, at which time Stockbroker sells, realizing a $48-per-share profit for her clients. Although Investor has made a handsome profit, he sues Stockbroker for the unrealized $2 per share.

In this case, Stockbroker is certainly not morally at fault, and only a really bad decision could render her personally responsible. In this case, Stockbroker ought to be able to stand behind her asset protection plan against the claims of Investor. The same result might apply if Investor has a reputation for being a "career plaintiff" and has been a plaintiff in a dozen similar lawsuits. Few people would hold it against Stockbroker if she uses an asset protection plan to shield her wealth from such claims.

ASSET PROTECTION AND DIVORCE

Let's consider the most common arrangement that leads to financial strife and judgments—marriage. Far too many asset protection plans are created with the purpose of protecting the assets of one spouse against the claims of the other spouse. Often they are used as a poor substitute for a prenuptial or antenuptial agreement that neither is comfortable discussing with the other; or, about as often, after an incident of marital infidelity.

Is this sort of planning appropriate? Should a husband be able to shield his assets from his wife? Arguments that a spouse should be able to protect what he had before marriage are not relevant; the laws of most states already protect those assets.

Asset protection planning in the marital context has attraction because of the propensity of judges in divorce cases to divide assets mathematically with little regard to the equities of the situation. A spouse who cheats or otherwise destroys the relationship often is awarded the same value as the more innocent spouse. However, who can say who is really at fault in a failed relationship? Perhaps a purely mathematical division of property measured by lost opportunities, earning ability, or the duration of the marriage is a reasonable way to resolve property issues.

Consider a wife who supports her husband through college and while he struggles in business. After many years, he achieves financial success and takes his company public. Soon thereafter, his ego motivates him to "trade up" to a younger, more attractive wife. Should the husband be able to keep his ex-wife from sharing in the windfall of the public offering? How about a husband who worked at the pizza parlor seventy hours a week to put his wife through medical school? Shouldn't he reap at least a portion of the benefits of her successful medical practice?

At the extreme are the cases involving the classic "gold digger." The twenty-something stripper who marries the eighty-something oilman comes to mind. Is it true love, or is the Bentley the ultimate aim? However, even in these cases, property issues are best resolved in advance in prenuptial agreements. Asset protection plans are not intended to change the character of contracts, whether commercial or marital, after the fact. As a matter of morality, asset protection planning in the context of divorce probably should be undertaken only in extreme cases. For example, it could be used to protect against an ex-husband who holds lifelong grudges and continually repetitions the courts for new relief as a form of harassment to "get back" at the wealthy woman he perceives as having left him.

APPLICATION OF MORAL ISSUES

The lesson of these examples is simply that under certain circumstances asset protection is appropriate and morally right and under others it is inappropriate and morally wrong. The relative effectiveness of an asset protection plan before a judge may depend on where in the moral spectrum the facts falls when the plan is challenged.

An asset protection plan that is created to protect assets in morally indefensible circumstances should fail and is likely to do so. Asset protection strategies that effectively protect assets in morally indefensible circumstances cannot be expected to avoid changes in the law made by the courts or legislatures.

On the other hand, an asset protection plan that is created to protect assets in morally defensible circumstances is likely to withstand challenge. The best asset protection plan is, of course, the asset protection plan that is never challenged. Proper business planning, risk management, insurance coverage, and the like should be the first line of defense against creditors to avoid claims at the outset and to ensure that if a claim arises, the moral high ground is claimed early on.

The second lesson here is that no one can know the context in which an asset protection plan will be challenged. An asset protection plan that is created to protect a client who seemed in the right at the time might be used to defeat the recovery rights of a victim who, as a moral matter, ought to be made whole.

The case most often mentioned in asset protection seminars is that of the brilliant surgeon who is beset by frivolous medical malpractice claims. The asset protection gurus would say that this is the perfect client for asset protection planning, and to some extent they are right. However, assume that the perfect asset protection plan is created for the brilliant surgeon—a plan so good that no creditor could ever cut through it. A few years after the plan is established, the brilliant surgeon gets drunk and crashes into a car driven by a single mother and her two children. The mother is killed and both of the children are permanently disabled. Because the surgeon was drunk, his insurance coverage was voided. Should the two children be able to recover from the surgeon for their injuries, or should they simply live with their injuries while the surgeon spends the rest of his life enjoying his beachfront condo in the Cayman Islands?

The problem in this situation, of course, is that although the perfect asset protection plan was created to protect the brilliant surgeon against medical malpractice claims, it will protect him even when he is clearly in the wrong. He ought to pay for his bad conduct. As a matter of morality, the plan assumes that the surgeon will do the right thing and voluntarily pay the two children. But human nature being what it is, chances are better that the brilliant surgeon will rationalize that he has worked hard to obtain his worldly goods and should not have to forfeit them based on a single mistake.

In such a case, a court should invalidate the asset protection plan and allow the children to recover. Whether the planning was created to protect against malpractice claims shouldn't make a bit of difference. The morality of asset protection plans are measured by the circumstances in which they are challenged, not by the risks against which they were originally designed to protect. The situation must be that way to avoid injustice.

THE ASSET PROTECTION PLANNER AS FINAL ARBITER

Moral issues present perhaps the greatest challenge in asset protection planning. No planner can accurately predict what his clients may do in the future, or whom they may harm. The problem is that a good asset protection planner can protect his clients' assets from nearly all creditors in nearly all situations. So a good planner can effectively protect a client's assets when the client is in the wrong and should not be protected.

There is a natural lag by creditors' attorneys in identifying debtors' plans as having an asset protection effect, devising strategies to break through these plans, and convincing courts and legislatures to invalidate such plans. This lag means that a good asset protection planner who is "ahead of the curve" can expect a strategy to be effective for at least several years from the time the strategy is first employed. So long as the planner can keep coming up with new ideas, the planner will be able to stay ahead of creditors.

The power of the good planner thus makes the planner, and not the courts, the arbiter of whether or not the planner's client should pay on a particular judgment. In other words, the planner effectively becomes the judge. This creates a conflict of interest between the planner and the client. It also has the potential to create great injustice toward claimants who have been harmed by the client.

Issues such as these are ordinarily resolved by the legislatures, which usually regulate debtor-creditor relations by way of collection procedures, fraudulent transfer law, and bankruptcy law. The problem, again, is one of the time lag between the planner's creation of a strategy and the legislature's doing something about it. Within that time lag, the potential for injustice is great.

In the authors' experience in asset protection planning, we try to resolve these issues by being closely involved in our clients' affairs, working to keep them out of trouble so that these moral issues do not arise. We encourage our clients to maintain adequate insurance, including umbrella liability insurance. We try to provide mechanisms in our planning so that the client can be encouraged to settle on reasonable terms if a claim arises. Nevertheless, we continue to struggle with these moral issues, and bring them up for discussion in our speaking engagements before the American Bar Association and other professional groups.

IS THE "PERFECT CASTLE" REALLY SO PERFECT?

The issues of morality in asset protection planning have a very important effect on plan design. This effect is that asset protection plans must to some degree be discriminating about how they will be effective. Very simply, an asset protection structure that protects the assets of all persons, no matter how illegal or despicable their conduct, cannot be expected to last long before changes in the law defeat such structures. If an asset protection plan is effective in protecting the assets of securities fraudsters and drunk drivers, don't expect that strategy to last very long.

A common misconception among asset protection planners is that certain structures will work for their clients, even though these structures have been invalidated in regard to criminals or others who from a moral standpoint should not be allowed to protect their assets from the people they cheated or harmed. Their rallying cry in the face of these defeats is, "Bad facts make bad law!" And of course, their clients "do not engage in that sort of conduct." But if a defendant had "good facts" he would not be in court! In our legal system, however, concepts of right and wrong are determined by whether a judgment is issued against one party or the other. If a judgment is issued against a debtor, the debtor is in the wrong, and the system wants to see the debtor pay the judgment, not wriggle out of it.

These concerns are difficult, often impossible, to reconcile. Where the "good" client should prevail is not in the postjudgment defense of an asset protection plan but at trial to avoid the judgment in the first place, or, even better, by entering into a favorable settlement. As we will next see, an important goal of asset protection planning is to facilitate such settlements.

CHAPTER 4

Goals of Asset Protection

A good asset protection plan does much more than just place assets out of the reach of creditors. It is an overall and comprehensive personal and business risk management strategy that furthers a variety of goals such as prompting the end of litigation or transferring the onus of wrongdoing to others. In fact, the best asset protection structure is one that simply is never challenged because litigation is avoided altogether or contentious matters are settled prior to judgment.

The primary goal of asset protection is to allow clients to rid themselves of creditors' claims while retaining a substantial portion of their assets. Good asset protection planning creates an environment that promotes settlement on terms favorable to clients, which creditors are willing to accept as settlement in full of all outstanding liabilities. A good plan will thus facilitate an end to the litigation, and it will allow debtors to get on with their business.

FAVORABLE PSYCHOLOGY OF SETTLEMENT

An asset protection plan should act as a lens to focus the creditor on the idea that any judgment he might obtain may not be collectible as a practical matter. Reaching a settlement favorable to the debtor requires convincing the creditor that the debtor's proposed settlement will result in the largest recovery for the least risk. We call this the *psychology of settlement.*

To understand the psychology of settlement, think like a creditor. Can I prevail at trial? If I lose at trial, can I win on appeal? If I get a judgment, can I collect on it? Creating uncertainty in the answers to these questions is how asset protection planning works best. If the creditor has doubts about his ability to win the case or to ultimately collect on the judgment, the case is much more likely to settle, and the more favorable the psychology of settlement is to the debtor. At the point where such doubts are maximized, other factors are brought into play to create the criticality of settlement, which is that convergence of events that finally causes the matter to be resolved (see Figure 4-1). Settlements concluded on the basis of a single factor are rare. Rather, most settlements are achieved because many conditions exist from the viewpoint of the debtor and the creditor so that settlement makes sense for both parties.

SUBTLETY

The psychology of settlement is not a one-way street. If the asset protection plan is too brazen, the creditor may hold an advantage. If evidence of the asset protection planning comes before the court, the judge or jury may deduce that the defendant knew she was guilty of some sort of wrongdoing. They may think, "Why else engage in such planning?" Blatant asset protection planning may

FIGURE 4.1

Criticality of settlement.

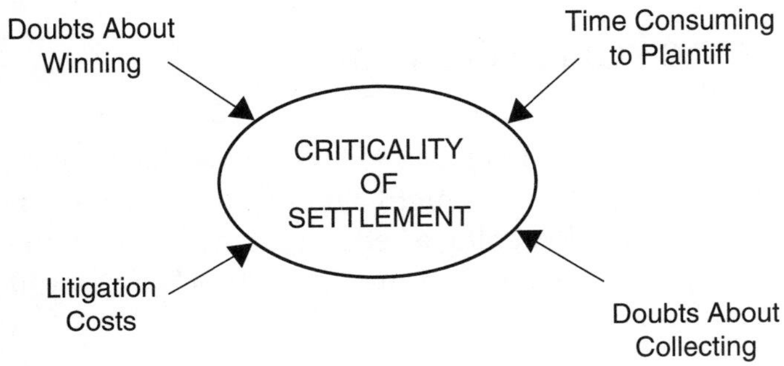

have a negative affect on the psychology of settlement. A creditor may believe the odds of obtaining a favorable judgment are higher because the asset protection plan is so blatant, even if collection may be difficult. Subtlety in planning is critically important so that a creditor cannot use the existence of the plan to his advantage in court.

The in-your-face asset protection planning mentality of the 1990s was anything but subtle. Telling a creditor, "I've got an off-shore asset protection trust in place, now go away!" was a short-sighted and often counterproductive tactic. When these strategies were later tried, they sometimes landed the debtor in jail for contempt and left the creditor emboldened. Yet, even with the documented failures of offshore trusts, some promoters continue to pursue this form of overt planning. After all, the brash and exotic has marketing sizzle; subtlety does not.

Even if a creditor has concerns about collectibility, he may be encouraged about his prospects of winning a judgment because of the inference that the debtor knew she was at fault because she had implemented an asset protection plan. The creditor can use the same arguments used to win the judgment to gain the help of the court in penetrating the asset protection structure and collecting. A principal goal of asset protection is to keep the creditor from drawing inferences based on the planning that is done.

Ideally, the asset protection plan should allow the creditor to ascertain that a judgment will be difficult to collect, but it should not be so brazen as to give the creditor an advantage in court. In other words, asset protection planning should not appear to be done for asset protection reasons. Instead, asset protection planning should be done within the context of other planning, such as financial planning, business planning, overall risk management planning, and tax planning.

CREATION OF OFFENSIVE OPPORTUNITIES

If possible, the plan should allow the debtor to take the offensive, drawing the creditor into a situation that may create the possibility of liability from the creditor to the debtor. While this potential liability may be offset by the underlying judgment, the prospect of costly litigation over a new claim in addition to continuing litigation costs for the existing claim militates toward settlement.

Alternatively, the debtor may explore means to expose the creditor for liabilities to third parties, including tax liabilities. While exposing the creditor to third-party liabilities does not benefit the debtor financially, it will add to the creditor's expense of time and money, and thus facilitate settlement. It may also help to deter the creditors from aggressively pursuing the debtor's assets, since the creditor will be wary of falling into traps.

Tactics that shift the creditor's focus from what he may gain in pursuing a claim to what he may lose in pursuing a claim are important. In the jargon of litigators, the creditor should be put in a position in which "he no longer wants the cheese, but just wants out of the trap." The importance of this psychological shift in the litigation cannot be understated.

TRANSFERENCE

Transference is another important goal of asset protection planning. An asset protection plan should be structured so that liability and, more importantly, culpability is transferred to a third party such as an insurer (see Figure 4.2). If the creditor can be convinced to pursue the debtor's insurance coverage rather than the debtor's assets, often the focus of the creditor on the "bad guy" can be shifted to the insurer as well. Transference can be accomplished outside the insurance context as well. If fault legitimately might be transferred to any third party, such as to foreign parties not subject to the jurisdiction of U.S. courts, and to other parties to the litigation, the debtor should pursue such transference opportunities to his full advantage. By transferring fault to third parties, the debtor may also avoid the creditor's "extrajudicial" attempts at resolution, including personal and hostile vendettas against the debtor.

TOTALITY

An asset protection plan should be comprehensive, providing complete and total protection for all assets. Some planners recommend leaving some property outside of the realm of planning to avoid allegations that the debtor has rendered himself insolvent. However, from a tactical standpoint, this can be disastrous. Exposing a significant asset to creditors gives the creditor's attor-

FIGURE 4.2

Transference.

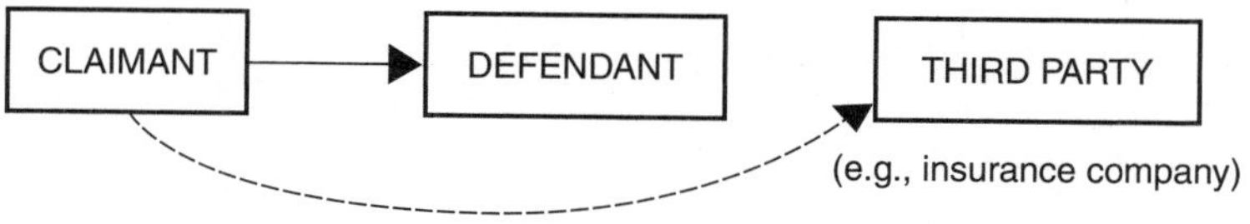

```
┌──────────┐        ┌──────────────┐      ┌──────────────┐
│ CLAIMANT │───────▶│  DEFENDANT   │      │ THIRD PARTY  │
└──────────┘        └──────────────┘      └──────────────┘
      \                                   ▲ (e.g., insurance company)
       \                                 /
        `─────────────────────────────`
```

Transference involves shifting the moral obligation to pay to
a third party, such as to an insurance company.

neys the opportunity to stay in the fight, financing litigation on the run, knowing that there is the prospect for at least the recovery of attorneys' fees. Having that knowledge, the creditor is allowed the opportunity to wear down the debtor and given time to devise a plan to successfully defeat the asset protection plan in court.

One usually harmless tactic is to exclude from the asset protection plan those assets having little value to the creditor for which cost-effective protection cannot be provided. Indeed, the creditor may incur more costs in terms of time and effort to pursue such assets than they are worth. One example of such assets is heavily leveraged real estate (generally, with a debt-to-value ratio of 90 percent or more) and equipment. Nevertheless, it is foolish to leave significant assets outside the realm of the asset protection plan simply because they are difficult to protect.

CONTAINMENT

Containing liabilities within subsidiary entities is a fundamental purpose of asset protection planning. Whenever an entity is used in an asset protection structure, consideration must be given to issues of containment. These considerations must include whether valuable assets are owned in an entity where liability is likely to arise and are, therefore, exposed to collection. An important precept of asset protection planning is never to mix dangerous assets (that is, liability-producing assets such as real estate and vehicles) with safe assets (that is, passive assets such as cash and securities). See Figure 4.3.

FIGURE 4.3

Containment.

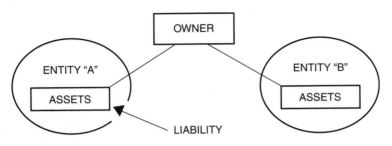

With proper containment, only the assets in Entity "A" will be
exposed to liabilities created by that entity. The assets in Entity "B"
will not be exposed to the liabilities of Entity "A."

Containment, particularly in asset-backed lending situations, sometimes includes the use of a *bankruptcy remote entity (BRE)*, usually a limited liability company, or LLC. The purpose of a BRE is threefold. First, the BRE's governing documents usually give the lender a voice in the management of the BRE and require the consent of the lender to file a bankruptcy petition. Second, it protects the lender from the bankruptcy of the BRE's owner. Third, it protects the owner of the BRE from the financial failure of the project for which the BRE was formed. Liability (other than debts guaranteed by the BRE's owner, of course) is contained within the subsidiary BRE and the lender is protected from the bankruptcy of its borrower. Of course, the BRE must be organized properly and its contracts drafted properly to minimize the risk of the BRE's liabilities attaching to the BRE's owner.

A word of caution is appropriate here. An asset protection plan should seek to avoid bankruptcy of any person or entity involved in the structure to the extent possible. At the very least, the asset protection plan should seek to avoid the personal bankruptcy of the owners of the entities. Bankruptcy courts have very strong and wide-ranging powers to set aside or ignore the attempts of debtors to avoid collection. Also, debtors may subject themselves to an accusation of bankruptcy fraud. Bankruptcy issues in asset protection planning are discussed further in Chapter 6.

FLEXIBILITY

Flexibility is also an important goal in asset protection planning. In the real world, there is no standard "predator plaintiff" who will attack an asset protection plan in a predictable manner. Instead, creditors may appear from outside or inside a structure, and they may assert a variety of claims such as negligence, fraud, breach of contract, statutory violations, and divorce claims. Rather than planning for a standard plaintiff, an asset protection plan should be flexible so that it can be modified later to offer the best defense against the specific creditors who do appear.

Most asset protection plans are meant to last for a long time. Over that time, inevitably changes in the law will occur. For instance, many offshore trusts were created before the Anderson and Lawrence offshore trust disasters discussed in Chapter 1. Many of the pre-Anderson trusts may be time bombs waiting to explode in court, as the plans using offshore trusts have not been reworked to avoid the defects identified in those cases. Tax law changes have made formerly legitimate offshore tax avoidance techniques ineffective. Proposals to change federal bankruptcy law to limit homestead exemptions may dramatically affect many asset protection plans for residences in Florida, Texas, and a handful of other states. They may also affect protected pension plans everywhere.

Factual circumstances also change. People marry and divorce. They have children, take on new responsibilities, and set new goals. Their businesses grow, reorganize, merge, and sell. Retirees substantially lower their liability exposure, while entrepreneurs forming new ventures take on new liabilities. If it is to be effective for more than a few years, an asset protection plan must be flexible and adaptable to changes in circumstance. As a result, the preferred methods of funding asset protection plans are by making investments that can be liquidated and by entering into business ventures or transactions that can be reversed or liquidated. For asset protection planning for oneself, the worst method of transfer is the irrevocable gift, because once it is made (and declared to the IRS), undoing that transfer is extremely difficult. To the extent that an irrevocable gift is part of a plan, it should be for the smallest amount possible. It should also usually be strictly limited to the initial gifts to fund a newly created trust.

REDUNDANCY AND DIVERSITY

Redundancy is another important goal in asset protection planning. Each important component of an asset protection feature should be redundant to some extent, and failsafe. Redundancy means that no single act of a creditor would be effective at reaching any of the debtor's significant assets (see Figure 4.4). Rather, a *defense-in-depth strategy* should be adopted and the strategy should be dynamic so that additional lines of defense are created even as a creditor attempts to penetrate the existing ones. Some might characterize asset protection as the digging of multiple trenches around assets, and this conception would not be far off the mark.

Redundancy is closely related to diversity, which is another important and interrelated goal. Diversity requires that asset protection planning be done in the many small pieces rather than in one large chunk. This is simply the maxim "don't put all your eggs in one basket" applied to asset protection planning. There should be diversity of the types of entities, funding methods, jurisdictions, and as many other elements as is practical and cost efficient. If one component fails, everything is not lost. Combining diversity with redundancy creates the strongest asset protection plans.

In developing an asset protection strategy, for every transfer, structure, and technique there should be an answer for "what if that component doesn't work?" After a couple of layers of protection, the answer usually will be that a variety of options exist based

FIGURE 4.4

Redundancy.

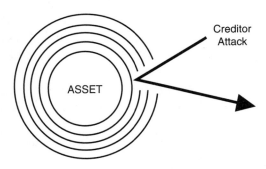

Even if a creditor gets past several layers, there are additional
layers the creditor still must contend with.

on the circumstances at that point, because in reality, the most effective planning cannot be done very far in advance because no one knows what the circumstances will require. Too much structuring in advance often will make the plan inflexible, expensive, and counterproductive.

The final goal of asset protection planning is cost efficiency. To the extent possible, the cost of an asset protection plan should be quantifiably justified by the protection it offers. Furthermore, it should fit within the client's existing or easily adaptable mode of business operations. Asset protection plans that are costly or cumbersome often go without necessary maintenance. This situation may negate the protection of the plan. Typically, if the plan blends in with and becomes a part of the existing business structure, the plan will be well maintained and thus be more likely to survive later challenges.

CHAPTER 5

Asset Protection Litigation

Assets are not protected in the Cook Islands or in Bermuda. Assets are protected in court. Thus, asset protection planning is fundamentally prelitigation planning. All of the offshore and domestic asset protection trusts, family limited partnerships, and other so-called asset protection entities should be formed in anticipation of one thing: that a creditor someday will put the entity's governing documents before a hostile judge who has just signed a judgment. These same documents might appear in a bankruptcy proceeding or in a civil conspiracy case against the debtor and the planner for conspiring to fraudulently transfer assets. The documents also might show up in the course of a state attorney disciplinary proceeding or in the hands of a U.S. attorney in a criminal money laundering case.

All of these situations represent cases in litigation. Everything an asset protection practitioner does must be done in anticipation of all reasonably conceivable types of litigation. The fundamental nature of asset protection planning as prelitigation planning cannot be overemphasized.

Remarkably, the great majority of those claiming to be asset protection planners have a very poor understanding of what really happens in litigation. Some of their sparse understanding comes from watching bits and pieces of high-profile cases on television. Others come from attending continuing education seminars taught by persons with equally meager courtroom experience. Sure, these planners can read cases and understand the theory behind the law, but there are important human facets of the litigation process that simply do not show up in court opinions.

Many of these planners are estate planners who figure that it likely will be a long time before any of their planning is tested, and by then the statute of limitations period for malpractice will have expired. But asset protection doesn't function this way. A fair percentage of the asset protection plans will be tested within several years of implementation. We are now beginning to see a surge of litigation arising from asset protection planning. Much of this litigation arises out of plans that have been around for some time, and we have yet to see if they will be effective or not. However, we are also starting to see a trickle of asset protection malpractice litigation (that is, litigation arising out of a faulty asset protection plan). We are also beginning to get a first glimpse of disciplinary and criminal actions against professionals who have assisted in the creation of asset protection plans.

Our purpose here is not to dissuade anyone from asset protection planning. We are very strong believers in asset protection, if it is done right and limited to appropriate cases. Furthermore, we do not believe that asset protection should be limited to "perfect" cases (that is, those cases where the client has nothing on the horizon and is not likely to be involved in litigation). Many self-proclaimed asset protection experts insist that they only take such "perfect" clients. However, do such clients even need asset protection planning beyond good insurance coverage? This seems somewhat like offering chemotherapy only to patients who have never had cancer and who are at low risk of ever getting it.

Rather, our purpose here is to provide a glimpse of how a hardcore litigator looks at asset protection from both the attack and defense perspectives. We will also provide some commonsense rules for creating asset protection plans.

The first thing to know about litigation is that rules do exist, but they vary in their application from case to case and from judge to judge. The same factual circumstances may be reviewed completely differently by two different judges and result in two completely different outcomes—or the same outcome may result, but for different reasons. Likewise, two cases with completely different facts may be treated alike by a single judge. What this creates is a system of quasi-random justice where, at best, one can only get a feel for what the outcome in a particular case will be, without really knowing.

Similarly, there are many different types of creditors, and many differences in the quality and experience of creditors' attorneys. One may be sued by an elderly pensioner who has little resources but is represented by a tough and savvy personal injury attorney who may take the pursuit of assets personally. On the other hand, one may be sued by a large corporation with practically unlimited resources but whose case is handled by a partner who passes off the work to a first-year associate attorney who couldn't figure out how to levy upon the cash in his own pocket.

So anything we say must be taken in the context of a specific case, before a specific judge, against a certain creditor, and against a certain attorney.

ASSET PROTECTION AND SECRECY

It must be presumed that in litigation *everything* comes out—all the dirty laundry and all the secrets. Even with attorney-client privilege and work-product immunity, hiding information in a lawsuit is very difficult. Furthermore, attempts to hide certain facts or circumstances are often counterproductive. Indeed, it usually doesn't take much for a judge or jury to suspect that someone is hiding something, and from there that person's credibility goes steeply downhill.

Secrecy can fail because of internal disclosures. Many people end up losing money in lawsuits to "insiders" (for example, to a spouse or an employee). These people are likely to know much more than is suspected, and even if they don't know everything, they can give their attorneys enough hints so that assets can be tracked.

Another internal threat is the carelessness, obstinacy, or plain stupidity of the defendant. Occasionally, a sophisticated offshore structure will result in a tax evasion prosecution because the client failed to make required tax filings and had his offshore bank statements delivered to his easily compromised mailbox at his U.S. address. Other schemes have collapsed because the client established trusts or made supposed gifts but insisted on retaining control over the assets.

There are also external threats to secrecy. These include actions of the creditors that actively extract information, such as depositions during the pretrial phase and debtor's examinations in the postjudgment phase. Defendants and debtors are asked, under penalty of perjury, whether or not they now have or had in the past any ownership or control, direct or indirect, of certain assets and classes of assets.

Postjudgment creditors in most jurisdictions can obtain the debtor's personal tax returns and the tax returns of all affiliated entities such as trusts or corporations. Even if the debtor asserts privacy concerns, this may mean only that the tax information will be turned over under a protective order so that only creditor and the court can see the information. But the creditor often still gets to see them, privacy concerns or not.

Creditors are not limited to asking questions or requesting documents from the debtor. They can also subpoena records, and the debtor can do little to stop these attempts. Telephone records are often the most valuable sources of information available, and it is probably impossible to keep a creditor from tracking phone calls unless a prepurchased calling card has been used and discarded. The information obtained from telephone records is usually a gold mine to creditors. Let's say that a creditor finds that you once called a Bahamian bank from your office. The creditor goes to the bank with a $50,000 check (fresh off the word processor) and the creditor tells the banker he is you, and he wants to make a deposit. However, he tells the bank, he forgot his (your) bank account number, which the bank gives him for purposes of making the deposit. The $50,000 check is, of course, worthless, which means that you will incur an expensive processing fee and may have to explain to your Bahamian bank why you tried to deposit a worthless check. Presumably, you could sue the creditor for doing this, but the creditor won't care because it is merely a setoff against the judgment held by the creditor.

Now the creditor has your account number and knows that you have an offshore account in your name. The creditor also has the telephone records of calls to the bank. You had better hope that you have reported this account to the IRS. Chances are that you didn't, however, because the creditor would have found that information in your tax returns rather than having to resort to sneaky tricks. In any event, the creditor's next call might be to the Criminal Investigation Division of the IRS. The creditor's call after that will be to the judge's chambers to advise the judge that you have committed perjury. The creditor will request a special hearing to force you to turn the funds in the Bahamian account over to the court for distribution to the creditor. If you don't, the court can hold you in contempt and make you sit in jail until you do.

In practice, this turn of events happens frequently, but the offshore banks, the planners, and the clients who get caught in this trap are not likely to tell much about it.

PRIVILEGES AND IMMUNITIES

If the planner is not an attorney, there is no chance of any documents being protected under attorney-client privilege. The new "accountant-client privilege" is completely worthless in creditor litigation. It only works in federal tax litigation, and even then the privilege is limited.

Usually, conversations and the documents drafted by an attorney for the confidential use of a client will be protected by attorney-client privilege. However, if a judge suspects that a fraudulent transfer has been made, she can invoke the crime-and-fraud exception to the attorney-client privilege and order the planner to turn over otherwise privileged documents. Depending on the state, engagement letters and billing statements are not protected by attorney-client privilege. Thus, a possible malpractice would be for an attorney engagement letter or billing statement to reference asset protection or to discuss in detail what was done for the client. For this reason, the better planners bill on a flat-fee basis, and their engagement letters reflect business or estate planning purposes but not asset protection.

Sometimes, unsophisticated planning attorneys will claim their documents are also protected by *work product immunity*. Unfortunately, this immunity often is restricted to documents that the attorney creates "in anticipation of litigation" (for example, the notes containing his trial strategy). Ironically, if the planner claims that the documents were created in anticipation of litigation because of a potential later creditor, the court may take that as an admission of an actual intent to defraud creditors. It would then set

aside a transaction related to these documents under the fraudulent transfer laws.

MARKETING MATERIALS OF THE PROMOTER

More than any other evidence, clients are most likely to be
harmed by the marketing materials of their asset protection planner. These are readily discoverable and not protected by any privilege or immunity. The contents of much of these marketing materials often will make both the client and the planner look horrible
in front of a judge or jury. It will be very unpleasant to be in front
of a judge with a planner who advertises that his plans are entirely immune from the judgments of U.S. courts. The judge is likely
to disagree and take her disagreement out on the client as well as
the planner.

Even worse is being in front of a jury in a tax case where the
planner put out marketing materials touting "offshore bank secrecy" or the ability to "hide your money from Uncle Sam."
Nevertheless, the books of a number of promoters promising exactly those benefits are still on bookstore shelves. While the reading
may be entertaining, and the first few low-tax years will seem
enjoyable, the clients will not have fun when the Department of
Justice raids the promoters' offices and seizes their client lists.

In litigation, the planners' marketing materials might be the
client's worst enemy. So might a planning memorandum drafted
for the client that describes how assets may be hidden and legitimate creditors defeated. All of these materials potentially can be
used by the court as actual evidence of intent to defraud creditors.

DUTIES OF PLANNER

Many planners do not consider themselves to have any duties to
the client once litigation commences. However, the conscientious
planner must provide immediate assistance to his client. If the
planner will not handle the litigation himself, he must see that the
client retains a competent litigator to handle the case. The planner
must act quickly, keeping in mind that lawsuits, like battles, are
won by fast marching and hard fighting. Often actions can imme-

diately be taken that will deflate or slow a case at its inception, such as a counterclaim or collateral attack.

The planner must also assume that in any case where his asset protection plan is implicated, he will be made a co-defendant with his client. The theories for such a cause of action are easy enough to identify, usually civil conspiracy to fraudulently transfer assets or something similar.

Why would a creditor's attorney bring such an action? The intent is to drive a wedge between the planner and his client and to pressure the debtor to assist the creditor's attorney to locate or recover the assets. Of course, the planner will not want to cooperate with the creditor, at least initially. Between the client and creditor, the planner's loyalty will be clear—until the planner's insurance company gets involved.

What often happens is that the creditor's attorney will sue both the client and the planner. If the planner doesn't cooperate, the creditor may make a favorable settlement offer to the planner but make the offer contingent on the planner helping to locate and recover the assets. The planner's insurance company will look upon this as a great opportunity since it will pay out very little under the planner's policy and the insurance company can stop paying the planner's defense costs. The planner's insurance company can employ a number of tactics to pressure the planner to accept the settlement, from an initial reservation-of-rights letter to a flat-out refusal to honor coverage.

So, the planner is caught between loyalty to the client and the real possibility of losing the benefit of his insurance coverage. The planner's loyalty can quickly shift and the story may suddenly become something like "the client lied to me and failed to disclose significant facts." The planner will then be firmly in the creditor's corner and arguing fraud by the client to try to avoid liability to the client and possible professional sanctions. In practice, sophisticated creditors know that this is what occurs and they seek to exploit these situations.

On the other hand, the client has a few tactics of her own to keep the planner's loyalty. The first tactic is to threaten to sue the planner for malpractice if he cooperates with the creditor. The client may even threaten to assign any claim against the planner for malpractice to the creditor in partial settlement of the underlying judgment. Of course, a creditor would prefer to chase a profession-al who is flush with assets, and probably has insurance that will pay something too, rather than to chase the debtor and to have to try to breach the asset protection plan directly.

Second, if the planner is an attorney, the client can file a com-plaint with the state bar and seek intervention by the bar. The fail-ure to support a client in litigating arising from a plan designed by an attorney probably is a breach of the attorney's continuing duties to the client. To abandon a client in his moment of need may result in professional sanction. This may serve to give the planner some backbone.

The planner also has some remedies against the planner's insurance carrier. One is to hire an attorney who specializes in bad-faith litigation to put the insurance carrier on notice that the client objects to its interference with the professional relationship between the planner and the client. A lawsuit can also be filed against the insurance company seeking to force it to fulfill its oblig-ations under the planner's policy. The client may also be able to sue the insurance company for intentional interference with her con-tractual relationship with the attorney.

Creditors also may attempt to pressure a planner by filing pro-fessional complaints against the planner. Typically, bar counsel will realize that these complaints are made by the creditor only to attempt to gain leverage in litigation. They will ignore them in all but the most egregious cases. Nonetheless, the bar has an interest in preventing ongoing fraud. If the creditor's attorney can convince bar counsel that there is an ongoing fraud to conceal or protect assets, the bar may begin immediate interim action to suspend the planner's license.

At this point, the planner really has to ask himself whether continuing to assist the client is worth risking his professional license in a battle. If that answer is "no," then the planner really never had the stomach for this sort of planning in the first place and should have stayed in more comfortable planning niches. The reason is very simple: Asset protection planners are planning for worst-case scenarios by their clients; therefore, they must be pre-pared to defend their clients and their planning to the fullest when the worst-case litigation does arise. This situation is very different from most business and estate planning practices, where litigation is relatively rare and not nearly as vicious.

THINKING OUTSIDE THE BOX VERSUS BEING CAUGHT OUTSIDE THE BOX

Asset protection litigation can be much different than ordinary litigation. The reason is that a smart creditor can sometimes ignore ordinary rules within which other litigants must stay. Why? Because most of the time any penalty that a creditor would pay is monetary, meaning that the creditor can just offset the penalty against the judgment.

For example, let's say a creditor has a judgment for $1 million. The debtor has stashed the money in a Belize bank account. So, the creditor hires someone who goes to the bank, impersonates the debtor, and convinces the bank to wire-transfer $1 million to the creditor's account. If the debtor sues, the odds of the debtor getting any real relief are low, since the $1 million was owed to the creditor anyway.

The point is that because the creditor has a judgment, the creditor doesn't have to care about whether the creditor harms the debtor or not, so long as any monetary harm the creditor causes is less than the amount of the judgment. At worst, the creditor simply will be able to set off that harm against the existing debt and there will be nothing the debtor can do about it.

Most asset protection planners don't realize this important fact: Creditors are not bound by Marquis of Queensbury rules, and to sophisticated creditors it may mean nothing to financially harm the debtor so long as the debt exceeds the harm done. This often makes asset protection litigation particularly nasty and is another reason why it isn't for the faint of heart.

Creditors generally consider law enforcement agencies to be their friends. A creditor chasing offshore assets may try to get U.S. law enforcement interested in the transfers that took place or in whether offshore accounts and entities were reported to the IRS. There is a definite tendency of law enforcement agents to view all offshore activity as inherently suspicious, without discriminating as to the subtleties of purpose. A creditor would have no difficulty persuading the IRS, the FBI, and the local U.S. attorney to start poking around in the affairs of the debtor and the planner in regard to offshore accounts and financial activity. This is a can't-lose situation for the creditor, who has the opportunity for these agencies to provide free discovery of offshore assets.

A rare, but occasionally relevant, practical problem involves extrajudicial remedies—vigilante justice. These situations arise where something very bad has happened, and the aggrieved party will not go away without some sort or redress or revenge, regardless of what the courts say. While this vengeance can include the ultimate sanction of terminating the wrongdoer, some extrajudicial remedies may be employed in a less drastic fashion. Some creditors believe that having a judgment in their favor means that they can act without fear of retribution.

Recall our earlier example where the creditor impersonates the debtor and has money wired from the debtor's offshore bank to the creditor's account? Has the creditor broken any U.S. laws? Probably not. Even if the creditor has broken a law, it is unlikely that a U.S. attorney would prosecute the creditor under such circumstances. Has the creditor broken Belize law by impersonating the debtor? Probably, but the local U.S. attorney or district attorney is not going to care much about what happened in Belize. It is also unlikely that Belize law enforcement authorities would attempt to remedy the situation in the United States.

The point of all this is that most asset protection planners think they are getting one step ahead of creditors by "thinking outside the box." These planners are assuming that creditors will not begin thinking outside the box, to come up with innovative and underhanded ways to recover assets or to get revenge against the debtor.

A party must have the will to fight to the end—the very end. This is the only way good settlements are won. A client who conveys a desire to settle to a creditor may never arrive at a good settlement, because the creditor will always want more. Conversely, the client who makes it known that he is willing to fight to the end has a much better chance of obtaining a reasonable settlement, since creditors really just want money and don't want to waste time litigating. On the other hand, being prepared and having the will to litigate to the end is much different than being so foolhardy as to pass up a good settlement offer if it arises. Fighting to the end may mean threatening or filing a bankruptcy action, the ramifications of which are discussed in the Chapter 6.

Fraudulent Transfer and Bankruptcy Considerations

Although planners place great emphasis on the structures that are used in asset protection planning, the method of transferring wealth to a structure is probably more important than the structure itself. If the transfer cannot be challenged as a fraudulent transfer or a preferential transfer, then it may be very difficult for the creditor to attack the structure. By contrast, if a court deems a transfer to be fraudulent or preferential, then the assets may be backed out of a structure even if the structure itself is otherwise impenetrable. Worse, as we shall see, if the transfer is fraudulent or preferential, the debtor, along with his or her planner, risks charges of contempt, bankruptcy fraud, and civil conspiracy. Thus, the effect of a bad transfer can be to put the debtor in a much worse situation than if he or she had done nothing at all.

All forms of transferring assets have something in common: Whether or not they will later hold up in court is primarily a function of the fraudulent transfer laws and federal bankruptcy laws. Yet, the manner in which asset protection planning interrelates with these laws is poorly understood and fraught with misconceptions. The authors are all too often called upon to fix asset protection plans that are defective because the planner involved lacked a thorough understanding of how fraudulent transfers and preferences are determined and what remedies were available to creditors. This area of the law provides creditors with the most effective tools to slice through defective asset protection plans and should be considered in some depth.

A *fraudulent transfer* (also known as a *fraudulent conveyance*) is a transfer in derogation of the rights of a creditor to satisfy his judgment against the assets of the debtor. For example, a debtor who "sells" everything to his brother for a dollar will likely see the transfer challenged as fraudulent. If a court determines that the transaction was designed to defeat creditors, either because the debtor was made insolvent by the transfer or because the debtor actually intended to defraud his creditors, the court will set aside the transaction. It will then order the person holding the assets (the *transferee*) to give them back to the transferor to be available to the creditor or simply to give them to the creditor directly.

THE UNIFORM FRAUDULENT TRANSFERS ACT (UFTA)

The *Uniform Fraudulent Transfers Act (UFTA)* is a statute that sets forth the fraudulent transfer laws of most states. (Those states that have not yet adopted the UFTA have similar legislation.) It allows a creditor of a transferor to challenge the transfer of assets to a transferee and, if successful, the creditor can reach the assets to satisfy its claim. Understanding how the UFTA defines *transfer*, *assets*, *debtor*, and *creditor* is important.

Anyone with a right to payment, even if contingent or disputed, is a *creditor* under the UFTA. The UFTA applies to existing and future creditors. A creditor does not have to prove that its claim existed at the time of the transfer in order to challenge a debtor's transfer as fraudulent. Similarly, anyone with a liability, even if contingent or disputed, is a *debtor* under the UFTA. A common misconception is that a transfer made while no claims are pending can never be a fraudulent transfer. To the contrary, UFTA has specific rules for when claims arise after a transfer has occurred.

The UFTA addresses *transfers*, defined to include every means of parting with an asset, including granting another creditor a lien (for example, a mortgage) in an asset or losing an asset in a foreclosure proceeding. An *asset* simply is anything that can be owned, but it does not include property encumbered by a valid lien, exempt property, and property held in a tenancy by the entireties (if not otherwise subject to the creditor's claim).

So nearly anyone can be a creditor, anything can be an asset, and every means of giving up total control over anything can be a transfer. So, how is a fraudulent transfer challenge analyzed? The critical factors in a UFTA analysis are timing, solvency, value, and intent.

The UFTA has a general limitations period of four years from the date of a transfer within which a creditor seeking to challenge the transfer must file a claim. A few states have shorter or longer periods, but the great majority uses a four-year statute of limitations. Thus, if more than four years have passed from the time a transfer was made, such a transfer usually will be safe. In that situation, timing is the sole determining factor.

In some cases, the UFTA provides for a limitations period of one year from when the transfer should have been discovered by the creditor, which applies to transactions involving insiders. Additionally, other special state laws regarding the timing of conversions of so-called *nonexempt assets* to *exempt assets* may be relevant. For example, in Texas, the limitations period for challenging conversions of nonexempt assets (such as cash) to exempt assets (such as a homestead) is two years. Exempt assets are discussed in great detail in Chapter 9. Lest the issue of timing seem a simple one, note that a few state courts have held that the limitations period under the UFTA does not even being to run until the creditor has obtained the underlying judgment.

Assuming the creditor challenges the transfer within the applicable limitations period, the transaction will then be scrutinized under the three remaining factors: solvency, value, and intent. As we will discuss later, *solvency* is determined by a balance-sheet test that simply adds up all the debtor's nonexempt assets and subtracts all of the debtor's liabilities, which liabilities include the creditor's claim even if it was unknown to the debtor at the time of the transfer. If the debtor was insolvent when the transfer was made, or if the transfer caused the debtor to be insolvent, the transfer will likely be deemed fraudulent, irrespective of the intent of the debtor in making the transfer.

The next element to examine is the *value* that the debtor received in exchange for the asset that was transferred. Value may also figure in the solvency element in the overall analysis of fraudulent transfers. Such transfers are sometimes called *constructive fraudulent transfers*, as opposed to actual fraudulent transfers.

The key to avoiding a constructive fraud claim is simply to ensure that *reasonably equivalent value* is received in exchange for any transfer. When a debtor is insolvent, a gift will always be a constructive fraudulent transfer under the constructive fraud theory. Thus, gifts must be ruled out as a method of transfer if either the debtor is insolvent or the gift will cause the debtor to be insolvent.

The UFTA does not define reasonably equivalent value, but many court cases have interpreted this phrase to mean basically what it says. Some courts have required nearly the full fair market value of an asset to be received by the debtor in order for the transfer to be found nonfraudulent. Other courts have blessed transfers as nonfraudulent when only half of the fair market value of the transferred asset was received by the debtor. The conservative route is to try to make all transfers for full fair market value.

Returning to the issue of insolvency, the UFTA deems a debtor insolvent if her debts exceed her nonexempt assets, at a fair valuation. On a balance sheet for UFTA solvency purposes, a debtor must include all of her liabilities but usually cannot include exempt assets or assets that the debtor has improperly tried to transfer, conceal, or remove to avoid creditors. An important reason to maintain insurance is that the face amounts of liability insurance policies are normally included as assets in a UFTA solvency analysis if the policy proceeds would be available to pay the creditor's claim.

Alternatively, a debtor is insolvent for UFTA purposes if he cannot pay his debts as they come due. This test takes into account the debtor's liquidity and cash flow. A good rule-of-thumb test is to calculate the ratio of current assets to current liabilities. Current assets would include assets that are currently liquid or expected to be liquid within the next year. They would include cash, receivables (including any reasonably anticipated self-employment income, salary, and bonuses), publicly traded securities, and prepaid expenses (such as insurance). Current liabilities are those that are to be paid within the next year such as a year's worth of mortgage payments. The more the ratio exceeds 1 to 1, the better. Even if a debtor is insolvent under the balance sheet test, a court may find him solvent if he passes the cashflow test.

Note that concepts of *intent* do not play a role in the solvency analysis. It simply doesn't matter if the debtor made the transfer in the utmost good faith if the transfer still had the effect of rendering him insolvent or unable to pay debts as they came due. Concepts of solvency are so important in asset protection planning that many planners require their clients to provide a sworn affidavit of solvency that memorializes their assets and liabilities on the date of a transfer so that contemporaneous proof of solvency is established.

BADGES OF FRAUD

If a claim is made within the limitations period and the debtor was solvent, or was insolvent but received reasonably equivalent value, the final battle will be fought over the issue of intent. The UFTA takes into consideration that debtors and debtors' planners are smart, and are likely to fabricate sophisticated stories to avoid an asset being seized. The UFTA also takes into consideration that it is unlikely that a debtor will confess to having made a fraudulent transfer. Thus, the UFTA allows for what amounts to a "smell" test: If the transfer "smells bad," the court can set aside the transfer if the court can point to certain circumstances that indicate a bad intent by the debtor. These circumstances are known as the *badges of fraud* and date back over 400 years in the case law. Over the years, the courts have identified literally dozens of circumstances as badges of fraud, including these most common ones:

- Was the debtor insolvent at the time of the transfer or soon afterward?
- Did the debtor know or suspect that a claim existed?
- Was reasonably equivalent consideration received by the debtor for the transfer?
- Was the transfer concealed from creditors?
- Had the debtor recently incurred a substantial debt?
- Was the transfer of all or most of the debtor's assets?
- Was the transfer directly or indirectly to an insider?

The weight to be given to any of any of these factors depends on the given case. A single factor might be enough to sustain the finding of a fraudulent transfer in some rare cases, while the existence of several factors in other cases might not be enough. The trial judge is given tremendous discretion in choosing which factors to consider, and what weight to give to each. Indeed, the intent test is often a results-oriented test, where the trial judge makes a determination on how the transfer "smells" to him, and then he looks for the badges of fraud to justify his decision. From the debtor's standpoint, the goal is thus to fashion transfers that are justified by legitimate economic reasons and that do not hint of a transaction meant to hinder creditors.

FEDERAL AND STATE BANKRUPTCY LAWS

Federal bankruptcy law has its own set of fraudulent transfer laws that meshes closely with the UFTA and actually generally incorporates the UFTA (by allowing bankruptcy courts to apply state law with regard to fraudulent transfers) with some special additions. Most importantly, under federal bankruptcy law, there is a one-year window prior to a bankruptcy filing during which any transfers made will receive special scrutiny. Any debts incurred within that one year that involve an actual fraudulent transfer will not be discharged in bankruptcy, often including transfers that convert nonexempt assets into exempt assets.

In theory, bankruptcy courts can go back in time nearly without limit to undo fraudulent transfers, but in practice bankruptcy courts rarely look back beyond a one-year period for potentially fraudulent transfers under the Bankruptcy Code or beyond a four-year period for potentially fraudulent transfers under the UFTA.

Federal bankruptcy law also automatically invalidates so-called *preferential transfers* (regardless of intent) to insiders within one year of filing, and to noninsiders within ninety days of filing. Thus, any transfer within these time windows can be automatically invalidated and the transferee can be forced to reverse the transfer. In practice, many such transfers may not be invalidated if equivalent consideration was received and is readily available to creditors. However, conversions of nonexempt assets to exempt assets and other debtor-favored transfers (such as transfers in exchange for partnership or limited liability company interests, discussed in Chapter 19) should be expected to be invalidated.

Bankruptcy can be thought of as the "neutron bomb" of asset protection planning and creditor remedies. The assets are left standing and owned by someone, but a lot of mutual destruction usually occurs to force the resolution of the debt standoff. Nevertheless, a debtor may choose bankruptcy or a creditor may force a debtor into bankruptcy. Therefore, it is important that asset protection planners have a basic understanding of bankruptcy law and planning tactics.

Asset protection planning usually contemplates that if the debtor is compelled to file for bankruptcy, it will be a total liquidation of the debtor's assets under Chapter 7 and the liquidation proceeds will be used to pay for the costs of the bankruptcy proceeding and to pay the debtor's debts owed to his creditors. Most debts that are not paid from the proceeds are eliminated ("discharged"). Some debts, however, cannot be discharged, including the following:

- Certain taxes under certain circumstances
- Debts arising from the debtor's fraud, embezzlement, larceny, or willful or malicious injury caused to another
- Debts that are not listed in the bankruptcy petition
- Alimony, support or maintenance, and educational loans
- Fines, penalties, criminal restitution, and death or personal injury caused by the debtor while intoxicated
- Debts for purchases of more than $1000 in luxury goods or services (or loans of more than $1000 on an open-end credit plan) from a single creditor within sixty days of filing for bankruptcy

A bankruptcy filing (under any chapter of the Bankruptcy Code, whether initiated by a debtor or a creditor) causes an automatic stay of any collection efforts by creditors. However, a creditor can request that the automatic stay be lifted with respect to it if foreclosure or repossession is certain. (So, this generally only applies to secured creditors.) This stay can be a valuable weapon in the debtor's asset protection arsenal, but it should be wielded with caution. Bankruptcy effectively eliminates much of the bargaining power on both sides, not just the creditor's side. Indeed, the debtor may end up attempting to negotiate with a bankruptcy trustee who is not as flexible as the creditors might have been outside of the bankruptcy setting.

Federal bankruptcy law, state law, or both provide that certain assets are exempt from this liquidation, as discussed below. The Chapter 7 bankrupt debtor typically retains these types of assets and continues paying on the loan. Unsecured creditors usually are left holding the bag once exempt assets and encumbered assets are removed from the pool of assets to be liquidated. As a result, unsecured debts generally are the ones that are discharged in bankruptcy.

All assets earned and received after the commencement of a Chapter 7 proceeding are excluded from the proceeding and are not required to be liquidated or otherwise used to pay debts involved in the proceeding, other than the following:

- Property received through inheritance
- Property received as a result of a divorce decree settlement
- Life insurance or other death benefits

These assets are brought into play if they are received during the proceeding or within six months of the final discharge.

Little that can be done to plan the timing of life insurance payments. However, other timing and planning opportunities may arise. For example, if a debtor anticipates a significant inheritance, prudence might dictate that he commence a Chapter 7 action quickly so that the inheritance would be received some time beyond the six months after discharge.

WHAT IS "ACCEPTABLE" PREBANKRUPTCY PLANNING?

The most common form of prebankruptcy planning is to maximize the use of a debtor's property exemptions. This type of planning is sanctioned by the legislative history of Section 522 of the Bankruptcy Code, which provides that the debtor will be permitted to convert nonexempt property into exempt property before filing a bankruptcy petition. The practice is not fraudulent as to creditors, and permits the debtor to make full use of the exemptions to which she is entitled under the law.

Defining the line between acceptable prebankruptcy planning and fraudulent prebankruptcy planning is often difficult. As long as such planning is not done to avoid a particular debt, however, prebankruptcy planning is usually accepted by the courts. The most common form of prebankruptcy planning involves converting cash to home equity (by paying down mortgages) in states that give substantial protection to homestead. Such strategies are not without their limitations, such as residency requirements. For federal bankruptcy purposes, residency is determined as of six months prior to filing. Thus, in order to use more generous exemptions than otherwise might be provided under the law of a debtor's current residence, he would have to move to the new, more generous state more than six months prior to filing.

PROPOSED BANKRUPTCY REFORM LEGISLATION

Pressure from creditor lobbies has led Congress to take up bankruptcy reform a number of times in the last several years. A major reform bill nearly passed in 2002, but was killed by political squabbling over minor provisions with little practical import.

Although nothing has happened as of the date of publication of this book, you need to be aware of what may be coming. The most recent bill, which nearly made it into law, included the following changes (among others) that would have had a major impact on the asset protection implications of bankruptcy:

- Debtors would be forced to file under Chapter 13, rather than Chapter 7, if the debtor would have at least $100 of disposable income available each month. In addition, the current three-year period for Chapter 13 repayment plans would be eliminated and only a five-year period would be available.
- The residency requirement that must be met to claim a state's exemptions would be increased from the current six months to two years. Of course, this would make it much more difficult to plan a move to Florida before bankruptcy in order to take advantage of Florida's incredibly debtor-friendly exemptions.

- State homestead exemptions would be capped at $100,000 for bankruptcy purposes.
- The retirement plan exemption would be extended to all retirement plans and IRAs.

CRIMINAL ISSUES IN BANKRUPTCY

An important problem with a bankruptcy filing, or being forced into bankruptcy, is that the matter has the potential to instantly go from a mere debtor-creditor case to one with federal criminal implications where a misstep or misstatement could result in a felony perjury or bankruptcy fraud conviction. Specifically, Section 152 of the Bankruptcy Code provides for fines, imprisonment, or both for any person who in connection with a bankruptcy action does any of the following:

- Knowingly and fraudulently conceals any property belonging to the estate of a debtor
- Knowingly and fraudulently receives any material amount of property from a debtor after the commencement of a bankruptcy action with the intent to defeat the provisions of the Bankruptcy Code
- In a personal capacity or as an officer of an entity, in contemplation of a bankruptcy case by or against the person or entity, or with the intent to defeat the provisions of the Bankruptcy Code, knowingly and fraudulently transfers or conceals any of his property or the property of such other person or entity

Note that Section 152 reaches "any person ... in connection with a bankruptcy action." This clearly could include the debtor's attorney or other persons involved (for example, family members) in a transfer. Also, note that if a debtor is found to have made a fraudulent transfer under Section 548, there is a violation of Section 152, although such cases are rarely prosecuted absent a showing of egregious facts.

Furthermore, a bankruptcy court has the power to imprison a debtor for contempt of court when the debtor fails to comply with an order of the court compelling the debtor to turn over assets to the court. At this point, the debtor must either turn over the assets or show conclusively that, after making all reasonable good-faith efforts, turning over the assets is an impossibility, and one that was not self-created.

Case Study: In re Stephen Jay Lawrence—Out of the Frying Pan and into the Fire

In January 1991, Stephen J. Lawrence settled an offshore trust in Jersey (a British Crown Dependency in the English Channel off the northwest coast of France), with an estimated value of $7 million. Two months later, a forty-two-month arbitration dispute with broker Bear Sterns resulted in a $20.4 million award in favor of Bear Stearns against Lawrence.

According to the trust instrument, Lawrence had the sole power to appoint trustees. Over time, several amendments were made to the trust. In February 1991, a spendthrift provision was added and the governing law of the trust was changed to the Republic of Mauritius, an island nation located some 450 miles off the coast of Madagascar. In January 1993, the trust was amended so that settlor's powers could not be executed under duress or coercion and his life interest would terminate in the event of his bankruptcy. In March 1995, an amendment was added declaring Lawrence to be an "excluded person" under the trust, thus proscribing his ever becoming a beneficiary of the trust. Finally, in 1999, the trustees issued a Declaration of Intent, stating that the excluded-person status was irrevocable.

In June 1997, Lawrence filed a voluntary Chapter 7 bankruptcy petition. The bankruptcy trustee objected to Lawrence's discharge. During that proceeding, a discovery dispute arose over the sufficiency of Lawrence's answers to interrogatories, which the court found to be incomplete and evasive. In granting the trustee's motion to compel, the court ordered Lawrence to appear at an evidentiary hearing at which the trustee would have an immediate, supervised opportunity to obtain responsive answers from Lawrence. After the hearing in July 1998, the court issued a default judgment, deeming the facts alleged in the trustee's complaint established. Furthermore, it found that the rights and obligations of the trust were governed by Florida law, not Mauritius law as chosen by the trust documents, and that the trust was property of the estate.

Several months later, the court further found that Lawrence had control over the trust, through his retained powers to remove and appoint trustees and to add and exclude beneficiaries, and it rejected Lawrence's impossibility defense. It then held Lawrence in contempt for failing to turn over the trust assets. Lawrence declined to comply, and in October 1999 the bankruptcy court ordered his incarceration, pending compliance, and also fined Lawrence $10,000 per day until he purged his contempt. In July 2000, the district court affirmed both the turnover order and the contempt orders. Lawrence appealed.

Lawrence claimed that in September 1999, he executed a document naming the bankruptcy trustee as trustee of the trust and advised the previous trustees of this action. He insisted that this is the limit of his power to turn over the assets of the trust to the bankruptcy trustee.

Lawrence claimed that he did all that he has the power to do by attempting to appoint the bankruptcy trustee as the new trustee. He insisted that the fact that this attempt was met with silence (presumably due to the duress provision in the trust instrument) was beyond his control. This contention was not persuasive to the appeals court for several reasons. In order to prevail on an impossibility defense, Lawrence must have demonstrated that he had made "in good faith all reasonable efforts" to meet the terms of the court order he was attempting to avoid. The Eleventh Circuit agreed with the district court that Lawrence's last-minute appointment of the bankruptcy trustee as trustee did not meet the requirement of "all reasonable efforts," nor did any of Lawrence's actions appear to the court to have been made in "good faith." He had to be aware that his attempted appointment would be ignored by the trustees under the duress clause. Furthermore, the district court simply did not believe Lawrence's testimony that he retained no control over the trust and that he had not maintained communication with the trustees. The Eleventh Circuit found no support in the record to warrant a rejection of that credibility determination.

Furthermore, the Eleventh Circuit found that Lawrence's claimed defense was invalid because the asserted impossibility was self-created. Because Lawrence himself was responsible for his inability to comply, impossibility is not a defense to contempt. Lawrence argued that his impossibility was distinguishable from other cases that found that self-created impossibility is not a defense. It was, he claimed, because his actions, if any, creating the impossibility occurred prior to the contempt action. The appeals court dismissed this argument summarily, finding that Lawrence created the trust in an obvious attempt to shelter his funds from an expected adverse arbitration award. In addition, at the time Lawrence became an excluded person under the trust he retained the ability to appoint a new trustee who would have the power to revoke the excluded-person status at any time.

Note that Lawrence essentially removed most of his settlement leverage in the case by transferring his assets to an offshore trust over which he may or may not have control. He could have pursued more comprehensive planning options like exemption planning, homestead (after all, he lived in Florida), life insurance, and annuities. Had he done so, Lawrence might have by now have settled the claim without resorting to bankruptcy and keeping most of the value of his assets.

The following chapter examines the allure of offshore planning that caused Lawrence to ignore common sense and to overlook the more fundamental and effective planning techniques that were available to him.

Offshore Planning

Asset protection is commonly associated with offshore planning, such as forming an asset protection trust in the Cook Islands. Indeed, a number of small countries make a business out of catering to the needs of judgment debtors and those who worry that they may be judgment debtors someday. Not coincidentally, these debtor havens are also tax havens. A few small, wealthy countries, such as Switzerland and Luxembourg, compete for asset protection business with the smaller, poorer countries of the Caribbean (for example, Anguilla, St. Kitts and Nevis, and the Bahamas) and of the Pacific (for example, the Cook Islands, Vanuatu, Nauru, and the Marshall Islands). Likewise, they also compete with various self-governing British protectorates and colonies scattered throughout the world (for example, Bermuda, the Cayman Islands, the British Virgin Islands, the Channel Islands, Gibraltar, and the Isle of Man).

As a practical matter, all of these jurisdictions offer essentially the same thing: U.S. judgments are not easily enforced, if at all, in their courts. This means that actions to recover assets in these jurisdictions usually must be started anew in those jurisdictions, despite the fact that the creditor already has a judgment in the United States. These jurisdictions have also padded their laws with debtor-friendly provisions, such as shortened statutes of limitations and very restricted fraudulent transfer laws. Additionally, these jurisdictions usually have strict confidentiality laws that prohibit, as a crime, a bank, trust company, or other financial institution from divulging information about its clients without an order from a court in that jurisdiction.

The goal of these jurisdictions is to be as debtor-friendly as possible in order to attract asset protection business. Indeed, these jurisdictions run a perpetual race to stay in front of one another in the competition for "the best laws." New amendments to the trust laws of the Cook Islands are matched by Nevis. Changes to the International Business Companies (IBCs) acts of the British Virgin Islands are met by the adoption of even broader changes to IBC legislation in St. Vincent. And so it goes, ad infinitum.

Similarly, the courts of these jurisdictions are typically debtor-friendly and routinely reach decisions that prevent creditors from reaching assets even in the most egregious situations involving securities fraud and consumer fraud. After all, it would be very bad for business if a court of one of these jurisdictions were to issue a judgment in favor of an onshore creditor in all but the rarest of occasions.

Just as offshore courts do not respect U.S. laws and the judgments of U.S. courts, neither do U.S. courts have to respect the laws of these debtor havens or the judgments of their courts. So long as a U.S. court has jurisdiction over the physical person of a debtor and can throw her in jail for contempt, it can order the debtor to bring back ("repatriate") her assets from the debtor havens to satisfy a creditor's judgment. This means that for offshore planning to work by the mere fact that the debtor's assets are offshore, the debtor must physically remove herself from the reach of the U.S. courts as well. While this solution might work for some, it is an entirely unworkable solution for a most of us, none of whom want to leave our families, careers, and comforts behind in the United States while running from a judgment offshore.

Good asset protection planning will take advantage of some of the features of the debtor havens without going so far as to expose the owner of the assets to the creditor's remedy of a repatriation order or contempt of court.

The strength of the offshore havens is that persons and things that are physically located there are not subject to the judgments or orders of U.S. courts. State courts must respect one another's judgments under the Full Faith and Credit Clause of the U.S. Constitution, and those of federal courts under the Supremacy Clause. Of course, offshore havens are not bound by the U.S.

Constitution and consequently they couldn't care less about judgments of U.S. courts. In fact, offshore courts seem to take great satisfaction in repudiating the attempts of U.S. courts to indirectly assert their judgments in the offshore haven.

But U.S. judgments are not the only things that offshore courts ignore. The offshore courts also ignore the discovery orders of U.S. courts. A subpoena issued to an offshore trust company may go unanswered, and the U.S. court is usually powerless to do anything about it. Only if the foreign entity has a U.S. branch against which a remedy can be fashioned will a U.S. court have a chance of seeing its order fulfilled.[1]

From a creditor's standpoint, this means that evidence will be, at best, very difficult to obtain (at least legally) in the offshore haven. Thus, a creditor may be denied a key witness to testify to certain issues regarding aspects of a transaction, or a party may destroy documents or simply refuse to produce them. Even where discovery is allowed (almost always meaning the debtor has consented to discovery), the discovery process in offshore havens is very time consuming and expensive. For example, a creditor seeking to take a deposition might have to fly a U.S. court reporter to the offshore haven.

A similar problem facing creditors is the difficulty in having a U.S. court assert jurisdiction over an offshore person or entity. This is important where the offshore person or entity may be deemed a *necessary party* to the lawsuit—that is, the lawsuit cannot go forward unless that party is brought into the case. If no basis for asserting jurisdiction can be found—or if service of process upon that party is impossible—the creditor may be stymied.

A popular use of offshore entities is as a manager or general partner for U.S. limited liability companies and limited partnerships. Even if a judgment creditor is able to obtain a charging order against the debtor's interest, the creditor will simply not be able to compel the offshore manager or general partner to make a distribution without extended litigation abroad.

OFFSHORE PLANNING AND CONFLICTS OF LAWS

Asset protection planning often seeks to take advantage of conflict-of-laws issues. (For example, what might be a fraudulent transfer in California might not be one in Florida.) Because the debtor havens have very debtor-friendly laws, planners naturally seek to import those laws to resolve debtor-creditor disputes in the United States. The mere presence of conflict-of-laws issues will create uncertainty for the creditor and promote settlement on terms more favorable to the debtor.

Some foreign laws will be respected, but other laws will be void for public policy reasons. The key is usually whether the U.S. jurisdiction where the court action is taking place has the same or similar laws as the offshore jurisdictions. For instance, because Texas has a Limited Liability Company Act, it is reasonable to expect that a Nevis LLC and the Nevis LLC Ordinance will be respected in Texas. In contrast, self-settled spendthrift trusts (for more on these, see Chapters 13 and 14)—asset protection trusts— are common in the offshore tax haven jurisdictions, but their protections for their creators are void as a matter of public policy in most U.S. states. However, in a state such as Nevada that respects self-settled spendthrift trusts and has specific legislation allowing such vehicles, offshore self-settled spendthrift trusts likely would be respected.

In other words, where the state and the offshore jurisdiction share similar legislation, the offshore entity itself should be respected. But the state court might not be as able to fashion a remedy where an offshore entity is involved as it might where a domestic entity is involved. For example, a court might order a domestic entity dissolved so that a creditor can reach the entity's assets, whereas the court would not have the power to enforce such an order with respect to a foreign entity.

Asset protection planners frequently attempt to import law into transactions, by using clauses that require that issues arising from the transaction be determined by reference to the debtor-friendly laws of the offshore havens, by the shortened statutes of limitations, or by requirements that the matter be litigated in the offshore haven. Not surprisingly, U.S. courts balk at importing such laws, especially where they were not required by the economics of the transactions, and especially where the creditor was not a party to the transaction at issue.

A recent development in asset protection planning is the use of entities in foreign countries that have similar laws to that of the

United States but that are not considered debtor havens. One example is the United Kingdom and its Limited Liability Partnership Act, described in Chapter 21. Since much U.S. law is derived from longstanding English law, a creditor would probably have difficulty contending that U.K. law, as a whole, is tainted in the same way that a court might view the laws of a Caribbean tax and debtor's haven as being tainted.

THE PERILS OF UNREPORTED OFFSHORE ACCOUNTS

Many people believe that the laws of offshore havens are so debtor-friendly that the mere use of a bank or securities account offshore will protect assets in such an account from creditors. If such assets are reported to the IRS (as required by law of U.S. taxpayers), this leaves a paper trail easily discoverable by creditors. Choosing not to report to the IRS simply is not an option. The failure to report offshore assets and income is punishable by severe fines and, in some cases, imprisonment. In cases that the IRS and the Justice Department choose to prosecute criminally, federal sentencing guidelines require judges to impose substantial prison sentences for tax evasion. The federal judge may even be required to enhance the sentence under the guidelines, adding more prison time due to the use of offshore transactions.

Furthermore, hiding accounts from the IRS is just a poor asset protection strategy. Ultimately, someone knows about the account; whether it is the offshore banker, trustee, or investment advisor. That person may be required to divulge account information if the secrecy laws of the debtor havens change or if they enter into tax information–sharing treaties with the United States. That person also may divulge the information negligently or maliciously, or may use the information to extort money from the noncompliant U.S. depositor. Indeed, many U.S. victims who have had their offshore funds embezzled simply are not willing to report the crime to anyone for fear that an investigation will lead to a tax fraud investigation as well. Offshore criminals know this, and it is one of the reasons why the potential for embezzlement of funds is a very real and serious problem for those attempting to hide money abroad.

In the late 1990s, a number of offshore banks and trust companies pitched the use of secret offshore accounts with access by offshore debit or credit card. This arrangement allowed funds—and otherwise taxable income earned on those funds—to be used by account holders in the United States without funds actually having to be transferred from an offshore bank to a U.S. bank. However, the IRS quickly became aware of the potential for abuse. In 2001, the IRS subpoenaed thousands of credit card records and began matching the credit cards and their users with offshore accounts. Recently enacted tax information–sharing treaties—forced on offshore havens under threat of economic retaliation—compelled offshore banks to cooperate with the IRS in U.S. tax investigations. A substantial number of successful prosecutions have followed. There perhaps is no better example to illustrate that what is a secret by law today may not be a secret tomorrow. Furthermore, tax evaders who tried to use offshore bank secrecy and who have not yet come clean face the prospect of prosecution for the rest of their lives, since there is no statute of limitations for tax fraud in the case of unreported income.

Of course, compliance with the law requires reporting income, foreign accounts, foreign trusts, and foreign entities to the IRS. This reporting creates a paper trail to offshore accounts and activity that is relatively easy for creditors to follow. So, the choice is to gain questionable secrecy protections by committing felony tax fraud or to comply with tax laws but give up any significant secrecy protections. The smart choice is not to rely on offshore secrecy, but instead to structure affairs so that they can withstand challenge even when fully disclosed.

Furthermore, money doesn't just appear in offshore accounts from nowhere. The days of hauling suitcases of cash to Switzerland are over, as banks run scared from anything that possibly could appear to involve money laundering. Funds have to come from somewhere, usually by check or wire transfer, which leaves easily traceable paper and electronic trails. Creditors' attorneys know what to look for in bank statements—one day there is $1 million in an account and the next day it is gone. In a postjudgment debtor's examination, questions about such transactions and about the existence of offshore entities and accounts must be answered honestly. If they are not, the debtor risks jail time for civil contempt of court for a refusal to answer and criminal prosecution on charges of perjury and criminal contempt of court for lying.

Furthermore, if a creditor discovers offshore financial activity that has not been reported to the IRS, the creditor may threaten to reveal the information if the debt is not paid. While this may be criminal extortion, the creditor may do it anyway; a prosecutor will be more interested in securing a tax evasion conviction against the debtor than in pursuing a relatively minor technical prosecution of the creditor who has turned in a tax cheat. Indeed, the only dispute between the prosecutor and the creditor may not be about attempted extortion but about whether the creditor is entitled to a reward for providing information relating to offshore tax evasion.

If offshore planning is to be part of an asset protection plan, it should be done so that, even when full disclosure is made to the IRS, and even if creditors gain access to all of the debtor's tax returns with details of all transactions, the plan will still perplex creditors. In asset protection planning, assume that every piece of paper and every conversation involved will eventually be entered into evidence. In other words, assume that planning that relies to any significant degree on secrecy likely will fail.

REPATRIATION AND CONTEMPT

Upon discovering the existence of offshore assets, whether or not the creditor knows precisely what or where they are, the creditor will next be likely to apply to the court for an order requiring the debtor to repatriate them, that is, bring them back to the United States. If the court issues the order, the debtor has three choices: repatriate the assets, flee the United States, or refuse to comply and, as a result, be held in contempt of court and jailed for an indeterminate time, perhaps years.

A creditor can also attempt to recover assets in the offshore haven. The difficulty in reaching foreign assets is touted as a benefit of offshore planning, and it is one claim that is quite true. However, in particular cases, a creditor may find a technical defect in a trust or company document that will allow the creditor to reach assets. Or a creditor may have success in obtaining a prejudgment asset attachment, known as a *Mareva injunction*, which will freeze the assets pending trial. If a creditor is successful in obtaining a Mareva injunction in an English Commonwealth jurisdiction (including many offshore havens), he has won a significant victory. That's because the injunction may be applied without further hearing in other Commonwealth jurisdictions in which there are assets in which debtor has a beneficial interest.

An aggressive creditor might resort to illegal remedies. After all, the creditor has no offshore assets and cannot be penalized by an offshore court. Some offshore havens are hopelessly corrupt, meaning that a bribe may lead to a result in favor of the creditor in a way not contemplated by local laws. The same is true for poorly paid offshore bank employees, who, for a price, might turn a blind eye to forged wire-transfer instructions, sending funds from a debtor's account to the creditor. If the debtor sues the creditor in the United States or offshore, there will be no real economic effect, because the debtor owed the money to the creditor in any event, and the debtor has suffered no real economic damages.

While, admittedly, the foregoing examples rarely occur, they illustrate an important point: Sophisticated and aggressive creditors are quite capable of devising creative solutions, including solutions that exploit the relative lawlessness of some offshore havens. A judgment creditor can take action that might harm a debtor economically without any significant risk of criminal penalties in the United States (since the acts did not occur within the United States). That creditor also has the ability to set off its judgement against any judgment won by the debtor in a civil action.

For most persons, a little bit of offshore planning can go a long way when it comes to financial accounts. For many clients, a single non-interest-bearing checking account with a balance always less than $10,000 (the limit above which Treasury Department reporting requirements are triggered) will suffice. Such an account probably will go undetected at least until a postjudgment debtor's examination. Essentially, that account is only for use as an emergency repository for funds in a creditor disaster situation, particularly if the debtor finds it necessary to leave the United States permanently.

OFFSHORE BANKING

Small offshore banks with potentially inadequate capital and reserves must be avoided. Some offshore jurisdictions, such as

Grenada, have been plagued by banking scams, such as the First International Bank of Grenada scandal, where con artist Van Brink set up a licensed bank, and then made off with an estimated $200 million of depositors' money. The scam artist even set up a phony "International Deposit Insurance Coporation" (IDIC) to give depositors the impression that the bank's deposits were fully reserved and insured!

Major multinational banks with offshore subsidiaries, on the other hand, are typically very well capitalized and have substantial reserves. In the better offshore jurisdictions, these banks are highly regulated by the local Central Bank or financial services commission, and are probably more fundamentally sound than some U.S. banks, though most offshore jurisdictions do not have any form of depositors' insurance comparable to Federal Depositors Insurance Corporation (FDIC) coverage in the United States. With the exception of high (sometimes exorbitant) fees and often extremely slow service, offshore banking is quite similar to U.S. banking.

Investing offshore, however, is very much different than investing in the highly regulated U.S. markets. Offshore investments are poorly regulated—often unregulated altogether. Due diligence and caveat emptor take on dramatically more important roles. Furthermore, most foreign markets, being smaller, are simply less efficient than U.S. markets. This results in higher trading costs and potentially lower liquidity. Similarly, money management fees and brokerage fees are typically considerably higher than in the highly competitive U.S. market

Novice U.S. investors often assume that offshore investments yield higher and safer returns than domestic investments, although the converse is almost always true. This misperception makes the offshore havens rife with fraud, particularly with regard to Ponzi schemes spinning tales of secret European banking systems and catering to greedy investors by offering "fully guaranteed" returns of 20 percent per month or more.

Offshore investment frauds sometimes assume a pseudolegitimate face. For example, some offshore hedge funds promise low-risk returns via arbitraged investments, but the fund managers are actually siphoning off the fund's assets via investments into companies controlled by their families or associates. The vast majority of regulated offshore investment funds, including hedge funds, are legitimate, but the loose regulatory environment offshore makes offshore investing outside of well-established institutional funds a dangerous hit-or-miss proposition. Offshore investors are wise to heed Will Rogers and to be "not so worried about the return *on* my principal as the return *of* my principal." When anyone is banking or investing offshore, investment safety must be the paramount concern.

Because of such concerns, most offshore asset holding structures are arranged so that assets are owned by an offshore entity, but the assets themselves are invested in the U.S markets. If a creditor cloud appears on the horizon, the offshore entity closes its U.S. accounts and transfers its investments abroad, perhaps into the relatively safe European markets. This arrangement provides relative investment safety while there are no creditor issues; it also provides for flexibility should circumstances change.

A more detailed discussion of the advantages, disadvantages, and frustrating quirkiness of offshore banking is beyond the scope of this book. An excellent resource for more insight into the offshore banking sector is *The Offshore Money Book: How to Move Assets Offshore for Privacy, Protection and Tax Advantage*, by Arnold L. Cornez (McGraw-Hill, 2000).

THE OFFSHORE STIGMA

Throughout this book we discuss various offshore strategies for asset protection. Keep in mind, however, that offshore asset protection has been heavily promoted, so much so that offshore strategies are strongly tainted in the eyes of many U.S. judges. The advertisements of offshore service companies and many aggressive and shortsighted offshore planners in the United States have unabashedly hailed the use of offshore planning to defeat the jurisdiction and power of U.S. courts. In other words, "Up yours, your Honor!" One cannot expect U.S. judges to be pleased with those who thumb their noses at them, and in fact, judges have responded harshly to blatant offshore anticreditor planning.

Because of this stigma, offshore planning should be used judiciously and cautiously. When possible, planners should avoid the more notorious debtor havens, instead using jurisdictions perceived as more legitimate, such as the United Kingdom and New

Zealand, which can give a fair degree of the practical benefits of offshore planning without the negative offshore stigma.

OFFSHORE TAX SCHEMES

Reinvoicing is an offshore tax evasion scheme in which many U.S. businesses have been caught. The concept, heavily promoted by offshore service providers and even some well-credentialed U.S. planners, involves establishing an offshore company in a tax haven. The offshore company submits invoices to the U.S. company for goods and services it supposedly provides to the U.S. company—and it may, in fact, actually provide those services. The U.S. company pays the invoices, sending funds to the offshore company's foreign account, where they disappear from the U.S. tax system. This scheme has been around for decades, and the IRS has strong powers to set aside these schemes. People caught in these schemes are regularly prosecuted for tax evasion.

A similar scheme involves a U.S. professional signing an employment agreement with an employee leasing company domiciled in a country that has a favorable tax treaty with the United States, such as Ireland. The professional's services are then leased back to his or her business in the United States at a rate substantially higher than the salary paid to the professional by the employee leasing company. The difference between the amount paid to the offshore employee leasing company, which is usually close to the total profits of the business (plus the salary paid to the professional by the offshore employee leasing company) is paid into an offshore "retirement" account controlled by the professional. This account purportedly accrues income tax-free to the professional, and is later transferred into another form of tax-free account, such as a Roth IRA, for easy and tax-free access by the professional. The IRS is on to these schemes as well, and those involved in them are now being actively investigated and prosecuted for tax fraud.

However, although arrangements like these fail from a tax perspective, they might still be effective from an asset protection perspective. So long as the U.S. person does not attempt to gain a tax advantage by using these schemes, it will be difficult for all but the most sophisticated creditors to identify and cut through these strategies. The key to success probably will be whether a creditor is able to ascertain that there is really no tax advantage to the arrangement. But keep in mind that the complexities of international taxation are not exactly the strong suit of the average tax attorney, much less the average creditor's attorney.

Judicious, tax-compliant offshore planning can provide significant advantages in asset protection planning. The keys to successful offshore planning include avoiding standardized cookie-cutter schemes, keeping away from heavily marketed strategies, staying clear of investment scams, and investing efficiently.

Certainly, offshore planning is an important part of many asset protection plans. However, it should not be the centerpiece. Effective asset protection planning is based on fundamental methodologies of planning—discussed in the next several chapters—with offshore components used to make those methodologies more effective.

ENDNOTES

1. See, for example, the *U.S. v. Bank of Nova Scotia* case in which the U.S. branch of an offshore bank was subpoenaed by a U.S. federal grand jury in a narcotics case to produce bank records from branches in Antigua, the Bahamas, and the Cayman Islands. The bank refused to turn over the records, citing its secrecy obligations, and it was fined $25,000 per day for noncompliance with the subpoena. Eventually, when the fines had reached over $1.8 million, the bank acquiesced and turned over the records. *U.S. v. Bank of Nova Scotia*, 740 F.2d 817, cert. den. 469 U.S. 1106.

CHAPTER 8

Methodology of Asset Protection

The processes by which an asset protection plan is developed and implemented, can be divided into two basic methodologies: *general methodologies*, which involve concerns common to most strategies, and *implementational methodologies*, which involve specific standalone strategies for protecting specific classes of assets.

An example of a general methodology is temporal methodology, which considers the effect of time in relation to asset protection planning. Time may limit or expand the range of available planning opportunities. Proper timing can significantly enhance a plan's effectiveness. Inappropriate timing can degrade or destroy a plan's effectiveness.

Time has a definite and measurable value in asset protection planning. For example, at some future time, a claim may arise against the client. Until that claim arises, the range of available planning alternatives to the client is broad. However, once a claim has materialized, the range of planning alternatives narrows as time progresses toward judgment and collection. Eventually, when the claim is reduced to judgment, there are scant few planning options. We refer to the decrease in the number of planning options available to the debtor as a claim materializes, is reduced to judgment, and is collected upon as the *time decay* of planning solutions (see Figure 8.1).

Time also impacts the implementation of the asset protection plan (see Figure 8.2). There is no reason to implement every part of an asset protection plan at once. Ideally, an asset protection plan is

FIGURE 8.1

Time decay of solutions.

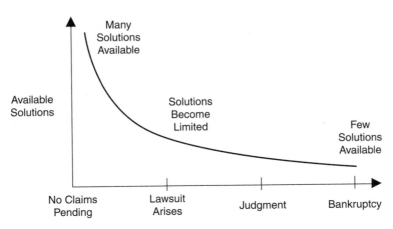

implemented in stages at different times so as not to suggest the existence of a grand scheme. Ideally, implementation occurs at about the same pace at which the client ordinarily conducts business and blends in with ordinary business decisions and transactions. By contrast, the sudden transfer of large amount of funds offshore soon after the client has been notified of a potential lawsuit is certain to generate scrutiny. However, a more subtle switch from domestic to foreign suppliers (perhaps related to the client in some manner) in the client's business operations may generate no scrutiny, even though this action could have the effect of transferring value in a way that is difficult for creditors to challenge or reach.

JURISDICTIONAL METHODOLOGY

Jurisdictional methodology involves importing favorable law into a transaction and exporting assets to more creditor-adverse jurisdictions. The essence of jurisdictional methodology is the manipulation of conflict-of-laws issues to favor the debtor.

The exploiting of conflict-of-laws issues is a core asset protection concept. Document drafting often involves importing favorable law—for example, providing that certain corporate issues will be construed under well-established Delaware law. Doubts that creditors may have about how certain conflict-of-laws issues might

FIGURE 8.2

Timing of implementation.

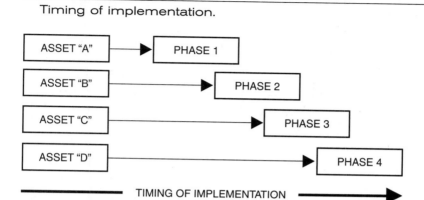

A good asset protection plan is usually spread over time to negate accusations of a "Master Plan" to shield all assets from creditors.

be resolved will strongly affect the psychology of settlement. In deciding whether to settle or go to trial, a creditor must first speculate as to which laws of various possible jurisdictions the court will apply. Second, the creditor must speculate as to whether the creditor will be successful under each of the various combinations of applicable laws the court might choose to apply.

When forming an entity, creating a trust, deciding where to invest or custody assets, or even choosing where to live, the choice of jurisdiction can significantly affect the successfulness of the asset protection plan. However, more often than not, choice of jurisdiction comes down to a simple choice of domestic, foreign (such as Canada or the United Kingdom), or an offshore haven.

The heavy marketing efforts of cookie-cutter asset protection planners and the offshore haven jurisdictions themselves could lead one to think the proper choice of an offshore haven jurisdiction is the crux of asset protection planning. The issue of whether the asset protection plan is a sound one then becomes somewhat of an afterthought. In practice, the choice of jurisdiction should be one of the last decisions made. Most structures can be moved from one jurisdiction to another; thus, assets in entities in more conservative jurisdictions can be moved to more debtor-friendly jurisdictions in times of duress. The soundness of the planning strategies is much more important than where entities and assets are initially located.

Fundamentally sound plans will survive whether assets and entities are initially located in a debtor haven or not.

INTEGRATIONAL METHODOLOGY

Integrational methodology deals with the processes by which asset protection planning is combined with the client's existing businesses and other planning. As we discussed in Chapter 4, one feature of a good asset protection planning is subtlety. This subtlety is most often achieved by integrating asset protection planning with business and estate planning. Indeed, the asset protection plan must be successfully integrated and efficient to work well in the long term. The plan must be something that can be used for other purposes on a regular basis, and not just taken out of storage when a creditor appears. The upkeep of a cumbersome or inefficient plan likely will be terminally ignored, and ultimately it will be ineffective.

Historically, asset protection planning and tax planning have had a symbiotic relationship. Asset protection plans are often said to have been created primarily for tax purposes, and many tax strategies are said to have asset protection as their economic motivation. How the plan is portrayed may depend on whether the case is being argued to the IRS or to a civil judge in a postjudgment collection proceeding.

Integrational methodology goes beyond simply creating a cover story or smokescreen. Integrational methodology involves a detailed analysis of how the client conducts her business and personal life. It involves structures and strategies that economically benefit the client beyond mere asset protection. A good asset protection plan allows the client to focus on the most important parts of her business and personal life. An ideal asset protection plan facilitates and enhances the client's ability to transfer wealth to future generations.

UNBUNDLING AND SEPARATION METHODOLOGY

Unbundling assets is an important asset protection device (see Figures 8.3 to 8.5). *Separation methodology* leverages the dichotomy of *simple assets* versus *complex assets*. Simple assets are those that

FIGURES 8.3

Bundled components of a typical business.

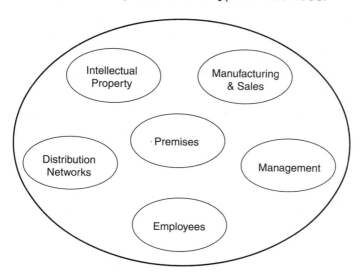

FIGURE 8.4

Separation of low-risk assets from liability-producing assets.

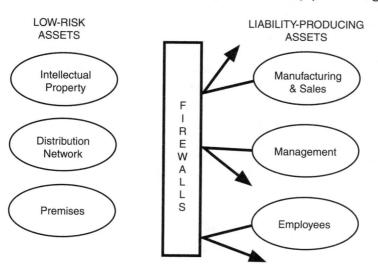

FIGURE 8.5

Unbundling of components.

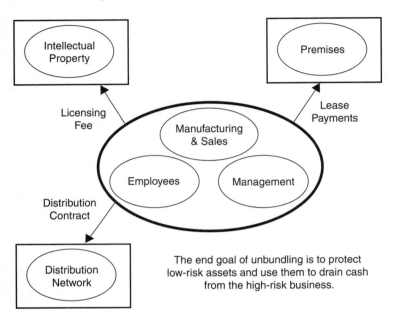

The end goal of unbundling is to protect low-risk assets and use them to drain cash from the high-risk business.

cannot be reduced to further component parts. Cash is a simple asset. So is a royalty stream from a patent.

Complex assets are those that are divisible into component parts. For instance, improved commercial real estate is a complex asset because it has (1) the value of the land itself and (2) rental value. Separation would involve protecting the value of the land separately from the rental value. Businesses have many component assets, including the market value and rental value of real property and equipment, customer contracts, customer lists, patents, copyrights, trademarks, key employees contracts, vendor contracts, and the like. Each of these assets can be valued, monetized, and protected separately. For instance, a business owner might set up an entity to own a customer list and rent it to the operating business. Real property and equipment might be contributed to other entities and leased to the operating business. Trademarks could be housed in another entity and licensed to the operating business. Yet another entity might contract with employees and lease their services to the operating business. Each contract would allow funds to flow from the operating business to each of the separate entities, where those funds are protected from the creditors of the operating business and from the creditors of the other component entities.

Separation methodology involves removing valuable assets from a liability-attracting operating business entity and using leases, rents, and licenses to continually bleed the business of assets. Thus, the operating business never accumulates significant value that could be exposed to creditors. The assets important to overall business success are spread across the component entities, so the value and profits in each entity is minimized but, when taken as a whole, in practical terms, the client is more wealthy and profitable than ever.

OPPORTUNITY SHIFTING

One of the most important concepts in asset protection planning is the concept of *opportunity shifting*. Opportunity shifting is an estate planning concept that allows future income and capital growth to accumulate outside of the taxable estate of a wealthy person by transferring or seeding new business opportunities in a family trust for children and grandchildren. This structure serves asset protection purposes as well by distancing the anticipated income and capital growth from the person who is likely to attract liabilities.

To facilitate opportunity shifting, new revenue-producing assets that would normally be created within or purchased by the business, such as new patents, should be placed into a separate asset protection structure so that wealth accumulates outside the liability-attracting business. To the extent that the business requires the new asset, the asset should be leased or licensed as necessary back to the business. This setup not only protects the asset from the creditors of the business, but it also provides another avenue of bleeding the business of its cash assets and thus depriving those assets to potential creditors. This form of asset protection is one of the safest and most reliable ones, and the best that a creditor can do is to make a valuational challenge to the amounts transferred.

STRUCTURAL METHODOLOGY VERSUS TRANSFER METHODOLOGY

Asset protection planning relies heavily upon choosing and forming structures (that is, structural methodology) and upon the means of transferring assets into those structures, such as gifts, sales, and capitalization (that is, transfer methodology).

Structural methodology tends to dominate the limelight. Most asset protection seminars and articles focus on the "latest and greatest" structures, whether new variants of domestic or offshore asset protection trusts, corporate and limited liability company law, foreign foundations, or whatever. Promoters want to be able to sell a single, easy-to-form structure to a client, pocket the formation fees, and then move on to the next client. Slickness sells, and exotic and new structures are slick, while the specifics of transferring assets to structures seem mundane.

From an asset protection perspective, however, the method of transferring assets into a structure often is more important than the structure itself. This is so simply because most of the laws that can negate asset protection planning primarily attack the transfer, not the structure.

As between a bad transfer into a good structure, or a good transfer into a bad structure, the latter is preferred. If the transfer method is well planned, the structure itself may not be challenged, and the creditor may be out of luck. On the other hand, if the transfer is poorly planned, both the transfer and the structure likely will be challenged with a greater chance of success.

The focus first should be on available methods of transfer, then on available structures. Only after those issues are resolved should the focus shift to less important concerns, such as specific document drafting issues and choice of jurisdiction.

Unfortunately, most planners get this backward and start in the reverse order—that is, choosing a jurisdiction, choosing a structure, and then finally figuring out how to transfer assets into that structure. As a result, the transfer often is not the best one for the circumstances and, under challenge, is the weak link that leads to the failure of the plan.

Structural methodology may encompass most, if not all, of the legal structures traditionally used to isolate or contain liability, including domestic and foreign corporations, trusts, and partnerships, limited liabilities companies, and variations thereof. Structural methodology encompasses very legitimate concerns about the structures that will hold assets. Unfortunately, the marketing and heavy use of standardized (or "cookie-cutter," to be less flattering) structures has plagued asset protection planning for over a decade. Certain structures, particularly offshore asset protection trusts, are fraudulently advertised as providing "absolute" protection to anyone with assets to protect (and the wallet to pay the fees).

In addition to the defects endemic to any cookie-cutter planning, a significant problem with these structures—if they work at all—is that they indiscriminately protect the assets of bad people who have committed bad acts as well as they protect the assets of good people. Congress, state legislatures, and courts will not allow these indiscriminate structures to remain effective for much longer. For example, proposed changes to bankruptcy laws would keep wrongdoing corporate executives from protecting money in their otherwise totally protected pension plans from defrauded shareholders. Furthermore, to the extent that any plan utilizes a standardized structure, the form of which has been defeated in the past, precedent exists for creditors to penetrate similar structures— even where the precedent-setting cases involved egregious situations, but later cases involve more favorable facts. "Bad facts make bad law," the saying goes, but bad law is law nonetheless.

CHALLENGE ANALYSIS

In rating the effectiveness of available asset protection strategies, a *challenge analysis* is useful. This technique involves categorizing strategies into those known to be effective, those in the process of being challenged, and new strategies (see Figure 8.6). The premise of challenge analysis is that the law is always evolving, usually in the favor of creditors. Just as asset protection planners devise new strategies that proliferate through the field, so are creditors' attorneys identifying asset protection strategies and ways to defeat them. No one should be surprised that creditors' attorneys have seminars, journals, and Internet discussion groups, too. The fact that an asset protection technique works today doesn't mean that it will work tomorrow. Indeed, to the extent that an asset protection technique has achieved popularity, it can be argued that the seeds

FIGURE 8.6

Efficacy pyramid.

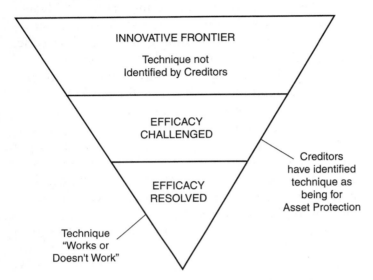

of its own destruction have already been sown. The key is staying one step ahead. Asset protection planners have been extraordinarily creative in developing new strategies, but at the same time they have been guilty of clinging to failed strategies beyond those strategies' useful lifetimes.

From the debtor's standpoint, challenge analysis is often a reverse popularity contest, with the most popular strategies often being the least desirable. Generally, in asset protection planning, new is good and popular is bad.

The first category in challenge analysis is Efficacy Resolved. Strategies in this category have been identified by creditors as having an asset protective purpose and effect, but they exist because of legislative or judicial recognition of important public policy reasons for protecting certain assets from creditors. The outcome of a challenge to these strategies can be predicted with a high degree of certainty by reference to existing law. Creditors rarely challenge these methods in the courts, because the law is clear. If creditors want to defeat these methods of asset protection planning, they must do so through legislative change.

Strategies in the Efficacy Resolved category generally are limited to *exemptional methods* (for example, planning involving state and federal exemptions for homes, retirement income, life insurance, and other assets), and *collateralization* and *securitization* (that is, burdening assets with debt). These aforementioned strategies are the most effective methods of protecting assets. Barring legislative changes or a broad judicial doctrinal change, these methods will continue to be effective, and the challenges of creditors will either be legislative or valuational in nature. The likelihood of change is low, because these laws have a strong basis in public policy. However, blatant abuse of these methods will ultimately bring legislative reform in favor of creditors. Recent attempts at bankruptcy reform in Congress, had they been successful, would have significantly limited some exemptions—for example, capping homestead exemptions in bankruptcy at $100,000. This attempt proves that the efficacy of even the most solid strategies are likely to deteriorate over time.

Strategies in the Efficacy Challenged category have been identified by creditors as having an asset protective purpose and are currently being challenged by creditors in the courts. The outcome of a challenge to these strategies cannot be predicted by debtors or creditors with reasonable certainty. Typically, these strategies start out being innovative and enjoy a period of unqualified success. As these methods are identified and studied, however, creditors develop more sophisticated tactics to attempt to defeat them. If a strategy remains effective after substantial court challenges, the strategy is reclassified into the Efficacy Resolved category. Creditors can then be expected to abandon court challenges and instead seek legislative changes. If a strategy fails in the courts, debtors should abandon the strategy. Failed strategies die hard in the asset protection world, however, particularly when a strategy has been heavily marketed. After all, many planners have vested financial interests in the continued use of the strategy.

Strategies in the Efficacy Challenged category are risky. A ruling in a case involving one debtor could render the strategy useless for all debtors. Furthermore, creditors can be expected to challenge these strategies in every case and to actively seek legislative changes. These strategies may be useful, but they should be used only when the strategy will be used merely as one facet of a larger plan, not as the lynchpin or the last-ditch layer. They should also be used only when the strategy can be structured flexibly in anticipation of later restructuring to accommodate changes in the law.

Dissociation methodology involves the transfer of assets from the debtor without consideration. Very simply, the debtor attempts to protect the asset by disassociating himself (and presumably also his liabilities) from it. These methods generally fall into the Efficacy Resolved category. Whether a transfer is to a brother-in-law or to a sophisticated foreign asset protection structure, the story from the debtor is the same: "I gave it away."

The efficacy of dissociative transfers is severely limited by the law of fraudulent transfer, discussed in Chapter 6. Dissociative transfers to trusts and related issues are further discussed in Chapters 11 through 15.

Transformation methodology involves converting assets from a form that is readily available to creditors into a form that is difficult or undesirable for creditors to attack. Typically, transformation methods seek to take advantage of local law that allows the asset to be protected, though often debtors import law and export assets (and sometimes themselves) to jurisdictions with more debtor-friendly laws. Transformational methods are discussed in Chapters 17 through 22.

The Innovative Frontier category includes new and cutting-edge asset protection strategies that have not been identified by creditors and thus have not been subject to challenge. These strategies are based on theory and have a good chance of protecting assets against the first few challenges to such methods. Strategies in the Innovative Frontier category generally are quite effective for a period of time. As they become more popular, they inevitably descend into the Efficacy Challenged category.

Advanced insurance and financial arrangements are at the leading edge of the Innovative Frontier. We discuss private annuity and private placement life insurance structures in Chapter 23. Captive insurance arrangements are discussed in Chapter 24. In Chapter 25, we provide an overview of other advanced methodologies.

Finally, we give an overview of the issues faced by several common types of asset protection clients, and the possible solutions for those clients, in Chapter 26, along with some final considerations about the practice of asset protection.

Statutory Exemption Planning

When attempts are made to place assets out of the reach of creditors, one of the first-line strategies is focused on the most effective uses of the asset exemptions allowed under federal and state codes. This exempted property is declared untouchable in the eyes of the law, should you find yourself in the undesirable position of having a creditor's lien liquidating your assets. As a general rule, exempt assets are not subject to the fraudulent transfer laws, and thus there is no such thing as a fraudulent transfer of an exempt asset.

Every state has a list of assets considered exempt from legal judgments and unreachable by creditors. This list of exemptions is contained in statutes and, for some assets, often in the state's constitution. In addition to offering protection in some amounts for one's home or automobile, the various state statutes also offer protection for such things as cattle, milking cows, farming implements, tools of the professional trade, and the family Bible.

The Federal Bankruptcy Act also has its own list of exempt assets. Most states have opted out of the federal exemption system. In these states, a debtor can only use the state's postjudgment asset exemptions in a federal bankruptcy proceeding. In the remaining states, a bankrupt debtor can choose between the federal bankruptcy exemptions and the state exemptions.

To effectively plan for maximum asset protection, you must understand the limits of exempt asset status and know the available asset exemption options. An asset protection planner must know how asset exemptions work, what they can and cannot do, and how to make them work best for their clients, including knowing how to use asset transfers to take best advantage of exemptions.

First, the exempt status of an asset—whether a home, a car, or any other asset—will not defeat a lender's security interest in that property. If a North Carolina debtor owns nothing but a home valued at $200,000 on which there is a mortgage of $160,000, the $10,000 North Carolina homestead exemption will not protect any of the value of the home as against what the mortgage lender is owed. The $10,000 exemption might be valid against unsecured creditors, but not against the mortgage lender.

Second, it must be understood that certain debts supercede statutory exemptions. The exemption laws of most states grant specific exceptions for federal, state, and local government claims; claims related to security interests in specific property; and claims for child support, alimony, and marital property divisions. For example, if the client fails to pay state property taxes, the homestead exemption will not protect any of the value of the home should the taxing authority foreclose the tax lien.

Third, exemptions apply only to natural persons. If a consultant forms an LLC to operate her business and contributes her car to the LLC, a statutory exemption for an automobile will not protect the car from the LLC's creditors, because the exemption for an automobile applies only to natural persons, not to business entities. The fact that the LLC is a single-member LLC and thus disregarded for federal tax purposes does not mean that the LLC can take advantage of the exemption. It can't because federal tax law does not affect the application of the state exemption statute.

HOMESTEAD EXEMPTIONS

Most states have statutory or constitutional protections for homesteads (that is, the residential real property and improvements of debtors domiciled in the state). However, the homestead exemption in many states is so small as to be useless for asset protection planning purposes. Homestead exemption planning is meaningful only if a client owns or contemplates owning residential property in a state with a large or unlimited homestead exemption, such as Texas or Florida.

In a recent significant case in Florida, *Havoco v. Hill*[1], the Florida Supreme Court ruled that although a bankrupt debtor purchased a $650,000 residence in Florida with the intent to protect the value of the home from his preexisting creditors, the home is still protected under Florida's constitutional homestead exemption. Mr. Hill owed Havoco $15 million from a 1990 judgment against him. A longtime resident of Tennessee, Mr. Hill purchased a "retirement home" in Florida for $650,000 cash in 1991. Then in 1992, he declared bankruptcy and claimed that the Florida property was exempt as his homestead.

After several appeals, the Florida Supreme Court noted that the intent to hinder, delay, or defraud creditors is not one of the three specific exceptions to the homestead exemption in the Florida constitution The court also held that state fraudulent transfer law is not applicable in the context of the homestead exemption.

Normally, transfers of nonexempt assets (such as cash) into an exempt asset (such as homestead) will be suspect, since the fraudulent transfer statutes might overrule the exemption statutes. However, Florida's homestead exemption is unique in that state's constitution, and thus trumps the fraudulent transfer statute. So, if all else fails, a debtor can move to Florida, converting as much nonexempt cash as possible into exempt homestead property. But caution is due, because potential changes to the federal Bankruptcy Act would significantly limit state homestead exemptions in bankruptcy cases.

When the homestead exemption is unlimited, or the amount of the exemption exceeds the value of the home, the debtor should consider paying off the mortgages on the property. But if the value of the home exceeds the exemption amount, the equity in the home should be stripped out by encumbering the home with an additional bank or finance company mortgage (or perhaps with a private mortgage from a client's business entity, preferably a protected entity, such as an asset leasing company). The cash can then be protected by purchasing exempt assets or by loaning the cash to a business operating entity. The note back from the operating entity will be available to creditors, but the note can be structured with *poison pills* such as balloon terms with all interest and principal payable at some distant date in the future, with high interest rates, or with both. This would cause a creditor taking the note to recognize taxable original issue discount interest income without receiving the cash to pay the tax.

Some states require that the homestead exemption be documented by recording a document with the county or state. If the exemption is not recorded, it may be lost. In some states, recording is optional. In the remaining states, there is no provision for recording of the exemption. In states where recording is required or allowed, best practices dictate that the exemption be recorded.

OTHER EXEMPTIONS

Many states provide significant protection for the cash value of life insurance and annuities. These protections are discussed in detail in Chapter 23.

Although many states provide no specific exemption for wages, federal law imposes a 25 percent restriction on wage attachment (except in the case of support orders, tax debts, and Chapter 13 bankruptcies). In other words, a judgment creditor can only attach 25 percent of a debtor's disposable income, which is defined as gross wages less amounts required by law to be withheld, including federal income and Social Security taxes. This federal law preempts state laws.

To ensure that a certain portion of the earnings of a client's business will constitute exempt wages, a self-employed business owner should take an authorized and regularly scheduled salary from the business, regardless of the form in which the business was organized. The failure to take a salary (for example, simply taking a distribution of profits from an LLC or S corporation) may mean that earnings from the business will not qualify for the wage exemption.

A *tenancy in common* is a form of joint property ownership in which two or more persons each has a separate, undivided, fractional interest in the property but all of them have common right to possession of the whole property. The ownership interest of any co-tenant is subject to the claims of the co-tenant's creditors. Thus, tenancy in common does not provide any asset protection to the owner. As a practical matter, however, since execution against jointly owned property of any kind can be a little problematic for creditors, especially for those with low-value claims, it may make the property unattractive to creditors.

A *joint tenancy* with right of survivorship is a form of joint property ownership in which two or more persons each has a separate, (presumed) equal, undivided, fractional interest in the property but all of them have common right to possession of the whole property. The interest of a deceased joint tenant passes automatically to the surviving joint tenants.

The ownership interest of any joint tenant is subject to the claims of that joint tenant's creditors, and a joint tenancy with right of survivorship may be severed by sale under execution against one of the joint tenants. However, no rights of a deceased joint tenant's creditors survive his or her death. Joint tenancy does not provide much asset protection, but since jointly owned assets of a deceased joint tenant pass to surviving joint tenants free of the claims of the decedent's creditors, it may be a better form of ownership than tenancy in common.

As with a tenancy in common, as a practical matter, with jointly owned property any execution against it can be a little problematic for creditors, especially for those with low-value claims, so it may make the property unattractive to creditors.

Tenancy by the entirety is a form of joint property ownership between spouses and is recognized by just under a third of U.S. jurisdictions.[2] Property held by a husband and wife as tenants by the entirety is considered to be held by the marital unit. In most states, property held as tenants by the entirety cannot be partitioned or conveyed by the unilateral act of either spouse. Consequently, in those states, an individual creditor of either spouse cannot reach any property held as tenants by the entirety. However, a creditor of both spouses can reach property held as tenants by the entirety. Some states allow tenancies by the entirety in personal and real property, while others only recognize tenancies by the entirety in real property.

Where both a husband and wife are actively involved in operating a business, caution must be exercised. This ownership form offers no protection for debts on which the couple is jointly liable. Thus, great efforts should be made to ensure that only one spouse guarantees the contracts of the business entity, if the business's creditor demands a personal guarantee. Conversely, if only one spouse is active in the business, the nonactive spouse should avoid any connection with the business, including service as an officer or director of a corporation.

Other than the potential for joint debts, there are two principal risks associated with planning using tenancy by the entirety. One is the death of a spouse, which would cause the property to be owned entirely by the surviving spouse, and to be completely exposed to creditors. The other is divorce, which would at best cause a severance of the tenancy by the entirety and creation of a tenancy in common, resulting in exposure to creditors. At worst, this could result in the loss of the client's interest in the property to the ex-spouse. Additionally, a tenancy by the entirety may not protect property from the claims of the federal government for taxes owed by one party.

CHANGING RESIDENCES

The ability of a state court to enforce a judgment is geographically limited by the state's borders, since the state has no powers or jurisdiction beyond its borders. A state judgment may, however, be taken to another state. This other state is required by the U.S. Constitution to give "full faith and credit" to the judgment and essentially treat the judgment as if it had been originally entered in that state. But this doesn't mean that the state where the judgment is taken must also respect the collection laws of the state where the judgment was originally entered. To the contrary, the state where the judgment is taken applies its own collection laws, and statutory exemptions from those laws, as if the judgment were entered in that state originally.

The consequence of this is that, just as creditors may often "forum shop" by choosing the jurisdiction most favorable to them to bring the original lawsuit, debtors may forum shop for the state where they will defend against the collection action. The differences among some states may be dramatic, since some states like Texas provide unlimited exemptions for homestead and do not permit garnishment of wages.

Thus, asset protection plans are sometimes designed as a passive contingency plan, with the idea that if the dark cloud of a possible creditor appears on the horizon, a move will be made to a debtor-friendly state. So long as residency requirements are met in the state to where the move is made, there is no reason why the debtor should not be able to take advantage of the more debtor-friendly laws of the state to which she moves.

For example, suppose a person living in California buys a life insurance policy while in California, and at a later time creditors appear. The person can move to Florida and expect that the cash value of the life insurance policy will be protected under Florida law, assuming that the necessary residency requirements are met.

Note that this strategy does not work in reverse: One could not take an asset that would be exempt in one state and move to another with the anticipation that the asset would continue to be protected by the exemption statutes of the first state.

RETIREMENT PLANS

Retirement plans come in many varieties, including employer-sponsored tax-qualified plans such as 401(k) plans, individual tax-qualified retirement plans such as individual retirement accounts (IRAs), and employer-sponsored nonqualified plans such as deferred compensation plans. Each has its own tax quirks and each also has its own asset protection quirks

Contributions made to an employer-sponsored tax-qualified retirement plan are tax-deductible to the employer, and they are not taxable to the employee at the time of contribution. The investment growth in the plan is tax-deferred. When the employee retires and begins withdrawing funds from the plan, the withdrawals are taxed as ordinary income.

The federal government and nearly every state have decided that protecting retirement benefits is an important public policy goal to prevent retirees from becoming a financial burden on society.

Several interrelated concepts work to exempt most employer-sponsored tax-qualified retirement plans from the claims of creditors. First, all such plans are subject to the Employee Retirement Income Security Act (ERISA). ERISA requires such plans to have an enforceable *anti-alienation provision*—a fancy way of saying that the participant in the plan cannot transfer her interest in the plan to a third party (such as a creditor) in any way. Second, the Bankruptcy Code specifically excludes from the bankruptcy estate property that is subject to a "restriction on the transfer of a beneficial interest of the debtor in a trust that is enforceable under applicable nonbankruptcy law." The anti-alienation provision required by ERISA is such a restriction on transfer. Finally, federal law preempts state law where both purport to cover the same ground. Where state law might otherwise subject an ERISA-protected retirement plan to creditors' claims in a state court postjudgment proceeding, the protections afforded by ERISA, which is a federal law, trump state law and the retirement plan assets are protected. Thus, ERISA qualification is key to the protection of many retirement plans.

To be ERISA-qualified, a retirement plan must be a type of plan that is covered by ERISA; it must be tax-qualified under Section 401 of the Internal Revenue Code; and it must include an anti-alienation provision.

Tax qualification is fairly straightforward. Once the IRS has made the determination that a plan is qualified, that decision is final unless it is revoked by the IRS. Likewise, the inclusion of anti-alienation provisions is straightforward. If a restriction on transfer is enforceable to prevent a transfer, it is valid.

ERISA coverage can be the Achilles' heel of a retirement plan. In order for business owners to benefit from ERISA protection for retirement plan assets, there must be at least one employee other than the owner and the owner's spouse also participating in the plan. If a tax-qualified retirement plan covers one or more employees other than the business owner and the owner's spouse, the owner, just as any other plan participant, qualifies for the protections ERISA affords plan participants, including protection from the participant's creditors. Conversely, if a business owner and the owner's spouse are the only participants in a tax-qualified retirement plan, the plan does not qualify for ERISA protections, and the plan assets of the owner would be subject to the claims of the owner's creditors.

Note that there are a few exceptions to the protection provided to ERISA-qualified retirement plans. Federal (but not state) tax liens may attach to a debtor's interest in an ERISA plan, which then may be garnished by the IRS. Also, Congress created an exception for a Qualified Domestic Relations Order (QDRO), which allows a participant's retirement plan assets to be assigned to a spouse, child, or other dependent.

Finally, ERISA protection does not extend to assets that have been distributed to or for the benefit of the debtor, including loans. In other words, although the assets may be protected while they are in an ERISA plan, they can become fair game for creditors once they come out. However, state exemptions may provide some protection, depending on the state.

If a retirement plan is not wholly protected by ERISA, it may be exempt from creditors' claims under state law. In particular, state exemptions become important with respect to employer-sponsored plans that cover only the business owner and his spouse (which are not protected by ERISA), IRAs [including Simplified Employee Pension (SEP) IRAs], and nonqualified plans.

IRAs are not covered by ERISA. Thus, the asset protection afforded to IRAs varies from state to state. Nearly all states have some level of protection for IRAs and other retirement accounts where the protection is not preempted by ERISA protection.

Only about half of all U.S. states exempt IRAs completely. Some states put a dollar limitation on the exemption. Other states do not exempt recent contributions. Some states exempt IRA balances that have been rolled over from an employer-sponsored qualified plan. Many states limit the exemption for IRAs and other retirement plans to what is "reasonably necessary" for the support of the debtor and the debtor's dependents. The determination of what is "reasonably necessary" depends on individual facts and circumstances and may itself be the subject of contentious litigation. Finally, although many states have updated their exemption statutes to protect Roth IRAs, some have not.

Some retirement plans are not tax-qualified. The typical non-qualified retirement plan is a deferred compensation plan in which an employee defers the right to receive some portion of otherwise current income until a specified future date or event. Such plans are referred to as "unfunded" because there is no segregated fund from which the deferred compensation is paid or the employee has no right to the deferred funds until the time specified in the plan agreement. The employer is not entitled to a tax deduction for payment of compensation until the benefits are actually paid to the employee or when the employee has an enforceable right to receive the benefits, if earlier. Likewise, the benefits are taxable to the employee when received, or if sooner, when the employee has the right to receive the benefits.

Although tax benefits are not among the benefits of nonqualified deferred compensation plans, there are other benefits. Primarily, they allow for retirement planning for highly compensated employees without having to meet nondiscrimination requirements. Also, the amount of compensation deferred for retirement is unlimited.

In order for deferred compensation benefits to be considered assets of the employer and not the employee, and thus not subject to taxation in the hands of the employee, the assets in a funded deferred compensation plan must be subject to the claims of the employer's creditors. Typically such assets are held in an irrevocable trust known as a *rabbi trust*, so called because the first IRS-approved arrangement of this type was established for a rabbi by his congregation. While assets in such trusts are subject to the claims of the employer's creditors, they are not subject to the claims of the employee-participant's creditors so long as the employee has no vested right in the plan assets.

Once the employee has a vested right in the plan assets and the assets are no longer subject to the claims of the employer's creditors, a nonqualified retirement plan is typically protected to some extent by state exemption laws, usually to the same extent that IRAs are protected under state law.

For any existing or new plan, ERISA and tax compliance should be reviewed by competent advisors. If the business owner and his spouse are the only participants in a retirement plan, they would be wise to bring in another employee-participant, such as a child, in order to obtain ERISA protection. At least one court has held that such a plan remains ERISA-qualified even after that other participant ended his employment and participation in the plan. Where an individual controls more than one business, all of the businesses will be combined in assessing whether at least one other person participates in any one of the businesses' retirement plans. Note that this rule can cut two ways. It may allow a plan to be ERISA-protected because it will bring other employees under the ERISA umbrella. However, it will also mean that all of the eligible employees of all of the businesses must be covered by the retirement plan under ERISA and tax rules that operate to prevent discrimination in favor of highly compensated employees.

SEP IRAs and SIMPLE (Savings Incentive Match Plan for Employees) IRAs are designed to allow small employers to offer retirement plans to employees with fewer administrative requirements and costs than more complex 401(k) plans or traditional defined benefit pension plans. Although SEP IRAs and SIMPLE IRAs feature an attractive simplicity in design and maintenance, they are not covered by ERISA and may be more vulnerable to the creditors of plan participants. While more complex to initiate and maintain, a qualified plan such as a 401(k) or a defined benefit plan may be more desirable from an asset protection perspective. Such plans also have the added benefit of allowing a participant to direct more compensation into the plan than SEP and SIMPLE IRAs.

Furthermore, if a participant is considering rolling proceeds of an ERISA-protected plan into an IRA, state law protections should be considered, including the possibility of changes in state law protection should the participant move to another state. Often, the best option will be to leave the assets in the ERISA-protected plan and structure the payout with asset protection considerations in mind. For example, some states exempt annuity payments from creditors' claims. An ERISA-protected plan paying a retirement annuity benefit will be considerably more protected in many states than a rollover IRA from which the participant is making voluntary withdrawals.

Nonqualified plans can be useful asset protection planning tools where the employee's asset protection risks are more significant than the employer's and the assets can be protected in a way that makes them technically available to the employer's creditors but difficult to reach. For example, a vulnerable employee may wish to defer significant amounts of compensation under a nonqualified retirement plan with the deferred amounts going into a rabbi trust established offshore. The trustee of the rabbi trust might hold the plan assets in one or more charging order–protected entities and further protect the plan assets by having the charging order–protected entities holding debtor-favored assets such as life insurance or structured financial products. Even if the offshore trust assets are subject to the claims of the employer's creditors, a creditor will have to get past the charging orders and the protections afforded to the underlying assets.

ADVANCED PLANS

Retirement plans are valuable tax planning tools and worthy of asset protection planning consideration, particularly once large balances have accumulated after a number of years. However, most qualified retirement plans and IRAs generally do not allow large enough contributions to be useful asset protection planning vehicles in the short term. There is one important exception to this rule: the 412(i) plan.

A *412(i) plan* is a type of defined benefit plan. There are two basic types of employer-sponsored tax-qualified retirement plans, defined contribution plans and defined benefit plans. A defined contribution plan specifies an amount of contribution (for example, 10 percent of salary, up to some maximum amount) that will be made during the participant's time in the plan. However, the amount of the retirement benefit that the employee will receive can vary greatly, depending on the amount of future contributions, time, and investment performance. A defined benefit plan specifies the amount of benefit the employee will receive at retirement. It is the old-fashioned pension plan, like those often offered by large corporations. The defined benefit might be a specific dollar amount (for example, $3000 per month for life, starting at age 62). It might be a percentage of salary (for example, 60 percent of the employee's last month's salary).

As with any other qualified plan, the employer gets a deduction for contributions made to the 412(i) plan and the employee is taxed when plan benefits are paid. A 412(i) plan is different from other qualified plans only in the requirements for funding the plan.

To meet the rules of Section 412(i), the plan must be funded exclusively with annuity contracts or a combination of life insurance and annuity contracts issued and guaranteed by a life insurance company. The plan must provide for level annual premium payments that start when the employee begins participating in the plan and are reduced by any policy dividends paid. (In other words, policy dividends don't increase the amount of funding; they simply decrease the amount of premium payable.) Finally, a

412(i) plan must not allow policy loans and must prohibit an employee from granting a security interest in plan assets to secure a third-party loan.

There are no limitations on contributions on 412(i) plans other than the amounts required by the insurance and annuity policies to fund them. So, for example, if the particular insurance and annuity contracts used to fund the plan require $400,000 premiums, the allowed contribution and attendant deduction is $400,000. This generally means that larger contributions are allowed than with traditional defined benefit plans, and much larger contributions are allowed than with defined contribution plans. Because 412(i) plans are ERISA-protected, they are excellent asset protection vehicles, because they often allow for quick funding with large amounts of cash.

Overfunding or underfunding of the plan isn't possible so long as it stays a 412(i) plan. The plan will be adequately funded for retirement and won't be subject to IRS penalties to which other types of defined benefit plans might be, if they are overfunded.

The assumptions underlying 412(i) plan funding are those guaranteed by the insurance company, so the plan should hold up to IRS scrutiny with no trouble. Beware, however, of abusive plans with assumptions that simply don't make sense. An example of such a plan would be one to which $1 million in premiums have been contributed over three years but which has a cash value of $100,000 at the end of the third year. This would be part of a design to allow a "roll out" the policies to the participant at a low tax cost. The IRS is actively looking for abusive 412(i) plans. But plenty of economically sound 412(i) plans are available. As the saying goes, "pigs get fat, hogs get slaughtered."

Benefits in 412(i) plans are guaranteed by the insurance company. The insurance company bears the investment risk and the benefits are not affected by market fluctuations. The guaranteed rates of return are almost always conservative, which means that high premiums likely will be required in the early years of the plan, which also means high deductions and the ability to protect large amounts of assets from creditors' claims.

Completely funding in a short period of time all of the benefits under the plan is possible. If, for example, a professional who made relatively little money in the first several years of practice begins to make considerably more money in the later years of his practice and wants to fund a guaranteed retirement plan completely as quickly as possible, the 412(i) plan would be an excellent choice. The ideal candidate for a 412(i) plan generally is age 40 to 75, has a stable or increasing annual income of $200,000 or more, and has few employees.

The 412(i) plan is a good example of a planning tool that is not intended for asset protection planning, but that has a significant asset protective effect. In the following chapter, we will see that debt financing arrangements can also have dramatic asset protective effects, although they serve important economic purposes other than asset protection.

ENDNOTES

1. *Havoco v. Hill*, 790 So. 2d 1018 (Fla. 2001).

2. The fifteen U.S. jurisdictions that provide for tenancy by the entirety are Delaware, District of Columbia, Florida, Hawaii, Indiana, Maryland, Massachusetts, Michigan, North Carolina, Ohio, Pennsylvania, Tennessee, Vermont, Virginia, and Wyoming.

Collateralization

Most property has some discernable value that can be used to secure a loan. Real estate is commonly used as collateral for loans, but it is not the only type of property that can be used to secure loans. Stock, accounts receivable, and equipment are just a few examples. When a lender loans money secured by property, the lender has first priority to realize the property's value in the event of default on the loan. The lender also has priority in the event of a disposition of the property, whether voluntary, as in a sale by the owner, or involuntary, such as a forced sale to satisfy a judgment. For example, if a bank loans $200,000 to a debtor secured by a $500,000 property, the amount available to the debtor's other creditors is whatever is left after the first $200,000 of sale proceeds.

If that debtor is being pursued by a judgment creditor, the creditor likely will pursue that property, which has something close to $300,000 of present monetary value.

The debtor and the creditor see this equity value differently, however. The debtor sees the potential for appreciation in value. The debtor may also realize intangible benefits from the property, such as may be the case with a vacation home that has been in the family for years. The creditor, on the other hand, sees only the immediate potential for the property to produce a lump sum of cash as soon as possible. That value is probably less than $300,000. If there is a forced sale of the property to satisfy the judgment, the proceeds will first be used to pay the expenses of the sale. Next, the secured lender will be paid its $200,000. Finally, the judgment creditor gets what is left. The judgment creditor cannot be assured that the sale will be for full fair market value. Under normal circumstances, properties listed for sale are marketed for several months, which allows time for the right buyer to find the property for a purchase at market value. In a forced sale, however, a number of factors generally cause the price to be something less than market value. One significant factor is that the sale takes place on a particular day at a particular time to the highest bidder who usually must produce cash or a letter of credit on the spot.

The difference between the viewpoints of the debtor and the creditor makes *equity stripping* an effective technique for protecting property. Equity stripping simply refers to encumbering property with legitimate debt to reduce its net value and make it less attractive to judgment creditors. Although the property is now exposed to the lender, it is no longer exposed to unsecured creditors and more importantly the debtor has the cash that would otherwise have been trapped in the property.

Cash is easier to protect than real or tangible personal property for two reasons. First, cash can be converted into more easily protected assets, such as life insurance or retirement plan assets. Second, cash can be moved. It can be moved out of the reach of creditors and into exempt assets or forms of investments that creditors will have a hard time getting at. Real property, on the other hand, is always subject to the jurisdiction of the court where the property is located and totally subject to local law and the orders of the local court. Attempting to protect real property by transferring ownership to an offshore asset protection trust, as some planners suggest, is foolish because the local courts simply may not recognize the validity of such trusts.

Realize that, from a purely economic standpoint, the rate of a property's appreciation is totally independent of how much equity is in the property. In other words, the property will increase at the same value regardless of how much equity you have in it. A property that is free and clear of debt will not appreciate any faster than one that is laden with debt. Free and clear property simply decreases the amount of cash available for other investments. Thus, it usually makes no sense to build up equity in property so long as the money could be invested with return rates greater than the borrowing rate for that money.

Debt financing is woven into the fabric of the American economy. A large body of law, including property law, the Uniform Commercial Code, and federal bankruptcy law, governs debtor-creditor relations with respect to secured lending. That law will determine with great specificity which creditors are first in line and which will fight over scraps.

Equity stripping can be divided into four basic categories: commercial, controlled, contingent, and cross-collateralization. They are not mutually exclusive. In fact, most equity-stripping plans use a combination of techniques.

COMMERCIAL EQUITY STRIPPING

Commercial equity stripping simply involves a commercial lender loaning cash to the property owner, with the property securing the loan. The owner receives cash, which is spent or protected, and a lien is placed on the property and recorded in a local government office. (See Figure 10.1, for a graphical representation of how this works.)

Faced with commercial equity stripping, a creditor will have nearly insurmountable difficulty in defeating the lender's lien. A commercial equity-stripping transaction is clearly for value for purposes of fraudulent transfer law. Furthermore, general property law and the UCC will protect the lender's lien. Essentially, the creditor's remedy is to chase the cash, not the commercial lender.

Commercial equity stripping is not without its downsides. The primary disadvantage is the debtor's lack of control over the lending situation. A commercial lender will demand regular loan payments. If payments are not made, a commercial lender likely will foreclose. Indeed, federal bank regulators will insist on this maneuver, in most cases. Of course, making payments is likely to be difficult in the asset protection context once a judgment creditor appears, because the owner may not be able to access cash to make payments. Even if the owner is able to make timely payments, under the terms of some loans, lenders have the right to foreclose if the debtor is deemed insolvent. These drawbacks can make commercial equity stripping impractical for assets such as a residence or where an operating business requires the use of the property.

Also, lenders typically loan only a part of a property's market value. For example, 80 percent is a common cap in the home equi-

FIGURE 10.1

Commercial equity stripping.

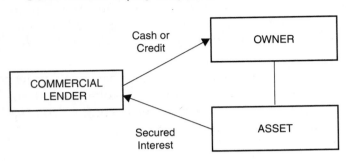

ty market. Loans of up to 100 percent or more of a property's value are available, but interest rates for such loans are usually very high. So, a substantial part of the property's value will be unprotected, and as the property appreciates, even more value will be exposed to creditors. Although subsequent refinancing or secondary loans are possible, these can be expensive, and often by the time the debtor realizes that it is time to act, it is too late and no lender will make a loan because of a pending or existing judgment.

CONTROLLED EQUITY STRIPPING

Controlled equity stripping involves the use of close, trusted persons to create entities to act as lenders to the owner. (See Figure 10.2, for a graphical representation of how controlled equity stripping works.) The private lender loans money to the debtor secured by a duly recorded lien against the debtor's property. If a judgment creditor appears, the private lender's lien will be superior to the judgment creditor's claim. Controlled equity stripping has significant advantages over commercial equity stripping.

Because the private lender's owner has a close personal relationship with the owner, there is considerably more flexibility in dealing with control issues. A private lender might, for instance, structure a loan as a long-term balloon obligation requiring little or no payments until the end of the loan term. If the debtor has problems with other creditors, a private lender might agree to suspend repayment for a period of time, giving the debtor time to deal with the creditor.

FIGURE 10.2

Controlled equity stripping.

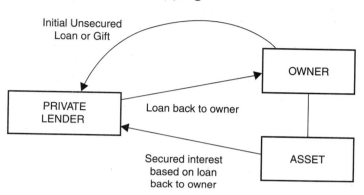

Controlled equity stripping can facilitate encumbering property up to its full market value, so long as the private lender is willing to risk a deficiency if the property is ever sold at less than the amount owed. It is possible and reasonable to consider loans for more than the current market value of the property, by incorporating assumptions about future appreciation into the loan agreement. Provisions in the loan agreement can make the property unattractive, such as penalties and a high interest rate upon default and high stated fees in the event of foreclosure. Controlled equity stripping thus can allow protection of the entire value of a property and more, including future appreciation.

Even if a judgment creditor is able to force a sale of the encumbered property, chances are that the controlled lender will end up owning the property. As a practical matter, the mere existence of the controlled lender's lien will deter all but the most determined judgment creditor from attempting a forced sale, because there is likely to be no value for the creditor to realize.

However, controlled equity stripping has some downsides. The first is that since the private lender has so much control over the situation, the private lender must be trusted. If the owner and the private lender are not on the same page, the lending agreement that is drafted to be very favorable to the private lender will put the private lender into a very advantageous situation where all the owner gets is the cash initially received.

Overt control of the lender by the debtor puts the arrangement at risk. A judgment creditor could assert that the granting of the security interest from the debtor to the lender was a fraudulent transfer. Or the creditor could contend that the arrangement is a sham with no economic substance and no purpose other than defeating the judgment creditor's claim. Ironclad controlled equity stripping requires a certain amount of real independence and separation between the lender and the debtor. This separation may be difficult to achieve, particularly for assets to which the debtor has an emotional attachment, such as a residence or family-owned business.

Controlled equity stripping requires the transfer of a large amount of cash from the lender to the debtor. In some cases, other measurably valuable assets may also be transferred to the debtor. But keep in mind that noncash assets allow for less planning flexibility, and the transaction then is more like an owner-financed sale than a loan. Generally, if the lender does not have sufficient cash to lend, the lender must find sources of liquid funds in order to carry out the loan transaction.

CONTROLLED DEBT FINANCING

Controlled debt financing bridges the gap between commercial equity stripping and controlled equity stripping. In a controlled debt financing transaction, a commercial third-party lender, such as a bank, extends a loan to the debtor. Next the promissory note is sold or otherwise transferred to a private finance company controlled by someone friendly to the debtor. The bank administers the loan for a fee. (See Figure 10.3, for a graphical representation of how controlled debt financing works.) The effect of this arrangement is that a judgment creditor sees a loan extended, documented, secured, and serviced by a commercial bank, with the debtor making payments to the bank. Of course, the creditor does not see that the payments are transferred to the private finance company (less the bank's servicing fee).

Secured loans are bought and sold daily. Lenders rarely keep loans that they originate. Therefore, a controlled debt-financing transaction is not likely to arouse a creditor's suspicion unless the creditor is aware of the private finance company, and perhaps not

FIGURE 10.3

Controlled debt financing.

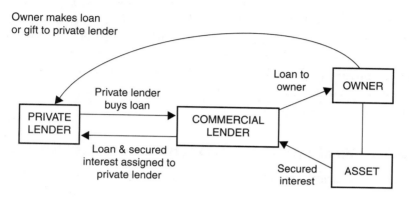

even then, because the transaction does have economic substance. The private finance company bears the default risk and interest rate risk in the transaction.

CONTINGENT EQUITY STRIPPING

Contingent equity stripping essentially involves the use of lines of credit secured by property. If a potential judgment creditor appears, the line of credit is exercised, stripping the equity from the property.

Contingent equity stripping can involve either commercial or private lenders. The most basic example of commercial contingent equity stripping is a home equity line of credit, which allows the homeowner to borrow cash on an intermittent basis up to a set credit limit, with the outstanding loan secured by the home. Fees for home equity lines of credit usually are relatively low, with no interest charges until funds are borrowed. There are usually little or no fees involved in this process until the line of credit is exercised. While a home equity line of credit provides an easy way to convert the value of real property into more easily protected cash assets, they are subject to the general limitations of commercial equity stripping.

Contingent controlled equity stripping provides many of the benefits of the typical controlled equity-stripping arrangement, with the added benefit that the private lender does not have to transfer cash immediately to the debtor. Of course, the private lender will have to transfer cash to the debtor when the private line of credit is exercised. For contingent private equity stripping to work, the lien or mortgage in favor of the private lender should be filed well in advance of the debtor's creditor troubles. A last-minute attempt to record a lien when creditors have already appeared may contribute to the arrangement being set aside as a fraudulent transfer or sham.

CROSS-COLLATERALIZATION AGREEMENTS

Cross-collateralization agreements entail using more than one property in a loan transaction. For instance, if the debtor owns a $500,000 property and wants a $500,000 loan secured by that property, a lender may require a security interest in an additional property as well. Although the equity of only one property has been borrowed out, the security interests encumber two properties. (See Figure 10.4 for a graphical representation of how cross-collateralization agreements work.) Cross-collateralization arrangements can cause substantial practical difficulties for creditors in reaching the equity value of either property, particularly if several lenders and liens are involved.

STRIPPING OTHER ASSETS

Although equity stripping is most common with real property, the same techniques can be used for other assets as well. For example, publicly traded securities can be equity-stripped by borrowing on margin using the securities as collateral. Margin credit is usually limited to 50 percent of the value of the stock. However, margin credit is often extended nearly up to the full value of bonds.

As with any other commercial lending arrangement, the debtor incurs risks. If the value of stocks or bonds declines significantly, the broker may require that some of the loan be repaid, usually by the owner selling some of the stock. Furthermore, margin loans are not free. The interest charges will negate to some extent the appreciation and the dividends or interest generated by the securities used as collateral.

FIGURE 10.4

Cross-collateralization agreements.

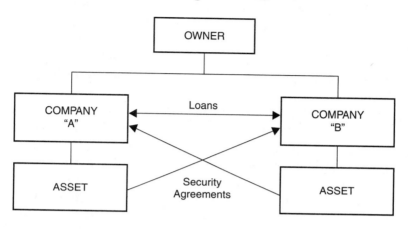

Margin credit is best utilized as a method of contingent equity stripping, simply by indicating on an account application that margin credit is desired. If stripping value from the securities in the account becomes necessary, the account owner can do so at any time, up to the margin limits of the account.

Accounts receivable are another form of property that can, and should be, equity-stripped. For a professional firm of physicians or attorneys, accounts receivable are often the firm's most valuable asset—and its most available asset as well. Accounts receivable can be equity-stripped by factoring (that is, selling the accounts receivable), usually at a discount, to a specialty finance company that then collects the accounts. Accounts receivable are best equity-stripped by means of loans. Specialty lenders will loan up to 100 percent of the value of a firm's short-term (for example, ninety-day) accounts receivable, requiring only periodic interest payments. The lender takes an ongoing security interest in the firm's accounts receivable. Thus, so long as the loan is not repaid, the lender always has a security interest in the firm's accounts receivable that is superior to a judgment creditor's interest. The cash from the loan is often used to purchase cash-value life insurance to fund supplemental retirement plans for the firm's professionals. If the crediting rate inside the policy is higher than the interest rate on the loan, this protection is free or even profit-generating. It is often so, because the lender also takes a security interest in the life insurance policies. This step allows the lender to make a low-interest-rate loan (for example, prime rate plus ½ percent), because of the low risks associated with the cross-collateralization involving both the accounts receivable and the life insurance policies.

Each professional in the firm receives an interest in a retirement plan funded with life insurance purchased with a portion of the loan proceeds. If the professional dies before retirement, his portion of the original loan principal is paid from the life insurance death benefit, with the remainder of the death benefit going to his family. If the professional retires, his life insurance policy is distributed to him, and he repays his portion of the original loan principal with his own funds, or by borrowing, tax-free, from his life insurance policy. Then, the professional can receive tax-free retirement income by borrowing cash value from the original life insurance policy (or a new policy obtained in an exchange for the old policy).

Because life insurance and even nonqualified retirement plans are protected in many states, this technique approaches the Holy Grail of Asset Protection status for many. Even without state protection of nonqualified retirement plans, however, the technique is one of the best available for protecting professional firms and their members.

CHAPTER 11

Trusts for Asset Protection

Trusts are a traditional asset protection tool. In the right circumstances, a trust can allow a person to give assets away in a controlled manner, protecting those assets from the claims of her own creditors, because the assets simply are not owned by her anymore. Even better, the assets are only "beneficially owned" by the person for whose benefit the transferor has given the assets. This means that if the trust is properly structured, in many states and foreign jurisdictions, the assets can remain free from the claims of the beneficiary's creditors as well. For these and other reasons, such as estate planning flexibility and estate and gift tax savings, trusts are a popular asset protection tool.

Indeed, to many people, asset protection is synonymous with the use of trusts and, particularly in recent years, offshore trusts. Ask many people about asset protection and they will mention trusts. After all, isn't hiding money in offshore trusts on obscure islands what asset protection is all about? The asset protection advertisements in the back pages of the financial magazines, the airline magazines, and the sports pages usually mention offshore trusts. Some savvy folks may even say that they have heard that offshore trusts "no longer work." Where is the truth in all this? Is there any truth in all this?

THE TRUST DEFINED

To understand how trusts relate to asset protection, you must first understand what a trust is, and as importantly, what a trust isn't. A *trust* really is just shorthand for "a trust relationship" and is little more than a legally recognizable agreement between two people that one will hold (be entrusted with) the assets of the other person for the benefit of someone.

Like corporations, trusts really don't exist in the physical sense of the term. Trusts fail our "beer and barbeque test." You simply cannot have a trust over to your house for a beer and barbeque. Now, you might have a trustee come over for a beer and barbeque, but not a trust. This is because a trust doesn't really exist; it is purely a legal fiction much in the same way that a corporation is a legal fiction. A trust is a legal fiction that has no existence other than what is recognized by the laws of the jurisdiction in which it has been created and also by the laws of other jurisdictions that recognize trusts, so long as it does not violate important public policies.

Trusts are a dissociative method of asset protection, meaning that the owner of the assets attempts to disassociate herself from them by claiming, "I gave them away." In our scale of relative method efficacy (see Chapter 8), the dissociative methods are typically unsophisticated and ineffective means of asset protection. Yet, trusts do have a legitimate place in asset protection planning, though they are often misused. The reason for this misuse is largely historical: Trusts have been used as a wealth-transfer vehicle for hundreds of years in England and the Commonwealth. They also have been well established in American jurisprudence. Trusts can be legitimate and efficient vehicles for transferring wealth. But they can also be used in ways that the laws of most states deem improper or abusive in shielding assets from creditors. As we shall see, the widespread abuse of trusts for asset protection is largely the result of historic anomalies.

ESTATE FREEZES

Asset protection planning is often done as a component of a client's overall estate planning. This strategy can be advantageous, because to be effective asset protection should generally not be done in a vacuum. Estate planners rely heavily on the use of trusts as wealth-transfer vehicles, so it seems logical for them to attempt to use trusts for asset protection purposes also.

The *estate freeze* is a popular and effective method of estate and gift tax planning. Generally, it involves transferring assets to heirs today, so that the assets' income and growth will be shifted to the heirs, thus "freezing" the value for estate and gift tax purposes at today's value. Familiar with freezing the value for estate and gift tax purposes, many estate planners try to implement an *asset freeze* for the client as well. They shift wealth to heirs so that the assets' income and growth (and, it is hoped, the assets themselves) will not be available to creditors. This is excellent planning, with one major caveat.

The problem is that the techniques used in estate planning and asset protection are often contraindicated by each other. In many circumstances, the best asset protection planning techniques and the best estate planning techniques are entirely incompatible. What may work well for estate planning may work poorly for asset protection planning, and vice versa. Primarily, this is so because estate planning relies heavily on gifting to facilitate transfers, and as we saw in Chapter 6, gifts are relatively easy for creditors to set aside under the fraudulent transfer laws. Nonetheless, the worry over future creditor claims (which for most people is merely a threat that never materializes) usually gives way to more financially immediate tax concerns of estate planning. The result is that the client ends up with estate planning utilizing trust structures that work very well from a tax perspective but which may be easily penetrated by unforeseen future creditors.

A related problem is that the historical roots of offshore trusts are heavily grounded in tax evasion. Trusts formed in low-tax or zero-tax jurisdictions have long been a device for persons in high-tax jurisdictions to avoid taxes. The ill-informed idea is attractively simple; if a taxpayer transfers assets to a trustee in a tax haven, the income and investment growth of those assets will not be taxable to the taxpayer in the high-tax jurisdiction. Unfortunately, that is a strategy that has not worked—at least legally—for decades. Nonetheless, the ill-informed taxpayer further assumes that since the IRS in the United States knows nothing about the offshore assets, there is no need to include them on federal estate tax returns on death. This strategy has never worked—again, at least not legally. To go a step further, offshore trusts are also often used to disguise ownership in offshore companies, which submit invoices to the taxpayer's business, creating phony deductions used to offset reported income. All of this activity is illegal and none of it works when challenged.

The commonly given reason for creating these schemes is "asset protection," although in truth asset protection was a far distant second to evading taxes. Thus, many trusts formed in offshore tax havens have been called *foreign asset protection trusts*, although asset protection almost always has been a secondary purpose of the trust. Eventually, an independent market developed for offshore trusts that truly did have asset protection as a primary purpose, but many of the inherent flaws of these structures for asset protection were overlooked, resulting in the disasters of the *Anderson* and *Lawrence* cases, discussed in Chapter 14.

MASS MARKETING OF OFFSHORE TRUSTS

The 1990s brought the mass marketing of offshore trusts by multilevel network marketers. Customers who bought into certain offshore marketing programs (Global Prosperity and Prosperity International League Ltd. were the most notorious) would get not only their own offshore trusts but also the opportunity to sell them to their friends and families. At the same time, a handful of attorneys and certified public accountants self-designated themselves as asset protection experts, the "Father of Asset Protection," and other such nonsense, and they started selling kits with which the "common man" could form his own offshore trust. These kits were pitched both at cheap seminars at local diners and for many thousands of dollars for a few days in exotic offshore locations. If you didn't have an offshore trust, you didn't have assets, or so it seemed. Asset protection and offshore trusts became, for a time, synonymous.

Overlooked in the hysteria of marketing asset protection trusts was whether they actually worked against creditors. In fact, using trusts for asset protection presents several significant problems, which substantially restrict their usefulness.

As we have already related, trusts are most typically funded with gifts; for example, you create a trust for your children and then you make gifts of cash or other valuable assets into it. However, the fraudulent transfer laws, including the Uniform Fraudulent Transfers Act, or UFTA, and its predecessor acts, have as one of their primary purposes to set aside gifts that have as their purpose or effect removing assets from the reach of creditors. In other words, the fraudulent transfer laws provide that you cannot do exactly what you want to do with trusts in the asset protection context—that is, give away assets to keep them out of the reach of creditors.

Even if transfers are made when no claims or creditors are known, the transfers will be at risk for some years. The limitations periods of the UFTA last for several years. They can last up to seven years in states like California that allow the suspension of the limitations period until there is a judgment. Furthermore, avoidance of specific creditors' claims is not an element of some fraudulent transfer tests. So, even if there are no known creditors or claims when a transfer is made, the transfer is potentially subject to being set aside for up to seven years or longer, depending on the circumstances under which the claim later arises. Few people with real asset protection concerns want to have their assets at risk for several years (much less seven years).

SELF-SETTLED SPENDTHRIFT TRUSTS

The fraudulent transfer laws are not the only laws that evidence a bias against trusts used for asset protection. In all but a handful of states, another set of laws prohibit what is known as the *self-settled spendthrift trust*.

A *spendthrift trust* is one in which the beneficiary cannot transfer his interest in the trust to a third party and where the beneficiary's right to distributions can be cut off if the distribution would otherwise go to a creditor of the beneficiary. These trusts also are usually *discretionary trusts*, in that whether or not to make distributions is entirely within the discretion of the trustee; the beneficiary has no right to compel a distribution of assets to himself from the trust. These trusts are designed both to preserve the trust assets of a beneficiary not wise enough to preserve them himself and to keep the beneficiary's creditors from reaching trust assets.

A spendthrift trust thus is specifically designed for asset protection, and in Chapter 12 we discuss their perfectly legitimate and effective uses in protecting beneficiaries' assets from creditors. Spendthrift trusts are so effective, in fact, the next logical question is "Why shouldn't everyone create a spendthrift trust for him- or herself?"

Most states do not allow the use of spendthrift trusts for the benefit of the person who originally set up the trust—those spendthrift trusts that are "self-settled." In other words, state law prevents a trust beneficiary from benefiting from spendthrift protections in a trust created and funded by that beneficiary. The rationale behind these laws is simply that people should be responsible for their debts; avoiding debts shouldn't be as easy as contributing assets to a self-settled spendthrift trust.

As we will see in Chapter 14, the offshore tax havens first attracted offshore trust business by specifically authorizing self-settled spendthrift trusts in new legislation, and in Chapter 13 we will examine how a handful of U.S. states now allow self-settled spendthrift trusts in order to attract trust business. However, the law in most U.S. states is that self-settled spendthrift trusts are not respected for the purpose of protecting the assets of the settlor-beneficiary from her creditors.

TRUSTS AND GIVING UP CONTROL

Another problem with trusts used for asset protection is that, for the trust structure to work, actual control of the assets must be totally ceded from the owner of the assets to a third-party trustee. If control is not totally ceded to the trustee, there is a substantial risk that a judge will determine that there was no real transfer made, and that the owner of the assets is only attempting to give the appearance of a transfer. In such a case, the judge will look through the arrangement and allow creditors of the owner access to the trust's assets. This is not a theoretical concern but one that has operated to defeat asset protection plans in several landmark cases involving foreign asset protection trusts.

The quite understandable concern of most people is that they do not want to give all their assets to a trustee, especially one who is prevented from giving the assets back by the clear language of the trust document. In Chapter 16, we will examine some of the ways that planners have devised to deal with this issue.

A major flaw of typical asset protection trust planning is that as litigation progresses, assets are liquidated into the trust or are transferred to the asset protection trust. Contrary to the goal of diversifying assets as litigation progresses, these trust structures create a large, singular target for creditors to attack. These structures create a winner-takes-all scenario, where the creditor has nothing to lose by attacking the trust and the debtor risks everything if the creditor is successful. To an extent, this is such a high-stakes situation that settlement may be promoted. However, the debtor is the one who bears the most risks since all of his wealth is in the trust, whereas the assets in the trust might be only a miniscule fraction of the net worth of an institutional creditor. In other words, an institutional creditor may have the freedom to gamble even where many millions of dollars of assets are a stake, but the debtor rarely has that same freedom.

So, these issues of fraudulent transfers, offending state law, retaining too much control, and asset consolidation are the primary concerns where trusts are used for asset protection purposes. They must be adequately addressed if a trust-based asset protection structure is to be effective.

LIVING TRUSTS

Widely marketed *revocable living trusts* provide absolutely no asset protection benefits. A revocable living trust is simply a trust that a person creates for her own benefit while she is alive, with the assets of the trust then passing to designated beneficiaries at death. Essentially, it is a will substitute. While generally effective as a will substitute and as a means of planning for flexibility in the event of disability, from an asset protection viewpoint, revocable living trusts suffer from three significant flaws.

First, as with all trusts, transfers to revocable living trusts can be easily set aside by creditors under the Uniform Fraudulent Transfer Act within the (usually long) limitations periods. In some states, the period during which a creditor may successfully challenge a fraudulent transfer may be seven years, or even longer in some circumstances.

Second, except in a handful of states as described in Chapter 13, living trusts cannot be spendthrift trusts with respect to the settlor-beneficiary. If a trust is not a spendthrift trust, a creditor can apply for a court order to distribute the assets to the creditor. Or the creditor can compel the single beneficiary to distribute the assets to himself so that they are accessible to the creditor. Usually, however, creditors do not even need to attack under this theory because of the third flaw.

Third, and worst of all, revocable living trusts are revocable, meaning that the creditor can simply apply for an order of the court compelling the debtor to revoke the trust and thus take the assets back, whereupon the assets are then accessible to creditors.

Of course, revocable living trusts are designed not for asset protection but for estate planning purposes. This fact hasn't kept some promoters from touting them as having special asset protection benefits, which is simply false, even with respect to third-party beneficiaries. It is true that, after the transferor's death, the terms of such a (formerly revocable living) trust can provide excellent asset protection for heirs, but the same trusts can be established under the transferor's will, and they will be just as effective to protect trust assets from the creditors of the heirs.

SHAM TRUSTS

A number of scam artists also sell their own version of a trust that they claim has asset protection benefits. These are so-called *pure trusts*, also known as constitutional trusts, common-law trust organizations (COLATOS and their foreign variant, FORCOLATOS), contractual trusts, and a number of other equally exotic and official-sounding names. Their promoters claim that the owner can transfer all family assets, personal and business, to the trust, and that creditors will be prevented from suing the trust, much less reaching the assets.

Pure trust structures are premised on the Contract Clause of the U.S. Constitution, which says that the states shall respect the sanctity of contracts. The promoters of these structures argue that since the trust relationship arises as a result of contract, pure trusts are not subject to the orders of state courts, nor are these structures subject to either state or federal income taxes. In essence, the claim is that these structures are entirely unregulated and are not subject to the jurisdiction of any court. This claim is of course complete nonsense, and many promoters of these structures and their clients have been successfully prosecuted for tax evasion and sentenced to lengthy prison terms. In short, pure trusts are disregarded under the tax code, meaning that any taxable activity in the trust is taxed to the person who transferred the property to the trust. The transferor must report and pay all the taxes for whatever taxable activity occurs with regard to trust assets. Unfortunately, however, based on the scam artists' advice, pure trust settlors attempt to treat the trust as a separate entity not subject to taxation, whereupon they are prosecuted for tax evasion. The IRS has never lost a pure trust tax evasion case. Anyone using such a trust to avoid taxes should contact a tax attorney as soon as possible and should make arrangements to come clean to the IRS voluntarily before the IRS discovers the existence of the pure trust. The IRS tends to be much more lenient on pure trust users in voluntary disclosure situations.

But what of the asset protection claims? The promoters' claims that creditors cannot sue the pure trust or its owners because of the Contract Clause is simply pure bunk. In addition to the Contract Clause interpretation being totally unfounded, pure trusts will almost always be treated as self-settled spendthrift trusts and thus not respected in most states. Even in those states that allow self-settled spendthrift trusts, these entities are usually susceptible to being defeated under other theories, including that the person who formed the trust retains de facto control and thus no true trust relationship was ever really formed, or that the trust is revocable.

CHAPTER 12

Spendthrift and Discretionary Trusts

Despite reservations about the efficacy of self-settled spendthrift trusts as asset protection tools for the settlor (as we shall discuss in Chapters 13 and 14), there should be no qualms about using trusts to protect assets against the creditors of beneficiaries other than the settlor. The use of trusts for making transfers to third-party beneficiaries, whether by means of lifetime gifts or at death, should always be considered.

BASIC CONCEPTS

The long-respected concept of the third-party trust is simply a means for one party, the grantor or settlor, to transfer the legal title (that is, the management and control) to an asset to another party, the trustee, while transferring the beneficial interest (that is, the economic benefits of ownership) in the asset to one or more third parties, the beneficiaries. Although the trustee is the legal owner of the asset, the trustee is obligated to exercise his control of the asset in the best interest of the beneficiaries of the trust. Although it is possible to have an oral trust agreement, the terms of the trust arrangement usually and ideally are spelled out in a written trust agreement.

A *living* or *inter vivos trust* is one established during the lifetime of the grantor. A *testamentary trust* is one established under the terms of the grantor's will. A *revocable trust* is one that can be terminated or amended by the grantor at any time. An *irrevocable trust* is one that cannot be terminated or amended by the grantor. Although revocable living trusts can have considerable utility as estate planning and probate avoidance devices, they provide no meaningful asset protection against the grantor's creditors. If the grantor can reach the assets of the trust at any time, so can the grantor's creditors, since the creditors can simply ask the court to order the grantor to revoke the trust. Not withstanding this obvious and fatal defect, amazingly some promoters sell living trusts as asset protection tools. Accordingly, the discussion here will focus on irrevocable inter vivos trusts and testamentary trusts.

SPENDTHRIFT TRUSTS

When a trust is created, the grantor can specify in the trust agreement that the beneficiary cannot transfer, in any way, her interest in the trust, and that the beneficiary's creditors will have no rights to trust assets so long as the assets remain in trust. Once distributed to the beneficiary, the assets are fair game to creditors, but so long as the assets remain in trust, creditors cannot reach them. A trust with such language is called a spendthrift trust.

Except in a handful of states, as discussed in Chapter 13, spendthrift clauses do not protect trust assets from the creditors of a beneficiary who is also the grantor of the trust. In other words, you can't form a trust for your own benefit and expect that it will hold up against creditors in most states. These types of trusts are known as *self-settled spendthrift trusts* or more popularly as *domestic asset protection trusts (DAPTs)*.

But as long as you are not forming the trust for your own benefit, you can create trusts that will stand up to the beneficiaries' creditors. Although a few states do not recognize the effect of spendthrift clauses and a few other states limit their application, in most states spendthrift protection is one of the most reliable forms of asset protection, albeit for trust beneficiaries other than the grantor and not for the grantor himself. The grantor of a spendthrift trust can provide formidable asset protection for trust assets for his children, as beneficiaries of the trust, but not for himself.

Some creditors have argued that spendthrift clauses should not protect trust assets from the claims of tort creditors—that is, where a trust beneficiary has inflicted physical suffering on a creditor, as for personal injury, wrongful death, or sexual assault. Courts have almost consistently rejected such arguments. In a case where the Mississippi Supreme Court did accept such an argument, the Mississippi legislature effectively negated the ruling for future cases by passing specific legislation preventing tort creditors from reaching a beneficiary's interest in a spendthrift trust. Note, however, that once the assets are distributed out of the trust to beneficiaries they become fair game for the beneficiaries' creditors to attack in all cases.

Spendthrift trusts are meant to provide for the basic needs of a beneficiary, and the creditor-protected status of the benefits of such trusts is a source of comfort to many grantors and beneficiaries. While the facts of particular cases may be unjust, courts are unlikely to change longstanding precedent favoring the enforcement of spendthrift clauses.

Despite these very solid protections, too many advisors allow their clients to make naked gifts and bequests to their heirs. This is probably the single biggest asset protection mistake made by estate planning advisors, and it can cost a client's family millions of dollars. Unless a client can absolutely guarantee that his or her children will never get divorced or sued, or unless the transferred assets are so small in value that the cost of an annual income tax return is prohibitive, there is rarely any reason not to transfer assets using a trust with a spendthrift clause.

DISCRETIONARY TRUSTS

As mentioned earlier, some states' laws limit or ignore spendthrift clauses. However, even where spendthrift clauses are valid, once assets have been distributed to a beneficiary they become available to creditors. If a trust mandates distributions or allows distributions only directly to the beneficiary, the beneficiary's creditors will be able to reach the distributed assets.

The solution to this potential problem is for the trust agreement to provide for distributions to or for the benefit of the beneficiary only at the discretion of the trustee. Even if a spendthrift clause is not effective to prevent a beneficiary's creditor from reaching her interest in a trust, the creditor will not have access to assets if they are not distributed. If a beneficiary has judgment creditors, the trustee can simply withhold distributions or can apply trust assets for the beneficiary's benefit. For example, the trustee could pay mortgages, medical bills, utility bills, educational expenses, and the like directly to the payee rather than distributing funds to the beneficiary to make those same payments. Creditors of a beneficiary simply cannot force a trustee to make distributions directly to the beneficiary if it is within the discretion of the trustee to withhold direct distributions to the beneficiary. Furthermore, creditors of a beneficiary cannot prevent a trustee from applying trust assets for the benefit of a beneficiary, to the exclusion of the beneficiary's judgment creditors.

Trusts for the benefit of multiple family members or classes of persons, such as children or grandchildren, can give the trustee the option to make totally discretionary distributions of trust assets to trust beneficiaries without regard to proportionality or equality among the trust beneficiaries. These discretionary distributions are sometimes referred to as a "spray" or "sprinkling" distributions, and correspondingly, such trusts are sometimes called *spray trusts* or *sprinkling trusts*. Sprinkling assets allows the trustee the flexibility to assist beneficiaries who need or deserve help and to withhold assets from beneficiaries who do not need or deserve help or who have creditor problems.

Note that estate planning considerations may factor into whether a trust is completely discretionary. For example, a trust for a grantor's spouse cannot be completely discretionary as to income and still qualify for the federal estate tax marital deduction. However, where asset protection is the primary concern, strong consideration should be given to the use of discretionary spendthrift trusts. Discretionary spendthrift trusts for the benefit of others provide very substantial asset protection. Assets in discretionary spendthrift trusts are protected from the creditors of beneficiaries in bankruptcy, in divorce, and in postjudgment collection proceedings in even the most egregious personal injury, malpractice, and wrongful death cases.

POWERS OF APPOINTMENT

For generation-skipping transfer tax reasons, sometimes the primary beneficiary of a trust will be given the power to give assets to anyone, including his estate, under his will, in order that the assets subject to that power will be included in the beneficiary's taxable estate (where it may be exempt or subject to a lower rate) rather than being subject to a higher generation-skipping tax. This power is called a *general power of appointment*. In some states and under federal bankruptcy law, property subject to a general power of appointment is subject to the claims of the power holder's creditors. In other states, such property is protected from the claims of the power holder's creditors. In most states, however, the issue has been addressed neither by statute nor at the appellate court level.

Some flexibility can be provided the trust instrument to afford an additional layer of asset protection in the event the beneficiary is given a general power of appointment. For example, an independent trustee can be given the power to toggle the general power of appointment on and off, as well as the power to restrict the terms of the general power of appointment. Consequently, the independent trustee can react to changes in the tax laws and changes in the beneficiary's creditor problems by modifying the general power of appointment accordingly. Furthermore, the trust might be drafted to give the primary beneficiary a general power of appointment that is exercisable only with the consent of the independent trustee so that, in any event, the independent trustee ultimately stands between the creditors and the trust assets.

A power of appointment that does not allow the power holder to give property to herself, her creditors, or her estate is known as a *limited* or *special power of appointment*. Limited powers of appointment can be useful in allowing the beneficiary of a trust to provide for others while excluding those assets from the reach of her own creditors and while excluding those assets from her own taxable estate at death. It allows the beneficiary to make tax-free gifts of assets that would otherwise benefit her or someone else. Furthermore, because the assets do not belong to the power holder, there can be no fraudulent transfer concerns for the power holder.

DYNASTY TRUSTS

Because of the powerful wealth-building and asset protection capabilities of discretionary spendthrift trusts, it is often desirable for a grantor to create a trust that will last for as long as is legally permissible, keeping trust assets in the family as long as possible. Trust assets are made available to or for the benefit of the beneficiaries; ownership of the assets is kept in the trust; and gift, estate, and generation-skipping transfer taxes are avoided to the extent possible (with these taxes often being completely avoided). Under an arcane rule called the *rule against perpetuities*, which will generally limit the life of a trust to three generations (about 100 years), most states limit the length of time that a trust can last. However, a number of states and offshore jurisdictions have abolished or modified the rule against perpetuities to allow trusts to last for a very long time. Trusts designed to last for many generations, which are established in one of these jurisdictions, are often called *dynasty trusts*.

Often the best wealth-building tool in a dynasty trust is a large life insurance policy. Many offshore private-placement life insurance policies, such as those discussed in Chapter 25, are owned by dynasty trusts. When significant assets have built up in the dynasty trust, it functions as a family bank or family asset pool. Distributions can be made to beneficiaries as with any other trust.

The best strategy is to keep assets within the trust, while making them available to the beneficiaries. For example, the dynasty trust might purchase a house, a vacation home, or boats or recreational vehicles for the use of trust beneficiaries.. The dynasty trust might also make secured loans to a beneficiary to purchase a home or to provide estate liquidity for the beneficiary. The possibilities are endless. A well-funded trust can provide for practically every need and want of trust beneficiaries without actually making distributions to the beneficiaries. Therefore, just about the only good reason to make a distribution is to allow a beneficiary to purchase life insurance for himself and his spouse to fund yet another dynasty trust specifically for his family.

Perhaps the best use of dynasty trust assets is to fund ventures that have the potential to build even greater wealth for the family inside the trust. For example, if a beneficiary of a dynasty trust wants to start a business and the trustee thinks it a good idea, the business can be started with trust assets used as seed capital. If the business venture takes off and the value of the business increases, it grows free of estate and gift taxes and the generation-skipping transfer tax inside the trust, where it is also protected from the creditors of the beneficiaries. This strategy is known as *opportunity shifting*, and it plays a significant role in contemporary asset protection, since the profits from the venture are protected within the trust. Of course, normal business asset protection considerations should be given to trust assets such as vehicles, real estate, and businesses, in order to isolate liability-producing assets from other trust assets.

BENEFICIARY-CONTROLLED TRUSTS

Trusts are often not used because of perceptions that trusts will cause loss of control. However, using the concept of the beneficiary controlled trust, a primary trust beneficiary may be given the functional equivalent of outright ownership, but without the assets being subject to attachment by creditors and without the trust estate being subject to estate taxes in the beneficiary's estate.

A *beneficiary-controlled trust* is a trust in which the primary beneficiary is either the sole trustee or a co-trustee. Often the beneficiary-trustee is given the ability to remove and replace trustees and co-trustees. But for asset protection purposes, it is best if decisions made pursuant to the power to remove and replace trustees is subject to the approval of a third party such as a trust protector. A beneficiary-controlled trust agreement would include broad investment powers so that the beneficiary-trustee can invest in anything just as she would be able to do with outright ownership. The primary beneficiary often is given a broad power to appoint trust assets to other persons (such as her spouse, children, grandchildren, or her children's spouses). This setup allows her to make nontaxable gifts and to eliminate potential interference by other beneficiaries (who effectively can be cut out of the trust by the primary beneficiary's exercise of this power of appointment).

A single beneficiary-trustee provides significantly less flexibility and protection than a co-trusteeship arrangement. It causes some potential difficulties or limitations from an estate and generation-skipping tax perspective. (For example, distributions to the beneficiary-trustee are required to be limited to an ascertainable standard, such as for reasons of health, education, maintenance, and support.) Having the beneficiary as the sole trustee may also be dangerous from an asset protection perspective. Some legal scholars argue that the creditor of a beneficiary-trustee should be able to reach whatever assets the beneficiary-trustee can properly distribute to himself under the terms of the trust agreement.

A more effective asset protection strategy is to use two co-trustees. The primary beneficiary is the investment co-trustee, who has the ability to make wide-ranging investment decisions. An independent co-trustee is given the sole power to make distributions to the beneficiary. With an independent trustee in charge of distributions, there is no need to limit distributions to an ascertainable standard. The primary beneficiary may also be given the power to remove and replace the independent trustee. However, this power should be exercisable only in conjunction with another independent party, such as a trust protector, so that the beneficiary could not be compelled by a court to name a trustee favorable to a creditor.

When a client tells her advisor that she wants trust property distributed to a beneficiary upon reaching a specified age, in most cases, the client has selected that age because of the belief that the beneficiary will be mature enough to prudently administer and use the assets. She may not necessarily do so because she wants the beneficiary to hold legal title to the assets at that time. The objective of control and use of assets can be accomplished by using a third-party-controlled discretionary spendthrift trust that becomes a beneficiary-controlled trust upon the beneficiary's reaching a specified age.

This beneficiary-controlled trust planning technique is clearly superior to making outright gifts or bequests and to making mandatory trust distributions at a specified age. Because this strategy creates a nearly insurmountable asset and divorce protection shield, the trust should be designed to continue as a dynasty trust for multiple generations so that the secondary and more remote beneficiaries also enjoy the benefit of a third-party-created spendthrift trust.

TRUSTS AND UFTA

The foregoing discussion of trusts presumes that there are no fraudulent transfer issues with the transfer of assets into such trusts. Although spendthrift and similar provisions provide solid protection for trust assets from the claims of creditors of beneficiaries other than the settlor, these provisions provide absolutely no protection against claims of the settlor's creditors that the assets were fraudulently transferred into the trust. The trusts discussed in this chapter are normally funded with gifts. As discussed in Chapter 6, gifts are relatively easy to set aside—for as long as up to seven years in some states—under the fraudulent transfer laws.

Gifting is not the only means of funding trusts. In Chapter 23 we discuss alternative methods of funding trusts, as well as means of holding assets in trusts, that mitigate these concerns. However, the bottom line is the same: Once assets are successfully placed into a trust with spendthrift provisions, it will be nearly impossible for creditors of beneficiaries other than the settlor to attack those assets.

Trusts are such powerful asset protection and estate planning tools that some people want to form spendthrift and similar trusts not just for their heirs, but also for themselves. In Chapter 13 we will consider the relatively new laws of certain U.S. states that allow persons to do just that. In Chapter 14 we will consider foreign asset protection trusts. In these two chapters, we will see that the courts and most state legislatures consider these types of trusts to be too good at protecting assets to be permitted.

The Domestic Asset Protection Trust (DAPT)

Courts have long perceived one particular type of spendthrift trust as abusive, precisely because it was used to defeat creditors in a way that seemed unfair. This is the *self-settled spendthrift trust,* by which a person creates an irrevocable discretionary spendthrift trust, naming him- or herself as a beneficiary. (For an idea of how these operate, see Figure 13.1.) The theory behind the self-settled spendthrift trust is that it allows a debtor to gift his assets to a trust, then to argue that those assets are the property of the trustee, not the debtor, when creditors come for those assets. Courts in the United States and in all English common-law jurisdictions have long since disallowed the protection of such trusts. In some places, the prohibition has been enacted into statutory law. Until very recently, legislatures have been reluctant to allow self-settled spendthrift trusts.

In Chapter 14, we will see that various offshore tax and debtor havens, in an effort to attract business, changed their trust laws precisely to allow self-settled spendthrift trusts to be effective. For a few years beginning in the mid-1990s, foreign asset protection trusts (FAPTs) became wildly popular and started to drain trust business away from U.S. trust companies. In 1997, Alaska became the first U.S. jurisdiction to adopt *domestic asset protection trust (DAPT)* legislation, which allowed self-settled spendthrift trusts. That legislation was soon followed by similar legislation in Delaware, Nevada, Rhode Island, and Utah.[1] This relative flurry of

FIGURE 13.1

Self-settled spendthrift trust.

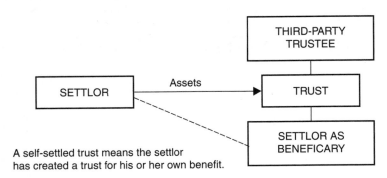

A self-settled trust means the settlor
has created a trust for his or her own benefit.

domestic activity is the direct result of the popularity of FAPTs and
the competition for trust business.

DAPT MECHANICS

The new DAPT laws authorize precisely what has been judicially
or statutorily prohibited for hundreds of years. They allow a person to create a discretionary spendthrift trust for her own benefit,
treating the assets of the trust as the property of the trustee and not
as belonging to the creator of the trust. Whether this is good public
policy is beyond the scope of this book. We will merely note that
laws prohibiting self-settled spendthrift trusts are entirely consis-
tent with the systemic underpinning of our economy that requires
that when debtors incur debt, they pay those debts.

The public policy issue is not merely an esoteric concern since
only a few states have adopted self-settled trust legislation and the
rest have not. The conflict is not merely a technicality. The states
that disallow the protection of self-settled spendthrift trusts do so
for the reason that they violate long-standing public policy as
expressed by their courts and their legislatures. This issue is every
bit as contentious as the issues between states that have legalized
gambling and those that have not. What seems libertarian and
open-minded in some states may seem immoral, illegal, or oppor-
tunistic from the viewpoint of the others. Although the courts of
one state usually show a degree of respect or comity to the laws of

another state, all bets are off where the court of one state decides that the law of the other state violates its public policy. This creates a classic conflict-of-laws situation between the few states that allow DAPTs and the majority that do not. This conflict presents opportunities, difficulties, and potential traps.

Adding to the confusion is the U.S. Constitution, which requires that the valid judgments of one state be given "full faith and credit" by the rest. However, a state might not even have to respect the judgment of another state if the law that produced the judgment would violate fundamental public policy in the state where recognition of the judgment is sought.

No state has jurisdictional powers beyond its borders. For example, an Oklahoma judgment recorded in an Oklahoma court is worthless against assets in North Carolina. The Oklahoma courts have no ability to compel a North Carolina person to do anything. However, the Oklahoma judgment can be registered in North Carolina. Thereafter the North Carolina courts would be required by the U.S. Constitution's Full Faith and Credit Clause to treat the judgment as if it were a North Carolina judgment all along. This would allow for all of the remedies that would otherwise be available to creditors in North Carolina.

Because of the Full Faith and Credit Clause, the remedies available to a creditor and the protections available for a debtor's assets depend on the state that the judgments are in, not the state where the debtor resides. This situation applies to trust assets too, since whether or not trust assets are protected depends on the creditors' remedies in the state where the assets are located, and not where the trust is formed or the trustee resides. For example, if assets of a Nevada DAPT are located in Kentucky, and if Kentucky does not recognized self-settled spendthrift trusts, the potential exists for a Kentucky court simply to deem that the Nevada DAPT does not exist. The assets would then be treated as those of the debtor, making them available to creditors.

Similarly, if the debtor is subject to the jurisdiction of a state that does not recognize self-settled spendthrift trusts, the potential exists for the courts of that state to require the debtor to bring the assets within the jurisdiction of the courts of the non-DAPT state so that the assets are made available to creditors. These *repatriation orders* have been the bane of those attempting to protect assets in offshore trusts, although the argument could be made that the creditors' remedy is to litigate in the DAPT state.

LIMITATIONS OF DAPTs

To the extent a DAPT can protect assets from creditors, both the assets and the debtor must physically be in a state with DAPT laws. However, even this arrangement is no guarantee that a DAPT will be effective in protecting assets from creditors.

In addition to state courts and state laws that may or may not respect self-settled spendthrift trusts, federal courts and federal laws can come into play. Under the Supremacy Clause of the U.S. Constitution, where federal laws and state laws conflict or cover the same legal ground, federal laws preempt state laws. So, if at some later time Congress decided to make a change to the federal bankruptcy laws to allow bankruptcy courts to ignore state laws relating to self-settled spendthrift trusts, that change would end the effectiveness of DAPTs. Another possible scenario is where Congress enacts legislation for a specific type of claim (for example, an environmental or maritime claim), to allow a regulatory agency or plaintiffs in a federal lawsuit to ignore the self-settled spendthrift trust and simply treat the assets as those of the settlor. Also, changes to the Federal Rules of Civil Procedure may authorize remedies that have the same effect.

Even in states that have adopted DAPT legislation, the original conveyance to the DAPT may be deemed fraudulent. DAPT legislation typically shortens the limitations period for a creditor to assert that a transfer to a DAPT was fraudulent. There are two problems with this scenario. First, there is still some period where even under the DAPT statute the transfer to the DAPT may be set aside as fraudulent. Second, as we saw in Chapter 6, which relates to fraudulent transfers, conflict-of-laws issues abound and may operate to defeat these shortened limitations periods.

For example, if a California resident makes a transfer of assets to a Delaware trust, which limitations period applies? Is it that of California or Delaware? The answer will probably depend on the type of property transferred and the method and timing of the transfer. Still, this is no easy question to answer. California might not even start the limitations period running until the creditor has a judgment. If the California limitations period applies, chances are good that the transfer to the DAPT will be negated, and the DAPT structure will fail to protect assets transferred to it.

The UFTA allows a transfer to be set aside in some instances even where the transfer occurred before the claim arose. Assuming that the DAPT will be effective against all creditors, simply because it was funded when there were no known claims may be wishful thinking. Certainly, advance funding helps. Indeed, advance funding is a necessity for a plan involving a DAPT. Nevertheless, a concern is that for a substantial period of years after the DAPT is funded it may not withstand an attack on fraudulent transfer grounds. DAPT legislation attempts to remedy this unfortunate situation by implementing stricter standards for judging whether or not a transaction is fraudulent. But here, again, a significant conflict-of-laws issue arises. If the transfer took place in another state, the other state's fraudulent transfer laws may apply, not those of the DAPT state.

A related problem is that while the trustee actually holding the asset may be protected in the DAPT state, the trustee may be exposed to judgments and court orders in other states, including garnishment and attachment orders. A smart creditor pursuing the assets of a Nevada trust, for example, might decide to register the judgment in New York and attempt to attach the Nevada trust company's assets held in a New York brokerage firm. In such a case, New York law would likely apply, not Nevada law.

DAPTs AND REPATRIATION ORDERS

A significant potential weakness for a debtor caught outside of the jurisdiction of a DAPT state is that a court of that state may attempt the *Anderson remedy* and order that the debtor-settlor be held in jail on contempt until he or she agrees to repatriate the trust assets to the non-DAPT state. The fraudulent transfer laws give courts tremendous latitude in fashioning remedies. Since the repatriation-contempt remedy is now ordinarily employed to reach assets in foreign asset protection trusts, a probable inevitability will be that someday a judge will employ the remedy against DAPT assets as well. The authors know of no constitutional grounds why such a remedy would not be successful in holding the debtor in jail until the assets are repatriated to the non-DAPT state so long as the court believes that the incarceration may still have a coercive effect. Indeed, some debtors have been in jail for several years for contempt for failing to repatriate foreign assets.

A significant weakness of DAPT assets as compared with their foreign counterparts is that DAPT assets are typically in the United States and are at least physically available to creditors. Indeed, some DAPT statutes require that some portion of trust assets be kept in that state. If a judge in that state interprets the law of the DAPT state in a way that benefits a creditor, the creditor may be able to reach the asset before the interpretation is appealed. Even if the judgment is later set aside, the debtor may have no means of relief against the creditor, especially if the creditor is domiciled in a state that does not allow self-settled spendthrift trusts. Until the asset protection benefits of DAPTs are validated in each DAPT state, and in a range of circumstances, serious questions remain about the viability of DAPTs, even in DAPT states.

DAPTs VERSUS FAPTs

One feature of a foreign asset protection trust makes it a much better tool than a DAPT. In the absolutely worst circumstances (keep in mind, such a situation is what asset protection is designed for), at least with an offshore trust, a debtor can physically leave the United States entirely and enjoy trust assets totally free from U.S. jurisdiction—so long as she or he doesn't return.

A less significant advantage of foreign asset protection trusts is that debtors may be able to take advantage of offshore secrecy and privacy laws. Or they can simply take advantage of the fact that getting information about offshore structures and offshore assets is difficult and expensive. In contrast, because a DAPT is in the United States, it is subject to the jurisdiction of federal courts, and the disclosure-oriented Federal Rules of Civil Procedure will take precedence over any state attempts at enhanced privacy. Although secrecy and privacy should never be considered effective asset protection tools, in some cases the difficulty of obtaining discovery abroad may help to facilitate an early settlement in a case involving a FAPT.

Like a FAPT, the DAPT has one particularly significant disadvantage for most trust settlors. The settlor of the trust is required to give up control to another person or institution located in the DAPT state. The skeptic's view of this situation is to realize that the settlor of a DAPT hopes to avoid having trust assets taken at some time in the future by an unknown creditor by transferring them to a trustee who may abscond with the assets now. If the settlor attempts to retain direct or indirect control over the assets, the entire arrangement risks being negated by a court as a sham. On the other hand, if the settlor yields total control—which he or she must for this to work—the assets may be "here today and gone to Maui tomorrow."

To avoid the problem of disappearing assets, most DAPT trustees are relatively large institutional trustees. The problem, however, is that these trustees are potentially subject to nationwide jurisdiction, and thus they are subject to the orders of courts in non-DAPT states. Under various rulings relating to personal jurisdiction, an institutional trustee that has, for example, an Internet Web site and solicits business from all fifty states could be subject to jurisdiction in all fifty states. Even if the trust is formed in a DAPT state and the trust company has its headquarters in that state, the trust company may be sued and be the subject of judgments in non-DAPT states. That trust company would thus be subject to considerable court pressure to turn over to the settlor's creditors the assets held for the trust.

OTHER POTENTIAL WEAKNESSES

A smart creditor may choose not to attack a DAPT structure straight on by arguing the fine points of the DAPT statute and Constitutional law. Instead, he may look for alternative plans of attack. The most obvious alternative attack available to a creditor is an action for civil conspiracy. While DAPT statutes attempt to limit these actions, these statutes cannot restrict such actions brought under the laws of a non-DAPT states, if the creditor can find a jurisdictional nexus there. For example, assume that a creditor in Iowa, which as of the time of the writing of this book does not have DAPT legislation, is able to assert jurisdiction over a debtor in Iowa who has settled a DAPT. The creditor would bring an action for civil conspiracy against the debtor and all involved (including persons and entities holding the trust assets) for a conspiracy to com-mit a fraudulent transfer under Iowa law. If the creditor obtains a judgment, he would then register the judgment in those states where trust assets are located, and pursue the judgment in those states. In theory, at least, Nevada courts would be required to recognize the Iowa judgment even if the Nevada DAPT statute specifically prevents such causes of action with respect to the Nevada DAPT.

In such a situation, the lack of flexibility of the DAPT structure becomes a potential hindrance. To work as a discretionary spendthrift trust, the DAPT must be irrevocable. However, being so makes it difficult to unwind the structure other than when distributions need to be made; those distributions are then made available to creditors. This constriction puts the DAPT in the posture of a boxer whose feet are glued to the mat. With business entities, on the other hand, there is greater flexibility to unwind or alter transactions to meet changing circumstances and to dodge or avoid creditor punches.

DAPTs also risk changes to DAPT legislation itself—changes that may or may not be grandfathered. All it takes to change the law is one high-profile case with unseemly circumstances. For example, suppose a drunk driver slams an oversized SUV into a school bus and causes significant injuries and fatalities. Further suppose the drunk driver avoids millions of dollars in liability for personal injury and wrongful death claims with a DAPT. (This is precisely the sort of result for which DAPT legislation, with little foresight, was enacted.) The resulting public outcry would be very likely to convince state legislatures that DAPTs aren't such a great idea after all. A subsequent change in the law to prohibit or substantially weaken DAPTs would almost certainly result. In a particularly egregious case like this one, such a change might even be effectively retroactive to past judgments. It would be, because after passage of the new legislation those creditors who previously were stymied could simply reattempt their collection actions, this time successfully.

Finally, changes to the federal bankruptcy laws have the potential to weaken or negate the effectiveness of DAPTs. Because federal law preempts state law, a creditor could possibly force a debtor into involuntary bankruptcy in order to take advantage of newly enacted federal provisions to reach assets in the DAPT.

For all these reasons, a decade or longer will probably be the time necessary before enough of these issues are resolved to give comfort to those interested in DAPTs as a primary asset protection tool. This assumes, of course, that there are no changes to the law, state or federal, that weaken DAPTs in the meantime.

Even then, a DAPT may never be a reliable asset protection tool. The primary reason is that DAPTs are not subtle at all. They are notorious and obvious attempts to change the debtor-creditor landscape by the brute force of legislation focused more on attracting assets to lightly populated or economically challenged states than on any fundamentally solid public policy purpose. DAPTs are indiscriminate in that they provide protection, to the extent that they do so at all, to the lifelong deadbeat, the deliberate environmental polluter, the drunk driver, the child molester, the securities fraudster, as well as the doctors and other professionals and entrepreneurs for whom these structures are ostensibly marketed. Some states have recognized this situation, and they have attempted to carve out statutory exceptions where the DAPT protection will not stand up, such as in the case of unpaid child support, while at least one DAPT state even protects against child support payments.

WHEN TO USE A DAPT

Even with the foregoing defects, a DAPT can be an appropriate part of an asset protection plan, so long as the planning is done with the aforementioned limitations in mind. Note that we said "part of an asset protection plan." Even if you decide to use a DAPT, that structure should not hold, directly or indirectly, more than a minor part of a person's total wealth. Our continuing emphasis on diversity of methods takes on a louder tone with regard to untested structures with many potential weaknesses, and DAPTs are a good example of this.

Generally, a DAPT should be considered only if the settlor resides in a DAPT state, and only if all the assets are held in the DAPT state, as it is unlikely that the courts of a state not having DAPT legislation will recognize the protections of the DAPT statute. Possibly, a person living in a non-DAPT state could form a DAPT and then, in the event of trouble, move to the state in which the DAPT was formed. (This would be much like a person attempting to utilize an FAPT for asset protection being prepared to leave the United States, for the FAPT to work.) But we think that such a person would be better off exploring other options that might work within his or her own state instead.

A DAPT should be merely one layer of an asset protection plan for the assets it is holding. Ideally, a DAPT should hold nothing but illiquid assets, so that if a creditor is successful in breaking through the DAPT the creditor still must cut through other layers to reach liquid assets. This setup may deter some creditors from attempting to challenge the DAPT in the first place.

A unique use of a DAPT may be for the *inbound migration* of a foreign trust—that is, moving a FAPT to the United States yet having most of its provisions remain effective. A person who lives in DAPT state may be able to utilize a FAPT, since the concept of a self-settled spendthrift trust obviously is not repugnant to the laws of the DAPT state. However, even if this is true, this FAPT is likely to be effective only if the debtor's assets are also located offshore or in the DAPT state. Of course, this whole scenario is ironic, because DAPT statutes were adopted after FAPT statutes, with the intention of making DAPT competitive with offshore debtor havens.

One potentially useful application of a DAPT may be to own a domestic private placement life insurance (PPLI) policy. At the time of the writing of this book, Alaska had a very low premium tax. Where millions of dollars of life insurance premium are involved, the premium tax savings may be quite significant—a few hundred thousand dollars perhaps. The person seeking to invest in the PPLI policy would first fund an Alaska DAPT, and then the Alaska trustee of the DAPT would purchase the policy in Alaska. If the state insurance regulators or tax authorities question why the policy was purchased in Alaska, the response would be that the DAPT was needed for asset protection purposes. (This would be yet another example of how asset protection can "cover" a tax transaction.) We have no opinion on whether such an arrangement to avoid premium taxes will avoid scrutiny, and we expect significant litigation over the issue.

DAPTs probably would not exist had not their foreign counterparts been so successful from a marketing standpoint. In Chapter 14 we examine foreign asset protection trusts.

ENDNOTES

1. As of the time of this writing, Alaska, Delaware, Nevada, Rhode Island, and Utah are the five states that have enacted self-settled spendthrift trust legislation, and they are actively attempting to attract trust business on this basis. Colorado and Missouri allow self-settled spendthrift trusts, with limitations. Other states are in various stages of considering similar legislation, but it is not the intent of this book to catalogue those states or the specific benefits of the legislation they have passed. A current list of these states and legislation is available on our Web site at http://assetprotectionbook.com

CHAPTER 14

The Foreign Asset Protection Trust (FAPT)

We began this book with the story of Mr. Steven Jay Lawrence. He was the bond trader who was wiped out in the crash of 1987 and pursued by Bear Stearns for a margin call. Shortly before an arbitration decision against him, Mr. Lawrence funded an offshore trust in Mauritius in the Indian Ocean and transferred most of his wealth there. Later, after he had filed for bankruptcy, the bankruptcy court demanded that he bring the assets back to the United States. When he refused, he was imprisoned for civil contempt of court, and his bankruptcy discharge was denied.

A bad result? Absolutely, except in one significant aspect. As of the time of the writing of this book, Bear Stearns has not been able to reach the assets in Mr. Lawrence's trust. The assets are protected, even if Mr. Lawrence remains in prison for failing to bring the assets back to the United States.

WHAT IS A FAPT?

The greatest advantage of *foreign asset protection trusts (FAPTs)* is that they work to protect assets. Once assets are in a FAPT, a creditor legally can do very little to retrieve the assets from the trust directly. The attack must be indirect, by the creditor convincing the court that the debtor has the ability to retrieve the assets himself. If the court is convinced and orders the debtor to retrieve the assets (and this is the current trend), the debtor faces imprisonment for contempt of court if he does not comply. So, in order to avoid this scenario, the debtor must leave the United States to avoid the jurisdiction of U.S. courts. This rather drastic downside to the use of a FAPT as a primary asset protection tool should dissuade most persons from using it. Indeed, many unscrupulous planners fail to reveal this practical tidbit of information to their clients, for fear of losing a sale. Despite this drawback, however, it does admittedly offer the potential for very significant protection and as such, it is worth exploring.

The FAPT is an offshore trust formed in an offshore jurisdiction that has specific trust and civil procedure laws designed to thwart creditors of trust settlors. These laws are the result of a business decision by the jurisdiction to attract trust business and trust assets. The FAPT jurisdiction generally will not recognize U.S. judgments. The courts of the jurisdiction are usually heavily predisposed to protecting the trust assets from creditors, since to allow creditors to invade the trust assets would effectively kill the offshore trust business there.

Offshore trusts have been used for hundreds of years to shield assets and income from creditors, albeit in a considerably more subtle manner than is evident today. In the mid-1980s, the Cook Islands, a tiny independent country in the South Pacific, attempted to establish itself as a significant offshore tax haven, a place for businesspeople to divert money away from U.S. taxation. Changes to the U.S. tax code and a number of defeats in court cases put an end to most offshore tax avoidance strategies involving offshore trusts. Thus, the Cook Islands adopted what would become the first "advanced" trust statute that was specifically designed to defeat the claims of creditors of the settlor-beneficiaries of Cook Islands trusts.

A number of lawyers wrote law review articles that celebrated the "absolute protection" virtues of FAPTs. They said that U.S. judges would be unable to find trust settlors in contempt of court for failing to obey an order to repatriate trust assets. The fight for assets, they explained, would have to shift to the Cook Islands where, for a number of legal and political reasons, no asset protection trust would be penetrated. Hopeful for asset protection trust business themselves, a handful of other offshore jurisdictions soon adopted FAPT laws, and then the race—to the bottom, it might be said—was on. Several more jurisdictions enacted FAPT laws, competing to see which could enact the most debtor-friendly laws.

FAPT/FLP STRUCTURES

Beginning in the early 1990s, FAPTs were combined with family limited partnerships (FLPs, discussed in Chapter 19) and were widely marketed as the ultimate asset protection tool, the fortress whose walls creditors would never breach. These structures were even marketed as the "family fortress" by various groups. The FAPT/FLP combination (we jokingly refer to it as the "combo platter") eventually became the most hotly marketed and commonly used asset protection tool for over a decade. It still remains popular, although its users and proponents likely are in for a number of rude awakenings.

A simplified explanation of the FAPT/FLP structure (see Figure 14.1) is that the client transfers virtually all of her assets to a domes-

FIGURE 14.1

FAPT/FLP structure.

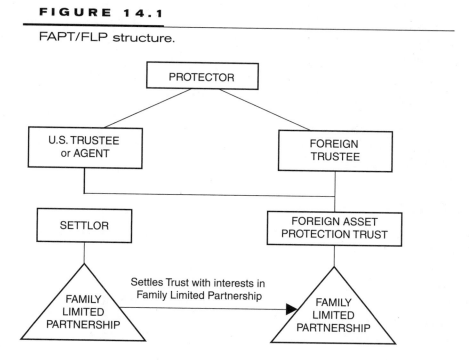

tic family limited partnership in exchange for a 99 percent nonvoting limited partner's interest and a 1 percent general partner's interest. The client would then transfer the interest in the FLP to the FAPT, as a gift. If estate and gift tax planning were part of the recipe, the client would "discount" the value of the FLP interests transferred to the trust to achieve estate and gift tax savings for lack of marketability and lack of control, in some cases. In theory, if a creditor came along, the FLP interest would be liquidated and all the assets "upstreamed" to the FAPT—effectively shipped offshore and out of the reach of U.S. courts. Even if the creditor were able to have the gift of the limited-partner interest to the FAPT set aside as a fraudulent transfer, the creditor would then be left with an "empty" and worthless partnership interest and no liquid assets.

The creditor's only chance to get assets (again, in theory) would be to bring a lawsuit in the jurisdiction where the trust then existed to have the transfer to the trust set aside under that jurisdiction's very restrictive fraudulent transfer laws. But even then, the creditor would be thwarted, because the trust would contain a migration clause allowing the trustee to move the trust to yet another offshore debtor haven. That would force the creditor to begin the fight again in the new jurisdiction. The trust seemingly could be moved from jurisdiction to jurisdiction until the creditor was exhausted and simply gave up.

This was the theory, and at the time it sounded quite good to a lot of people, especially estate planning attorneys interested in expanding their service offerings. However, in addition to the fact that the structure's underpinnings were purely theoretical, the "combo platter" suffered perhaps an even more fatal feature: It was too easy to implement.

THE OFFSHORE TRUST BOOM

Once an average estate planner or tax attorney could figure out how to create their first such structure, from then on it was just a matter of drafting a set of boilerplate documents (or modifying the form documents provided by offshore trust companies) that could be used for multiple clients with only minor modifications for each client. The combo platter became a cookie-cutter structure. Next, planners began using this as an exclusive asset protection methodology, generally ignoring more proven and fundamentally solid methodologies such as exemption planning and equity stripping. These other methods had been used successfully by debtors' attorneys for years, but they were relatively difficult to implement, because they required custom planning focused on each individual client. The path of least resistance, as it has been done so many times in tax and estate planning, led to poor planning.

As the economy kept chugging healthily through the 1990s, many of the workout specialists who were involved in the cleanup of the savings and loan debacles and the commercial real estate bust of the 1980s, who were the real elite in the asset protection sector, retired or went on to more lucrative transactional work. Thus, the asset protection sector came to be led by tax and estate planners who had not been in the debtor-creditor trenches of the courtroom. Most of them had never been before a hostile judge in a postjudgment collection proceeding. Not being concerned with what a judge might think, for these rather naive planners the lucrative cookie-cutter combo platter was a dream come true. Moreover, it felt like a natural fit, since these planners were already familiar with FLPs and family trusts as excellent and effective estate planning tools.

Indeed, by the late 1990s, the offshore trusts sector was filled with everybody from accountants to financial planners who were forming FAPTs for their clients often without any involvement by an attorney. The offshore trust companies kicked their operations into high gear and ground out FAPTs by the tens of thousands. Brokerage firms offered special funds and other financial products that were specifically designed for those who were hiding money in their offshore trusts. Offshore banks offered seemingly anonymous debit cards. These cards allowed easy access at all times to money locked away behind trust documents that for some planners had absurdly grown to over 120 pages in length because they were packed with every anticreditor clause imaginable.

Yet, as any passenger on the *Titanic* would testify, the theory that a ship can hit an iceberg without sinking and the practical results of the ship actually hitting the iceberg can be two different things entirely. As the century turned and cases involving FAPTs started to work their way through the U.S. courts, theory finally met reality—and reality won.

ADVANTAGES OF FAPTs

What makes FAPT so great? Over the years, planners have developed a number of mechanisms to make the FAPT, in theory, into a better and better asset protection tool. The advantages of the FAPT can be summarized in four major points.

First, a person can create for his own benefit a discretionary spendthrift trust that is effective to protect trust assets from the claims of his creditors. Such self-settled spendthrift trusts are not permitted to offer such protections as a matter of public policy under the laws of the great majority of U.S. states.

Second, the foreign trustee is not subject to the jurisdiction of a U.S. court, meaning that any orders of a U.S. court to the foreign trustee can be ignored. Similarly, in FAPT jurisdictions foreign judgments, including U.S. judgments, generally are not recognized. In order to defeat the trust, a creditor must bring a costly, risky, and inconvenient suit in the FAPT jurisdiction.

Third, there is a very short (usually two years or less) statute-of-limitations period within which to challenge transfers to the trust as fraudulent. This statute of limitations can preclude a creditor from suing even if a creditor who was a creditor of the settlor at the time the trust was created doesn't know about the existence of the trust until after the limitations period has expired. Also, in many FAPT jurisdictions, in order to prevail on a fraudulent transfer claim, a creditor must prove the elements of a fraudulent transfer by "clear and convincing evidence" or some other such elevated standard of proof. Getting this proof is difficult since issues of intent are often proved by circumstantial evidence, and few people will sign a confession stating that their intent was to make a fraudulent transfer.

Fourth, if the settlor of a beneficiary is forced by a U.S. court to do anything, such as to request a distribution from the trust or a to initiate a liquidation of the trust, then the trustee can simply ignore the instructions or requests of that person, as FAPTs nearly always contain a *duress clause* authorizing the trustee to do just that. The offshore trustee can also move the trust to another jurisdiction. So, if a creditor brings an action in the jurisdiction where the trust is located, the trustee can invoke the trust's *flight clause* and migrate the trust to another debtor haven, where the creditor must start the collection efforts anew.

CONTROL ISSUES WITH FAPTs

The biggest problems with offshore trusts have always involved settlor control. For the FAPT to work, the settlor cannot be the trustee. This usually means that a foreign trustee must have real control over trust assets. Most people, understandably, are uncomfortable about giving up control over most of their assets to a foreign trustee, and stories about trust assets disappearing offshore are too often true. Even if the foreign trust company is an entirely legitimate institutional trustee, settlors often fear (and not without reason) that once the institutional trustee has begun receiving management fees, that trustee is unlikely to willingly relinquish control of the trust or trust assets. That trustee will no doubt try to generate as many fees as possible.

If a U.S. settlor controls FAPT assets as a trustee, then the trust probably will not work from an asset protection standpoint. A court could simply order the settlor to make a distribution of trust assets to himself so that his creditor could reach the assets. The pro-FAPT crowd in the legitimate asset protection planning world generally agrees that the client cannot be a trustee. For a FAPT to work, a demonstrably independent person or institution must be trustee. But that situation leads us back to the fundamental control problem, which is to negate the possibility of an offshore trustee bleeding trust assets with high fees or, worse, embezzling trust assets.

In an attempt to avoid these problems, planners became creative with words and relationships to create a *trust protector,* who has no direct control over trust assets but who can hire and fire trustees, veto distributions, and the like.[1] The problem then becomes, who will be the trust protector? For years, many planners argued that the client could be the trust protector. Others argued that if the client was the trust protector, the court would simply order the client to use her powers to bring about a unanticipated remedy, such as firing the trustee and substituting the creditor as the new trustee. That action would of course allow the creditor to reach trust assets. When FAPTs began to be attacked, the court did indeed follow the latter course of action in one landmark case.

Some FAPT planners comfort clients by giving them behind-the-scenes arrangements (for example, making the client or the client's spouse the protector of the trust) by which they continue to exercise substantial indirect control over trust assets. Of course, these are the same trust assets over which the client supposedly has no control—or at least that is what the client will tell a judge. With these sorts of arrangements, some FAPT planners convince clients that significant wealth can be placed overseas without the risk of it disappearing in the hands of a corrupt or negligent foreign trustee. These sorts of protector arrangements thus became the center-pieces of foreign trusts. They were described at length in the professional journal articles written by FAPT planners and in their marketing materials.

This activity overlooks the simple fact that creditors and judges are as capable of reading professional journals and marketing materials as prospective clients. They know perfectly well what is going on. It was inevitable that a case would appear where the settlor would tell a judge with a straight face that he or she lacked the ability to bring the trust assets back, and the judge would look right back and exclaim "bull!" That is precisely what happened in several landmark federal court cases in which FAPT settlors have landed in prison. In some cases, those incarcerations have been followed by criminal indictments for obstruction of justice, bankruptcy fraud, and other wrongs. As a result, today, most, if not all, protector powers are *negative powers*—that is, the protector has the power only to veto trustee actions but does not have the power to cause an act to be undertaken. However, the subtleties of this arrangement, the benefits of which are wholly theoretical and not based upon any actual law, may very well be lost on the courts, which are as likely to view the protector arrangement as merely another form of co-trusteeship but with a more fancy name.

DISADVANTAGES OF FAPTs

FAPTs have not and will never find acceptance in U.S. courts for two reasons.[2] First, a FAPT is designed to and effectively does eliminate a U.S. court's power to give relief to a party that appears before it (that is, a creditor). No judge is going to tolerate something that is designed to deprive her of her power. The fact that the marketing materials of many asset protection planners essentially say that a FAPT settlor can "thumb his nose at the judge" doesn't help matters.

Second, offshore trusts simply have such a sleazy reputation that a FAPT could put a settlor into a worse position than if he had no asset protection plan at all. Juries tend to believe that "sunny climes are for shady people" and that only crooks and mobsters need offshore trusts. Thus, where a jury might not find a defendant without the offshore trust "taint" liable, the same jury might decide that because the same defendant has an offshore trust the person must have been doing something bad. Ironically, the existence of the FAPT could result in the very judgment against which it was meant to defend.

Despite being marketed as the "perfect" asset protection tool, FAPTs have been proven to have significant disadvantages—so much so that their use for asset protection purposes should be limited. One of the most obvious disadvantages is that the settlor of a FAPT may well land in jail for contempt if he doesn't obey a court order to bring trust assets back to the United States.

Prior to the *Anderson* and *Lawrence* cases, discussed below, the fundamental premise of FAPTs was that a court simply could not hold the settlor of the trust in contempt of court for refusing to repatriate trust assets so long as the settlor did not have the power to do so at the time of the court order. The theory was that the settlor could demonstrate that under the terms of the trust documents and the laws of the debtor haven he was unable to compel the repatriation of trust assets. Because he was unable to repatriate the assets from the foreign trust, it would therefore be unfair for the U.S. court to hold him in contempt. This theory was known as the *impossibility defense* and it has seen practical application in less contentious cases. The theory doubtless had a nice ring to anyone who had never been before a hostile judge. In truth, it merely evidenced the temporary divorce with reality rampant in the asset protection planning community.

The case that exploded the myth of the impossibility defense was the *Anderson* case.[3] The Andersons were telemarketers who established a FAPT in the Cook Islands. Shortly thereafter, the Andersons became involved in an aggressive telemarketing campaign with one of their clients to sell units of television airtime. Investors lost a great deal of money in the campaign. But the Andersons made a great deal of money, which was transferred to the Cook Islands FAPT. The Federal Trade Commission became involved. They sued the people behind the scheme, including the Andersons' company, Affordable Media, LLC, and the Andersons individually, seeking a return of substantial amounts of money lost by investors. The federal district court granted a temporary restraining order and a preliminary injunction that required the Andersons to repatriate any and all assets held for their benefit outside the United States. In accordance with the injunction, the Andersons faxed a letter to the Cook Islands trustee, instructing it to provide an accounting and to repatriate the assets to the United States. In response, the trustee notified the Andersons that the temporary restraining order qualified as an "event of duress" and removed the Andersons from the co-trusteeship. Because of the Andersons' failure to comply with the injunction, the district court granted the government's motion for them to be held in contempt of court.

The Andersons appealed the decision of the district court, arguing that they could not be held in contempt because compliance with the district court's order was impossible. The U.S. Court of Appeals for the Ninth Circuit disagreed. For the first time it set forth what we call the *doctrine of disbelief*, which will eliminate the impossibility defense in many future cases relating to FAPTs:

> While it is possible that a rational person would send millions of dollars overseas and retain absolutely no control over the assets, we share the district court's skepticism. The district court found, notwithstanding the Andersons' protestations, that: "[a]s I look at the totality of the scheme of what I see before me at this time, I have no doubt that the Andersons can if they wish to correct this problem and provide the means of putting these funds in a position that they can be accountable if the final determination of the Court is that the funds should be returned to those who made these payments."

Within several months, the *Lawrence* case, discussed at the beginning of this chapter and in Chapter 1, appeared. After having employed "*Anderson* relief" against Mr. Lawrence, throwing him in jail for contempt also, that court stated:

> Indeed, this Court's finding is based as well on the entirety of the record before the Court in this case and in the Adversary proceeding, and the Court's own common sense: it defies reason—it tortures reason—to accept and believe that this Debtor transferred over

$7,000,000 in 1991, an amount then constituting over ninety percent of his liquid new worth, to a trust in a far away place administered by a stranger—pursuant to an Alleged Trust which purports to allow the trustee of the Alleged Trust total discretion over the administration and distribution of the trust res. The Court declines to abandon common sense and to torture reason in the manner urged by the Debtor.

Thus, the impossibility defense, which was repeated as mantra in scores of asset protection seminars through the 1990s, was itself defeated in the *Anderson* and *Lawrence* cases by the doctrine of disbelief. Whether or not the settlor actually has given up control over the trust or trust assets may simply not matter. If the facts of the case are such that a rational person giving up control of nearly all of her assets in exchange for nothing in return does not make sense (and it rarely does), then the court simply can choose not to believe the settlor. It will then treat the settlor as if she still has control. The consequence is that a settlor may be held in jail for contempt of court even if she in fact does not have the power to repatriate the assets from the FAPT—a very bad result indeed.

The upshot is that in most circumstances, the FAPT likely will fail when it is aggressively challenged in court unless the settlor also flees the jurisdiction of the U.S. courts. Note that if the settlor's plan is to flee the country, then the FAPT still may prove to be a disadvantage. In certain circumstances the settlor may have to fight a legal battle in a foreign court to get the assets back from the foreign trustee or to receive distributions from the trust. After all, the settlor likely is under duress as defined in the duress clause of the trust document.

There is a lesson here about other asset protection schemes as well. The strengths of the FAPT were theoretical. The Cook Islands statute was relatively new. Since most cases involving asset protection plans never reach the point of being challenged, significant asset protection cases appear only rarely in court. Indeed, although offshore trusts were heavily marketed and sold through the 1990s, not until the *Anderson* case in 1999 were FAPTs significantly challenged in the U.S. courts. But when FAPTs were challenged, the theory was also challenged. And the FAPT was essentially declared unacceptable by the U.S. court. Only then did the real-world defects of the FAPT became too apparent to those who might attempt to stand behind them (see Figure 14.2)

Another problem with FAPTs is that they are indiscriminate. Because FAPTs protect assets irrespective of the good intentions or bad acts of the settlor, they might be considered immoral tools. True, FAPTs can protect the assets of the head of the family who desires to create an offshore nest egg in case of political uncertainty in the United States or elsewhere. But they can just as easily protect the assets of the narcotics trafficker and the securities fraudster. Suffice it to say that the criticism of FAPTs within the academic legal community has been nothing short of caustic, with some writers calling for criminal sanctions to discourage their use.[4]

PLANNING USES OF FAPTs

Despite the foregoing, a FAPT might play a legitimate role in asset protection planning in some circumstances.

For example, if the settlor has a legitimate interest in expatriating from the United States at some future date, an FAPT may provide a vehicle to facilitate the transfer of assets prior to or during

FIGURE 14.2

Defective FAPT

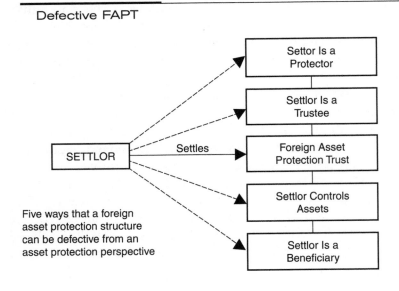

Five ways that a foreign asset protection structure can be defective from an asset protection perspective

the expatriation process. By the time a creditor approaches a judgment, the expatriation should be completed or else the settlor risks incarceration for contempt.

FAPTs can be useful to hold foreign investments, such as foreign life insurance and annuity products, discussed in Chapter 23, or foreign investments where the foreign investment company will not allow a U.S. person to invest but will allow the foreign trustee to invest. In such circumstances, the settlor can articulate a solid economic reason for having a foreign trust as opposed to a domestic trust. And, even if the FAPT is unwound, the creditor is stuck with a financial product that may be impossible or unattractive to liquidate.

A FAPT may be used in cases where a dispute over the settlor's testamentary disposition is anticipated. The problem is that a person who is exercising undue influence over a settlor may attempt to use an offshore trust to foil what would otherwise be a quite legitimate testamentary dispute, and thus cheat the settlor's heirs out of their rightful inheritance.

The use of an FAPT might also be warranted in other circumstances. But even in these cases, the FAPT is only one component of an overall asset protection structure and absolutely should not be the last line of defense, as is the case with the FAPT/FLP combo platter. This is a common flaw in many asset protection plans: using the FAPT as the centerpiece of the overall client strategy, thus creating a large and irresistible target for creditors.

In this post-*Anderson* era, some of the asset protection crowd has abandoned the FAPT in favor of the domestic asset protection trust (DAPT), which potentially has even more serious flaws as we discussed in Chapter 13. At least with a FAPT, the settlor can flee the United States and he and the assets will be out of reach of U.S. courts. This recent marketing retreat from FAPTs has allowed us to begin evaluating ways to use some of the beneficial features of the FAPT to create a structure that would not draw the ire of U.S. courts but which still would be effective to protect and transfer wealth. In such cases where it makes sense to use a foreign trust, the trust document should not be filled with typical anticreditor provisions, as the court will quickly identify it as an FAPT and try to pigeonhole it as an *Anderson* situation. Instead, planners should find more subtle ways to structure the overall arrangement.

Arrangements involving both U.S. and foreign trustees may create opportunities for FAPT structures that may emigrate or immigrate as the circumstances require. A trust that is formed in the United States and then moved offshore at the sole discretion of the trustees (and without any input of the U.S. settlor) may have a better chance of withstanding scrutiny than a trust that was formed offshore initially.

One of the biggest problems with FAPTs is the need to trust someone in an offshore haven with a large amount of valuable assets. That is the very thing that must happen for FAPTs to be effective when creditors come calling. In the next chapter, we will discuss alternative methods of maintaining control over trust assets.

ENDNOTES

1. The concept of the trust protector is an excellent idea for nonasset protection reasons to keep the trustee honest. The use of a trust protector is often a good idea for all trusts, both foreign and domestic.

2. A discussion of the technical reasons why the federal courts have refused to accept FAPTs can be found in several articles written by the authors, including "Ninth Circuit Eviscerates Foreign APTs in the *Anderson* Case," *Offshore Finance U.S.A.* (Sept./Oct. 1999); "Walking on Thin Ice— and Falling Through: The Perils of Offshore Trusts (*FTC v. Affordable Media LLC*)," *Asset Protection Journal* 22 (Spring 2000); and "A Conversation on the Anderson Case Between Jay Adkisson and Denis Kleinfeld," *Asset Protection Journal* 15 (Spring 2000).

3. *FTC v. Affordable Media*, LLC, 179 F.3d 1228 (9th Cir., 1999)

4. S. Sterk, "Asset Protection Trusts: Trust Law's Race to the Bottom?" 85 *Cornell L. Rev.* 1035 (2000).

CHAPTER 15

Foreign Trust Control

The most immediate challenge when anyone deals with a foreign trust is simply to ensure that the trust assets will not disappear. Another challenge is to ensure that the assets will be applied for the beneficiaries as the creator of the trust originally intended. To some degree, domestic trusts have the same problems, and many of the solutions discussed here may apply with equal advantage.

The normal purpose of an asset protection trust is to create an *asset freeze*, whereby certain of the settlor's assets are conveyed to the trust for the future benefit of some persons designated by the settlor, including the settlor himself. This asset freeze will create a legal separation between the settlor and the assets and thus remove the assets from the reach of creditors. But for this strategy to work, the settlor must give up legal title to the assets, so that after the assets are conveyed to the trust they truly no longer belong to the settlor.

Prior to the *Anderson* case, some planners thought that a person could transfer assets to himself as the trustee of his own offshore trust. The legal title would thereby be separated to the satisfaction of U.S. courts, which would simply leave the debtor alone. Such was the self-delusion of the offshore trust boom years. In the *Anderson* case, the Andersons started out as the trustees of their own Cook Islands trust, but they later resigned. Nevertheless, as a significant factor in determining that they still had control over their trusts, the U.S. court emphasized that the Andersons at one time had been trustees of their own trust. The documents did say that the Andersons had no control at the specific time they were ordered to repatriate the trust assets back to the United States. Still, the Andersons ended up spending six months in jail for contempt, pondering the ineptness of their planner in, among other things, making them trustees of their own trust.

So, the settlor must be ruled out as a candidate for controlling the trust. Who does that leave as a likely controller, and what assurances can be given that trust assets will not be stolen?

One obvious solution is to have U.S. trustees actually hold the assets of the trust. Yet, if the trustees are living in the United States, they are potentially subject to the orders of U.S. courts. They may be compelled to comply with the court's wishes regarding the transfer of trust assets. Because most trusts are funded by gifts, which may be set aside relatively easily under fraudulent transfer law, a potentially difficult situation exists for U.S. trustees of foreign trusts.

Another problem is that significant amounts of money are usually involved. Often the amount is great enough to make normally honest people contemplate dishonest acts. It simply doesn't make economic sense to create a FAPT for negligible assets. Instead, FAPTs are typically funded with millions of dollars' worth of assets. This creates a tempting target for embezzlement or fraud, such as causing the trust to invest in companies owned by persons indirectly controlled by the trustee. Since the trust assets may be placed offshore, where embezzlement and fraud occur with disturbing regularity, very real concerns arise about protecting the trust assets from the trustee and anybody else who comes into contact with the trust assets.

Next, the trust laws of the offshore haven may limit who can be a trustee. The offshore haven may require, for instance, that the trustee be a licensed trust company or a bank. Often, the reason for this requirement is not concern about the safety of trust assets, but rather to create local jobs. The question of who should be the trustee or trustees of a foreign asset protection trust is often resolved by the process of elimination of unsuitable candidates. The choice is then between relative evils among the options that remain.

TRUSTEE ARRANGEMENTS

Naturally, the client will always want to be the trustee of her own trust. This desire is perfectly understandable. It would allow the client, by the simple device of switching hats from owner to trustee, to distance herself legally from her assets while keeping total control over them. But the fact that the settlor of the trust is also the trustee (or one of the trustees) is strong evidence that the entire arrangement is simply a sham to avoid creditors. If a U.S. court does determine that the settlor's gifts to the trust is fraudulent and voids those transfers, the settlor-trustee can be easily ordered by the court, under threat of imprisonment for contempt, to bring the assets back to the United States to satisfy creditors. Thus, unless the settlor-trustee is prepared to flee the United States to avoid the repatriation order and its consequences, a FAPT arrangement in which the settlor is also a trustee is severely compromised.

The beneficiaries of the trust also should not be trustees. If the beneficiaries are also trustees, the spendthrift protections of the trust may be compromised. Furthermore, if the beneficiaries are within the jurisdiction of the U.S. courts, then they too are subject to repatriation orders.

Having eliminated herself and her beneficiaries as candidates for trustee, the settlor will next want her immediate family and friends in the United States to be the trustees. These persons, however, are also subject to the orders of U.S. courts and will be unsuitable as trustees once a creditor has a judgment and is attempting to enforce it. This vulnerability does not mean that these persons can never be trustees. They can be, so long as it is understood that in the event that a creditor gets a judgment against the settlor or any beneficiary, that person will resign in favor of a foreign trustee. Of course, this proviso should not be in the trust document or otherwise in writing.

See Figure 15.1 for suitable controlling U.S. trustee arrangements.

Depending on the jurisdiction where the trust is established, a foreign trustee is probably required. The purpose of the debtor haven in enacting aggressive FAPT legislation is to promote business in that country. If a FAPT were allowed to have trustees who would be entirely outside the FAPT jurisdiction, this arrangement would defeat the haven's purpose in trying to create jobs. In fact, if there is no foreign trustee in the FAPT jurisdiction, and if assets are not kept there, a serious question arises about whether the pur-

FIGURE 15.1

Controlling U.S. trustee.

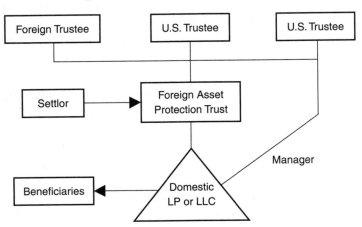

ported law of the trust, as indicated in the trust instrument, is indeed the law of the trust. In such a case, where would be the nexus between the trust and the jurisdiction? A U.S. court could easily conclude that it should apply the law of the jurisdiction of the U.S. settlor's residence, the law of the location of the trust's U.S. assets, or the law of the jurisdiction of the U.S. trustee's residence.

So, a foreign trust probably will be required to have at least one foreign trustee. If the settlor has trusted foreign friends or relatives, then this issue often is easily resolved. Otherwise, the settlor must rely upon a hired unknown trustee. In hiring a foreign trustee, the settlor basically has two choices. First, the settlor can use a foreign trust company. Unlike U.S. trust companies, which are usually strictly regulated, foreign trust companies are relatively loosely regulated. If trust assets disappear in the hands of a small trust company in the less-sophisticated FAPT jurisdictions, which is nearly every aggressive FAPT jurisdiction, there likely will be no effective recourse for the settlor and the beneficiaries. Often foreign trust companies in these jurisdictions are shoestring operations run by one or two people with little banking or trust experience.

These types of trust companies frequently provide "wink and a nod" trustee services, where they sign on as the foreign trustee in name only, with the settlor or somebody close to the settlor actually administering the trust. Sometimes, these small trust companies are merely fronts for U.S. legal or financial advisors, who use the allure of offshore planning and FAPTs to attract legal or investment business. Although the foreign trustee signs all the documents, the U.S. legal or financial advisor is really the one in charge (see Figure 15.2).

In these arrangements, while the foreign trustee administers the paperwork of the trust, the U.S. advisor directly manages the assets. The comfort in this type of arrangement is that the foreign trustee can't run off with the assets without the U.S. advisor knowing about it and giving the settlor the opportunity to do something about it. One problem is that while a U.S. advisor may be in charge as a practical matter, the foreign trustee still has legal control over trust assets. If the foreign trustee and the U.S. advisor ever begin to see things differently, the foreign trustee may assert himself in the process and attempt to take over control of trust assets, probably successfully.

Another problem is that the foreign trustee and the U.S. advisor could collude and loot trust assets without the settlor knowing about it. For example, long after the trust assets had been looted, the foreign trustee could tell the client that all is well. The U.S. advisor could continue to send impressive brokerage statements that show that the wealth is safe and growing at a generous rate. If the client needed some small distribution of cash, the U.S. advisor could pay it from the trust assets of new victims who are coming into the scheme. Where the trust has been used to evade U.S. taxes, the embezzlement often goes unreported, as the settlor would

FIGURE 15.2

U.S. custodian.

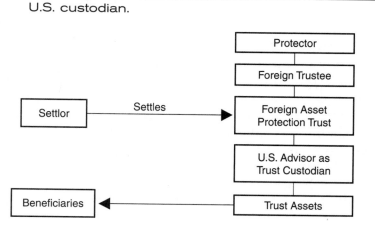

rather see the trust assets disappear than to spend several years at Club Fed.

INSTITUTIONAL TRUSTEES

The best candidates to act as a foreign trustee are the large banks and financial services firms that have branches in the debtor havens. These firms will help to create and administer the trust, and they can provide total management of the trust assets. These firms are typically well managed and have capable staffs. Better yet, they will have a system of checks and balances to ensure that the trust assets are neither embezzled nor misused. These institutional trustees provide one-stop shops that take care of all aspects of the offshore trust from the day it is formed to the day it is wound up. They are usually well capitalized, meaning the risk of their collapse or sudden disappearance is unlikely. Even if they were to collapse, the trust assets would be administered without regard to the institution's creditors by a receiver appointed by the local jurisdiction.

Use of institutional trustees does have several disadvantages. First, they are relatively expensive. Trustee fees and asset management fees in offshore havens tend to be 50 percent to 100 percent more than fees for comparable services in the United States. Second, once a trustee gets on board the trust management gravy train, getting it off is sometimes very difficult. If a trustee can figure out a way to keep its trusteeship and its management fees, it will do so. To prevent self-serving decisions by the trustees, the trust document should be very clear as to when distributions to the beneficiaries should be made.

On the other hand, a FAPT will contain spendthrift provisions and discretionary distribution provisions to protect the trust assets from creditors of the beneficiaries. These provisions can thwart a beneficiary from access to trust assets as easily as they can thwart a creditor. When the beneficiaries are children and young adults, this arrangement is probably a desired check on unwise spending, but at some point this limitation may become a point of frustration for the beneficiaries. The result could be, ironically, that trust assets are depleted by litigation costs in defending against attempts of the beneficiaries to reach them.

Still, for all of the downsides, placing trust assets with a large institutional trustee is a better solution than placing the assets with small trust companies and then attempting to retain indirect control via a friendly advisor or asset manager. As with all asset protection planning, there is safety in diversity. First, the amount of wealth placed into the offshore trust should represent only a part of the estate. Second, a better arrangement is to have several smaller offshore trusts in different jurisdictions with diverse institutional trustees than to have one large trust in a single jurisdiction with a single institutional trustee. This diversity will be more time-consuming and more expensive than using one trust with a single trustee in a single jurisdiction, but it will also be much safer.

Another possible solution to the trustee problem is to have a committee of trustees, with some of the trustees being close U.S. friends and family and at least one trustee being foreign, whether a private trust company or an institutional trustee. The advantage of this arrangement is that it allows the foreign trustee to provide the nexus to the offshore trust jurisdiction so that the law of the offshore jurisdiction should apply; but it also allows control to remain with the U.S. trustees, at least until a potential creditor problem appears.

The disadvantages to this arrangement are relatively few. The U.S. trustees will be responsible for filing certain reporting forms to the IRS as the trustees of a foreign trust. The U.S. trustees will have to agree on the administration of the trust, and the foreign trustee will have to agree to be bound by the decision of a majority of the trustees. If a creditor appears, the U.S. trustees may have to resign so that a U.S. court could not force them to make decisions contrary to the purposes of the trust. Only at that time, if it ever occurs, will it be necessary to rely on the foreign trustee. And this is where the concept of the trust protector becomes particularly important.

Before moving on to a discussion of trust protectors, you need to be aware that the trust document should identify in detail both the persons who will serve as substitute trustees and a method of selecting substitute trustees and new trustees as the circumstances dictate. Also the document needs to spell out who may not be a trustee. The reason for this is that courts can be quite ingenious in ordering the trustees to replace themselves with, for instance, a creditor who then takes over control of the trust for its own benefit. The trust document should thus have a list of persons to be excluded from the realm of possible trustees, beneficiaries, and protectors. That list needs to include creditors of the settlors, trustees, beneficiaries, and other persons whom the settlor absolutely does not want to be a trustee.

TRUST PROTECTOR ARRANGEMENTS

A *trust protector* is a person or entity identified in a trust document who has certain delineated powers, either over the trust terms or the trustee, but who is not a trustee. Often a trust protector will be given the power to fire and replace trustees as circumstances dictate. Recently, the powers of trust protectors in FAPTs tend to be limited to negative powers—for example, the power to veto trustee decisions but not to compel any particular trustee action. The concept of the trust protector is an excellent one and should be used for foreign trusts and domestic trusts. Only in the rarest of cases will the appointment of a trust protector not make fundamentally good sense.

The best arrangement is to give a trust protector full discretion to act rather than requiring that certain circumstances be met before acting. The latter requirement might well result in the trustee claiming that the circumstances have not been met, a situation that often requires costly and lengthy litigation to resolve. Trust protectors can dictate which of the trustees can or cannot be signors on particular accounts held by the trust. A protector should not, however, be given such broad powers that it can be deemed to be a trustee or co-trustee of the trust, or can hijack the trust for its own benefit.

A trust settlor or beneficiary should not be the trust protector. If the settlor is a protector, and the settlor has creditor problems, the court might order the settlor to use his powers as protector to unwind the trust. Or it might force the settlor to fire the existing trustees and appoint somebody friendly to creditors as the replacement trustee. A similar risk exists if the protector is a beneficiary.

Often, the trust protector is a member of the settlor's family or a close friend. Sometimes, the trust protector is the settlor's attorney or another trusted advisor. Some trust agreements will provide for a committee of protectors. Regardless of who is the initial protector, the trust document needs to clearly name substitute protectors and a method of selecting new protectors. The trust document should provide for the possibility of foreign protectors who will not be subject to the orders of U.S. courts.

We are now squarely back to the problem we had with trustees and with foreign trusts in general. For FAPTs to work, the settlor ultimately will be required to trust one or more persons or institutions offshore. An offshore law firm or another offshore trust company is probably the best choice as an offshore protector, so long as it does not have close ties with the institutional trustee with which it might be tempted to collude for illegal gain.

PRIVATE TRUST COMPANY

An option in complex trustee and protector arrangements is the *private trust company (PTC)*. Some jurisdictions—most notably Nevis—allow a corporation formed in that jurisdiction to act as the trustee of a FAPT formed there. The corporation is not required to be licensed as a trust company, although it still must have a local agent for service of process. Because there are no ownership restrictions on the corporation, it can be owned by anyone.

Ideally, a close family member or friend of the settlor will form the offshore corporation that will act as the trustee for the foreign asset protection trust. The corporation, as the foreign trustee, enters into the trust agreement with the settlor, takes possession of the assets that are transferred to the trust, and thereafter administers the trust just like any other trustee. See Figure 15.3 for how a PTC is set up.

Since the PTC is owned or controlled by family or close friend, the settlor does not have to jump through the complicated series of hoops involving U.S. co-trustees and protectors. Also, the settlor doesn't have to attempt to retain indirect control over the trust. In fact, the PTC arrangement probably allows the settlor to cut out much, if not all, of the blatant anticreditor language that so infuriates U.S. judges.

FIGURE 15.3

Private trust company.

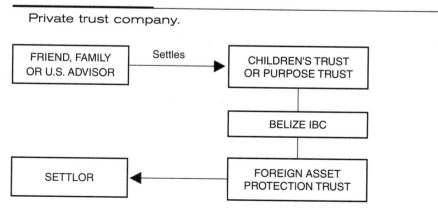

Even if the creditor is able to figure out everything about the structure, the creditor may have a very difficult time prevailing in his pursuit of trust assets so long as the settlor genuinely has nothing to do with the PTC or any structure that owns it. Of course, the shares of the PTC are subject to the claims of the creditors of its owners, so the ownership structure of the PTC is critically important. A *purpose trust*, which is a form of trust with no beneficiaries that serves some specific purpose, such as a charitable purpose, is often an excellent vehicle to own the PTC.

CHAPTER 16

Introduction to Share Structures

Share structures are entities, such as corporations, in which the owners hold shares in the entities; they may buy, sell, and trade the shares (unless they are restricted by company rules or by securities laws). The incorporated company is the most common form of share structure. Other forms of share structures exist as well, particularly foreign share structures. A company is formed under the authority of legislation in the jurisdiction in which it is formed, and this formation, effected by *articles of incorporation*, is registered by the appropriate government agency. Once a company has been formed, it takes on a legal life of its own. It has the ability to enter into contracts and to sue, or be sued, in its own name. The hallmark of a company is thus a legal existence separate and apart from its owners. That state of existence is a legal fiction, to be sure (like a trust, it won't be attending our barbeque), but for many purposes it is a very real entity that provides very tangible benefits.

Most share structures require a contribution of capital to the company that is used for the company's stated purposes, whether those purposes are to generate profits, to hold assets for investment growth, or to promote charitable purposes. So that companies can attract investors, company legislation usually provides that the liability of the company's shareholders will be limited to the amount of their contributions. For example, if a shareholder purchases $100 of stock from the company, the most the shareholder can lose is that $100 and any undistributed profits generated by that $100.

A company's articles of incorporation may allow for one or more classes of shares to be issued. Two classes of shares are typically issued. First, there is *common stock*, shares that represent the right to receive distributions of profits, called *dividends*, and liquidation proceeds after all other obligations of the company have been met. Second, there is *preferred stock*, which represents the right to receive preferential distributions of profits at a specific rate of investment return, and liquidation proceeds, which are paid after company creditors are paid but before the holders of common stock are paid. Both types of stock also may carry with them voting rights, but both types of stock also may be issued with no voting rights. Usually, preferred stock carries limited voting rights or no voting rights at all.

For asset protection purposes, care should be taken so that no shares—shares of voting stock, in particular—fall into the hands of creditors. If a creditor attaches the company shares, the creditor becomes an owner of the company, with all of the rights that go along with that status. The creditor can make enforceable demands upon the company for the payment of dividends. The creditor may be able to demand an accounting of the company's finances, and it may have the right to inspect the company's books and records at any time. Contrast these rights with a creditor's rights with respect to a debtor's interest in partnerships and limited liability companies. In the latter situations, creditors usually are entitled only to a charging order, if distributions are made, and they usually have no rights to demand distributions or accountings or to inspect the books and records.

In addition, creditors, as shareholders, may be able bring legal claims on behalf of the company against the officers and directors of the corporation. Sometimes they can do so against other shareholders and third parties with which the company has done business. These *derivative actions* give the creditor the legal means by which to conduct extensive investigations of all of the parties involved with the company. They can seek recovery for perceived bad acts, to be paid back into the company's coffers. In many jurisdictions, aggrieved shareholders can petition the courts of the jurisdiction of incorporation to have the company dissolved and wound up and its assets distributed to the company's creditors and shareholders. That group to which assets are distributed may include creditors of shareholders or former shareholders.

From an asset protection standpoint, the foregoing company traits can be very bad. Thus, among other things, governing documents of companies at the very least should contain detailed *poison pill* buyout provisions (see Figure 16.1). These provisions allow at least certain shareholders of the company to buy out hostile shareholders at a predetermined price. Or, even better, they allow the shares at a predetermined price to be paid in an unfavorable manner. Such a disadvantageous purchase could be over a long period of time at a low rate of interest. Or it could be a balloon note that will require the selling hostile shareholder to recognize taxable income on deemed interest even though that shareholder has not received any interest payments yet. Other measures developed primarily in the heyday of hostile corporate takeovers in the 1980s can be useful as well.

A *golden parachute* provision offers lucrative benefits (for example, stock options, severance pay, and bonuses) to company executives who lose their jobs if the company becomes controlled by third parties. The *macaroni defense* is a strategy that can be deployed when the company sees a hostile shareholder coming. It is called the macaroni defense because when the danger of a takeover appears, the company issues a large number of bonds to friendly creditors, with the redemption price of the bonds expanding—like macaroni in a pot of boiling water—if the company becomes controlled by third parties.

Dilution provisions allow additional stock, stock options, or warrants to be issued by the company in the future. So, if it appears that a creditor will be able to successfully attach an owner's stock, those shares can be diluted by the issue of additional units of ownership in the company. Ideally, this procedure can be accomplished

FIGURE 16.1

Poison pill.

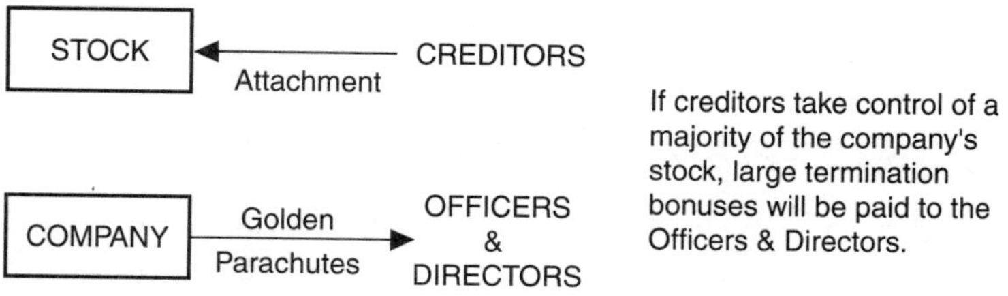

If creditors take control of a majority of the company's stock, large termination bonuses will be paid to the Officers & Directors.

before the creditor attaches the debtor's stock in accordance with provisions in the company's governing documents that have been in place for some time. If so, the creditor likely will have difficulty reversing the dilution in his capacity as an allegedly aggrieved minority shareholder. He also will have difficulty arguing that the dilution was a fraudulent transfer.

Most company legislation allows great flexibility in structuring shares. In the right circumstances, creative drafting can create share classes with inherently creditor-unfriendly features, shares that pay no dividends, shares convertible by the company into long-term unsecured debt, and the like. The key to using this technique successfully, as usual, is subtlety as well as the ability to articulate an economic purpose for the share structure. Such is the art of advanced corporate structure design.

CONTAINMENT OF LIABILITIES

From a risk management and asset protection perspective, limited liability is a powerful tool. With few exceptions, it allows an investor to invest a finite amount of capital, with her personal liability for debts of the company limited to that amount, but with an infinite potential for investment return. Liability is contained within the company. Even better, this containment extends beyond the company's profit-making activities to all of its related activities, including employment practices, products liability, and many other types of tort and regulatory liability (see Figure 16.2).

Limited liability entities, such as companies and charging order protected entities, or COPEs (for more on COPEs, see Chapter 19), should be used whenever practical for investment arrangements, commercial operations, or simply for ownership of risky assets that have the potential to produce liabilities for their owners such as real estate and vehicles. Rarely, if ever, does it make sense to conduct business personally or to own a liability-producing asset personally any time that a limited liability entity could be used for the same purpose.

RESPECTING THE CORPORATE SHELL

To obtain limited liability protection, a company must have a legal identity separate from its owners—that is, it must be more than a

FIGURE 16.2

Containment.

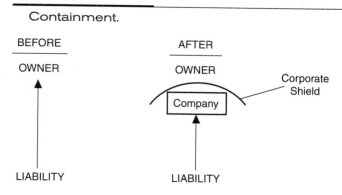

mere shell. Its owners must respect its character as a separate entity. Company owners, officers, and directors are required to follow formalities established by company legislation. Normally, companies are required to make decisions in a strict hierarchy, with shareholders electing directors, who in turn guide the business in its overall mission, and who elect officers to deal with the daily affairs of running the company. Sometimes, shareholders who wield sufficient power can force the consideration of issues by the directors or remove directors and replace them with more sympathetic directors. However, all of these actions must take place either by means of formal meetings or by written consent in lieu of a meeting. Additionally, most company acts require that shareholders and directors hold annual meetings to deal with company matters. These meetings must be preceded by formal written notice to the shareholders and directors.

Most small companies avoid the requirement for actual meetings by having all parties waive notice of meetings. They then circulate for approval minutes of a meeting not actually held or written consents to actions in lieu of a meeting. Alternatively, some companies fulfill meeting requirements by holding meetings via telephone or Internet conferencing. In any event, however, the meeting or action in lieu of a meeting must be memorialized in the books and records of the company.

Although meetings may be required by statute to be held only on an annual basis, good practice is to hold meetings, or to memorialize actions taken in lieu of meetings, whenever a major decision is made. Such major decisions include entering into an important contract such as a lease, borrowing money from a bank, issuing stock or debt, electing directors and officers, and establishing salaries and benefits.

A company's failure to follow corporate formalities can cause a court simply to disregard the company (known as *piercing the corporate veil*) and deem that it legally does not exist. This subjects the company's owners, officers, and directors to unlimited personal liability for the debts of the company. Companies with few owners are especially at risk of having the company disregarded for liability purposes. Plaintiffs in cases against small companies, in efforts to pierce the corporate veil, often assert as a matter of course that the company is merely the alter ego of the owners. In order for the plaintiffs to succeed in their endeavor, two elements usually must be met. First, there must be unity of interest and ownership between the company and its owners such that the separate personalities of the corporation and its shareholders do not truly exist. Second, the entity must have been used to perpetrate a wrong (sometimes specified to be "a fraud") for which it would be fundamentally unfair to allow the owners to avoid liability simply by hiding behind the limited liability veil of the company.

There is no bright-line test to determine when unity of interest and ownership exists, but the basic issue is whether the company was respected as a separate entity by its owners, directors, and officers. The following are some of the factors common in successful veil-piercing cases:

- Commingling of company assets and personal assets
- Diversion of company assets for personal use without adequate payment
- Treatment of company assets as personal assets of the owner
- Inability to keep transactions between the company and its owners, officers, and directors at arm's length
- Failure to maintain company books and records
- Lack of shareholders' and directors' meetings
- Identical ownership in two entities
- Having some of the same directors and officers in both parent and subsidiary companies

- Common business locations
- Use of the company as a single-purpose entity
- Employment of the same employees by the company and its owner
- Failure to maintain capitalization and insurance adequate to meet the reasonably anticipated business needs of the company
- Concealment of ownership, management, and assets
- Concentration of the assets of related entities in one company and liabilities in another
- Use of the company for illegal activities

The presence of one or two factors is usually not enough to convince a court to pierce the corporate veil. Indeed, some of the factors, when viewed separately from the others, are arguably good business practices, such as using single-purpose entities, separating assets and liabilities, and legally concealing ownership or other company information for privacy purposes. Normally, several factors must be present and the second element of fundamental inequity also must be met in order for an alter ego claim to succeed. However, the avoidance of as many factors as possible is crucial.

Because unity of interest and ownership is often much easier to demonstrate in the case of single-owner companies, they usually are undesirable for most asset protection purposes (except as subsidiary companies, as discussed in Chapter 20). Although the laws and cases from nearly every state respect the concept of the single-owner company, a creditor that can successfully assert the inequity element likely will succeed in proving the element of unity of interest and ownership, allowing the creditor of the company to reach the assets of the company's owner.

VEIL PIERCING

Relatively little risk of liability flows from the company to the shareholders. The role of shareholders in a classic corporate structure essentially is to contribute capital, elect the directors, and collect dividend checks. Small companies, however, simply do not work that way. As a result, particular attention should be paid to prevent the corporate veil from being pierced.

Certainly, there is a degree of asset protection afforded by the company's limited liability character, even if the client is the sole shareholder. However, with the single-shareholder arrangement the creditor will find it considerably easier to successfully pursue a veil-piercing claim. Keep in mind: Finding other persons or entities to be additional owners is not difficult. While the existence of other owners will not defeat a creditor's claims of unity of sole ownership, it will make the creditor's argument that there is unity of interest and ownership more difficult. That uncertainty might make the critical difference in a close case. The greater the proportion of ownership held by the additional shareholder, the less likely the corporate veil will be pierced. For example, if the owner transfers some stock to an irrevocable trust formed for the client's children, the case that the corporation and the owner are not really one and the same is strengthened. The more stock the trust has, the less likely that the corporate veil will be pierced. If the owner is not also the trustee of the trust, or better yet, if the owner did not settle the trust (perhaps the grandparents settled the trust, for example), the corporate veil is stronger yet. The goal is to diversify ownership so that the primary owner will not be responsible for the corporation's debts as the result of a veil-piercing claim.

One method that may alleviate all of these problems is to finance the company with debt rather than by contributing equity capital. This method is especially useful if the owner has heirs he wishes to benefit through equity appreciation. If the heirs (or, better, a trust for heirs, which owns shares via a COPE) contribute a small amount of seed capital in return for equity ownership, and the owner lends money to the company, the owner has achieved several good things. First, he has distanced himself from the company and from the possibility of a veil-piercing claim. Second, he will have priority over company shareholders in the event of a liquidation or bankruptcy. Third, if the owner's loans are secured by company assets, he may have priority over all of the company's other creditors in the event of a liquidation or bankruptcy. Finally, if the value of the company's stock in the hands of the heirs appreciates at a rate greater than the rate of interest on the debt, the owner will have achieved a tax-free transfer of wealth to his heirs.

However, if the owner wants to participate in the company's potential future equity appreciation, yet another solution is available. The corporate debt held by the shareholder can be issued in a fashion such that it is convertible into company stock. Options and warrants can be used similarly.

DIRECTORS' AND OFFICERS' LIABILITY

To the extent possible, persons with significant assets should not serve as officers or directors of corporations that are conducting active business, since this has the potential to create significant liability even if the corporate veil is respected. As the ultimate human actors who will be held responsible for the negligent acts of a company, officers and directors face significant potential personal liability for events occurring both inside the corporation (for example, in a sexual harassment lawsuit by a disgruntled employee) and outside the corporation (for example, an environmental or tax claim that may provide for strict personal liability for the company's officers and directors). A person known to be wealthy may be a lighting-rod for litigation against the company, as claimants will presume that the wealthy person ultimately will be responsible for judgments.

Ideally, a client should be an indirect passive investor through a holding company structure (see Figure 16.3). In a simple holding company structure, two tiers of companies exist. The lower tier consists of the companies that are actively conducting business, holding business assets, employing people, and the like—that is, they are the liability-prone companies. The upper tier consists of one or more companies that has few or no employees and conducts no business other than owning stock in the lower-tier entities.

Holding companies have in the past been utilized by tax planners to create situations involving interlocking ownership. That arrangement drives down the percentage of ownership held by a taxpayer yet still allows the taxpayer to retain control. For U.S. persons, the Internal Revenue Code has attribution rules that seriously restrict the effectiveness of these structures. However, interlocking ownerships may have asset protection advantages, mostly in defusing alter ego and corporate veil issues.

FIGURE 16.3

Holding company.

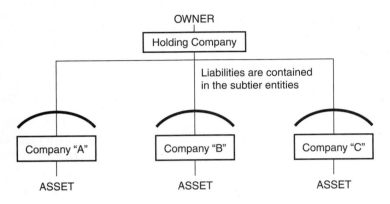

For instance, assume that Company A is owned 50 percent by Company B and 50 percent by Company C. Next, assume that Company B is owned 49 percent by Company A, 50 percent by Company C, and 1 percent by Company D. Similarly, Company C is owned 49 percent by Company A, 50 percent by Company B, and 1 percent by Company D. The ultimate beneficial owner owns all of Company D. This relationship is shown in Figure 16.4.

In this case, effective ownership and control is held by Company D. However, if Company A is sued, a creditor will have difficulty arguing that Company A is the alter ego of either Companies B or C since neither of those company have a majority ownership in Company A. The same holds true for creditor attacks on Companies B and C, since neither of those companies have a majority owner. Company D, which does have effective control, is distanced two layers from Company A and one layer from Companies B and C. If a creditor attacks only one of Companies A, B, or C, the creditor will have difficulty getting past any of the entities to the others.

The creditor's remedy, of course, it to attack all the companies simultaneously on the grounds that they are interrelated and are alter egos of Company D and its owner. However, especially early in litigation, a creditor may not be able to obtain discovery as to these ownership issues, and by the time the creditor reaches the bottom of the structure, the limitations period for suing the other companies may have expired. While these interlocking maneuvers

FIGURE 16.4

Attribution games.

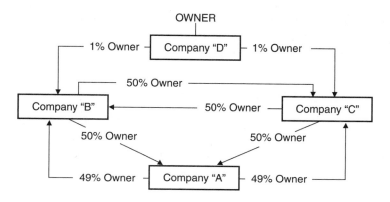

will not benefit the company being directly sued, they may deter a creditor's attempts to reach the ultimate beneficial owners.

ADVANTAGES OF DEBT FINANCING

Companies regularly borrow from individual investors by issuing bonds. These bonds may be secured by the company assets; thus, their holders will have a claim to priority over most other creditors of the company. Bonds also may be unsecured or subordinated to other indebtedness of the company. In either case, bondholders and creditors will have priority in bankruptcy and liquidation over the company's equity owners.

The issuance of debt by a company strips equity from the company. If the company is forced into liquidation by an unsecured judgment creditor, bondholders will have priority claims to the company's assets, before unsecured creditors (including the judgment creditor) and before shareholders. In an asset protection scenario, a distressed small company might issue zero-coupon bonds to someone friendly to the company's owners, and because the company is a small distressed company, the bonds will probably be sold at a deep discount. The company would then use the proceeds of the bond issue to purchase asset-protected assets or to effectuate another asset protection technique. If an owner of the company loses her stock to an unsecured judgment creditor who then liquidates the company, the bondholder will have priority over the creditor in the distribution of liquidation proceeds.

Bonds can also be issued in a convertible form so that they can be exchanged for stock. Such bonds can be designed to be convertible by the bondholder or by the company. Thus, a useful strategy might be to issue debt to friendly parties so that if a creditor of an owner becomes a shareholder, the bonds can be converted to equity, diluting the creditor-shareholder's interest.

CORPORATE STOCK OPTIONS

Stock options and warrants can play a significant role in corporate planning. First, the issuance of options and warrants by the corporation for services provides the alternative of diluting shares if circumstances so dictate. Options and warrants are typically issued on terms that allow them to be exercised to purchase stock at a relatively low price. This arrangement keeps cash contributions to the company upon exercise at a minimum.

For the owner of a small business who may have potential creditor problems, virtual ownership by way of options is an excellent alternative to owning shares. An option has a fixed expiration date. If an option is not exercised by the expiration date, the option is worthless. This gives a person who is concerned about creditors some time to see if a creditor threat materializes. If a creditor threat does not materialize, then the options can be exercised and the holder becomes a normal equity owner in the company. However, if the creditor threat does materialize, the person simply can allow the options to expire, and the creditor has no avenue for pursuing the assets of the company.

Options are also unique in that they have a value that generally decays over time. That amount definitely becomes zero, if the options are not exercised by the expiration date. An option generally will have a value roughly equal to the difference between the price at which the option may be exercised and the price of the company's shares on the date the option is exercised. However, as the expiration date approaches, the option loses value because the time available to exercise the option shortens. There will be a significant decrease in the value of the option if the company's stock has not increased in value since the issue of the option. This allows (or forces, as the telling of the story requires) the holder of the option to sell the option at a heavily discounted price, but it will be difficult for a creditor to claim that this sale was a fraudulent transfer because of the valuation issue surrounding the discount caused by the time decay.

Options can also be a vehicle for wealth transfer to an asset-protected entity if they are never exercised. A client who wants to transfer value to the entity purchases options from the entity. The company immediately realizes that value and has the equity to pursue business projects. If the options holder does not exercise the option and the option expires, wealth has been transferred from the client to the company. The option technique will be difficult for a creditor to show as a fraudulent transfer because the options holder did in fact get valuable options back from the company, even if they were never exercised.

CHAPTER 17

Domestic Corporations

Historically, the most commonly used entities for asset protection in the United States have been corporations formed under the laws of one of the States—that is, domestic corporations. With few exceptions, most of the entities whose shares are traded on the various U.S. stock exchanges are domestic corporations. Most of their subsidiaries are domestic corporations. Even mutual funds, some of the largest owners of wealth in the United States, are organized as domestic corporations.

Likewise, most U.S. small businesses are organized as domestic corporations. Although the number of limited liability companies has dramatically increased in recent years, and is likely to overtake the number of corporations in the relatively near future, the legal landscape for all U.S. businesses is still dominated by domestic corporations. Corporate law in the United States is well developed and over time has proven largely successful in insulating shareholders from corporate liabilities.

So long as the corporation's separate identity is maintained and the corporation is not used to perpetrate a fraud, shareholders of domestic corporations have little reason to fear that the corporate shell will be penetrated by the corporation's creditors to make the shareholders personally liable for the corporation's debts. Even corporate officers and directors are shielded to a significant degree from corporate liability.

DELAWARE GENERAL CORPORATION LAW

The starting place for an examination of domestic corporations is the Delaware General Corporation Law, which many U.S. states have copied to a significant degree. Even some foreign jurisdictions, such as Nevis and Panama, have copied Delaware's General Corporation Law. The Delaware courts have addressed and resolved more important issues of corporate law than have any other U.S. courts. Hence, most of our discussion in this section references Delaware law, except where noted.

From an asset protection viewpoint, what needs to be kept in mind is that because a corporation is a legal fiction, a company's books and records will be critically important in establishing whether the company should be respected for veil-piercing purposes. A corporation is formed by filing articles of incorporation with the Delaware Secretary of State. These articles typically are simple and generic, but they will list the original incorporators of the company and the name and address of the registered agent for service of process in Delaware. At this point begins the company's paper trail. It must be assumed that all filings with the Delaware Secretary of State can be easily obtained by creditors.

Depending on how the corporation is to be used, the choice of incorporators may be important. The incorporators—that is, the people who bring the corporation into being by filing the articles of incorporation—are the first names appearing in the paper trail. The incorporators need not be the original shareholders. So, for example, if some distance between the corporation and an owner is required, then neither the owner nor any person identifiable with the owner should be the incorporator. Often, the owner's attorney is the incorporator. Keep in mind that because articles of incorporation are publicly filed documents, they are not protected from disclosure by the attorney-client privilege.

The corporation will have by-laws to govern its operations. Like articles of incorporation, by-laws should contain little information that will be useful to creditors, because it should be assumed that creditors will be able to access a corporation's by-laws with relative ease.

The corporation laws of all jurisdictions, domestic and foreign, require that the corporation maintain a registered agent in the jurisdiction of incorporation. One very important consideration is that the registered agent be competent and trustworthy. The registered agent's function is to accept service of process on the corporation. If the registered agent does not notify the corporate officers and directors that a lawsuit has been filed, the creditor likely will be able to obtain a judgment against the corporation by default.

Under state law, having a registered agent in the state of incorporation creates nexus sufficient to allow the corporation to be sued in that state. This fact alone may affect the decision where to incorporate. A jurisdiction where jury verdicts tend to be very conservative may be preferable to one with a reputation for runaway jury awards. The cost of defending a lawsuit may also be a significant factor in this decision. Defending a lawsuit in the owner's home state will be substantially cheaper than defending the same lawsuit across the continent. This may be a factor in deciding where to incorporate.

The choice of company directors often presents practical difficulties. From a purely objective perspective, the best arrangement is for the owner not to be a director of an operating business. Preferably, the owner should be distanced from the company's operations through use of a holding company. Instead, the directors of an operating company should be other trusted persons. Ideally, the owner should not be an officer of the company, as this may expose the owner to various potential liabilities. Trusted persons other than the owner are the best choice as company officers.

CORPORATIONS AND BANKRUPTCY REMOTE ENTITIES

From a risk management perspective, the principal use of a domestic corporation is as a *bankruptcy remote entity (BRE),* which allows owners to stop complex litigation by reorganizing or liquidating the company. A bankruptcy filing triggers an automatic stay of any litigation in which the corporation is involved. A plaintiff then is forced to attempt to have the stay lifted in separate litigation in bankruptcy court or to abandon its lawsuit.

In the case of reorganization under bankruptcy laws, the corporation can put off creditors for many months while the corporation prepares and submits a plan of reorganization for approval by the bankruptcy court. In the meantime, the original officers and directors of the corporation remain in charge unless the creditors can force the appointment of a receiver. If creditors of shareholders are involved as well, which is not an uncommon situation, particularly with small corporations, and those creditors have seized stock, any derivative actions that a creditor-shareholder may bring on the corporation's behalf against its officers and directors or other parties are treated as assets of the corporation. If it is to proceed, the creditor must convince the appointed bankruptcy trustee to bring the case. Usually, this sell is a hard one, because the trustee will be more concerned about liquidating existing assets than in pursuing something that may not pay off.

The importance of long-term prebankruptcy planning cannot be overstated. Transactions occurring within a year of a bankruptcy filing will be considered suspect, and they will be susceptible to being set aside by the bankruptcy court. However, if a transaction involving the corporation has matured beyond a year, preferably several years, and at the time was supported by consideration, a creditor will have difficulty setting aside the transaction as a preferential transfer. This has important practical ramifications, because bankruptcy laws assign priorities to various classes of creditors. Holders of secured debt typically have priority over all other classes of creditors. Therefore, if a note of the corporation received in a transaction structured well in advance of a bankruptcy filing was secured by the corporation's assets, the party holding that note will be in a superior position to any subsequent creditors and effectively can guide the course of the bankruptcy. Unsecured creditors will have little say in how the corporation is reorganized. If the corporation ultimately is liquidated, secured parties will receive the assets of the corporation that were used to secure the debt it holds, and the unsecured creditors receive what is left, which usually is nothing.

For this reason, corporations should be substantially financed by debt and the financing should be secured by the corporation's valuable assets. Essentially, the corporation is equity stripped so that in the event of a bankruptcy, no value will remain for creditors.

Note that last-minute attempts to tie up a corporation's assets are likely to backfire. They may result in additional liability for all involved, as well as possible allegations of bankruptcy fraud. The downside to corporate bankruptcy is, of course, that some conduct that would simply lead to a transaction being set aside under fraudulent transfer laws can become criminal in the bankruptcy context. When a court suspects fraud, it will often bring in a specialist: an independent bankruptcy trustee. At that point, life can become miserable for anyone involved in poorly planned corporate transfers.

CHOOSING THE STATE OF INCORPORATION

In forming a domestic corporation, several states will be considered suitable candidates for incorporation purposes. The available states are usually where the business of the company will be conducted, where the assets of the company will be held, and then several states such Delaware and Nevada that have advanced corporation laws and whose courts tend to respect the sanctity of the corporate entity against those who would set it aside.

If the corporation is meant to hold real estate, the state where the real estate will be held usually makes the most sense for the state of incorporation. The reason is simply that for a corporation to hold real estate, it must be registered in that state. If the corporation is formed elsewhere, the corporation will still have to be registered in the state where the real estate exists. A balancing must be done as to whether the added protection of the other state's laws will outweigh the duplicative costs of having the corporation domiciled in one state and registered in another.

To a lesser degree, this analysis applies to states where the company intends to conduct business. If the company fails to register in the state where it is doing business, a creditor may be able to succeed in obtaining corporate assets on the argument that the corporate shell should not be respected in that state. However, questions as to whether an unregistered company was doing sufficient business in a state that the corporation shell should be ignored are sometimes difficult to resolve. For example, if a company's sole business is holding the stock of another company, or holding passive investments, a creditor may have a great deal of difficulty arguing that the company was doing business in a state other than the state of incorporation. But if a company is regularly entering into contracts in a particular state, and if its owners are concerned about liabilities arising from those contracts, then the company should probably register in that state.

Problems of registration can usually be solved by having the company simply register as necessary. If the company's contacts with a particular state are so significant that the courts of that state will be able to assert personal jurisdiction over the company, then the company should probably register there. But note that registration will submit the company to jurisdiction in that state. If a company does not want to be dragged into court in Alabama, notorious at the time of this writing for its huge plaintiff awards, the company should not register in Alabama, and it should also avoid doing business there.

RIGHTS OF CREDITORS

The biggest disadvantage to domestic corporations is that issues relating to shares of the corporation are within the jurisdiction of at least the state wherein the corporation is formed. These issues may be within the jurisdiction of other states as well. If the court makes a decision regarding share ownership, that decision is binding upon the corporation even if the shareholder and the physical share certificates are outside the jurisdiction of the court. The reason is that the court can simply order any change of ownership be entered on the books of the corporation.

The effect of this capability in the debtor-creditor context is dramatic. It means that a court can give the equity in a corporation to a creditor, even if the court has no jurisdiction over the affected shareholder or the physical share certificates. So the creditor can immediately become a shareholder of the corporation, with the full rights of any shareholder of that class of stock. From an asset protection perspective, this would be disastrous.

Under the corporate law, the creditor can demand the right to inspect the corporation's books and records and to get an accounting. The creditor can also bring a derivative action against the officers and directors of the corporation for any malfeasances. A derivative action doesn't benefit the creditor directly, since any damages won by such a suit are paid into the corporation. But, of course, such awards increase the asset base of the corporation and make it potentially more valuable to the shareholder.

Since privately held corporations by their very nature often have many *insider transactions*, the remaining owners can thus personally become exposed to derivative claims that would otherwise never have been asserted. Thereby, leverage would be created for the creditor to force the remaining owners to buy the creditor out or to liquidate the corporation. In the worst-case scenario, a derivative action by the creditor could have the effect of reaching other "deep pockets" in the persons of the directors and officers of the corporation.

A derivative action brought by a creditor could also potentially affect other planning by the original shareholder. If the creditor is successful in asserting a derivative action against the original shareholder whose shares the creditor has taken, because of an insider transaction, a court may deem that the original shareholder had a claim for that amount as of the date of the transaction. This claim could potentially factor against the original shareholder's balance sheet for purposes of determining solvency under the fraudulent transfer laws. Thus, other planning that might have otherwise survived scrutiny under the fraudulent transfer laws might become susceptible to being set aside because of the derivative claim.

PROFESSIONAL CORPORATIONS

Because the corporate shell shields the owners from liabilities, most states will not allow professionals to operate their professional practices, such as medicine or law, from a typical corporation. Instead, professionals are allowed to form *professional corporations*. These corporations are very similar to typical corporations, but they may have only designated professionals as shareholders. In some cases, they may have nonprofessional shareholders, but they must be controlled by professionals.

It is important to recognize that, just as with any other corporation, a professional corporation does not protect an individual from liability for her or his own actions. Just as a shareholder who is at fault in an auto accident that occurs on company business is not protected from personal liability, neither is a professional who commits negligence. Instead, a professional corporation only shields the professional owner from the ordinary liabilities of the business, such as contractual liabilities for office supplies, equipment leases, etc.

REGISTRATION OF FOREIGN CORPORATION

If a corporation is to own and lease real estate in a particular state, the corporation typically must either be incorporated or registered as a *foreign corporation* (that is, formed under the laws of a jurisdiction other than that state) in that state. Registering, which typically includes the appointment of an in-state agent for service of process, as well as the doing of business in the state, submits the corporation to jurisdiction in that state. By incorporating in one state, and registering in another so as to be able to hold title to real estate, a corporation subjects itself to the imposition of a second layer of state and registered agent's fees.

However, the fact that the corporation has its assets in a state other than the one in which it is incorporated may present obstacles to the creditor. While issues relating to the property itself will be resolved by the courts of the state in which the property is located, most corporate issues will be resolved by reference to the laws of the state of incorporation. Issues relating to whether the corporate veil may be pierced present difficult conflict-of-laws questions. Should corporate veil-piercing issues be resolved according the laws of the state in which the real estate is located or according to the laws of the state of incorporation?

Conflict-of-laws issues may come into play when new theories for penetrating the corporate structure are being developed by the courts of some states, while the theories have not yet caught on in other states. Virginia, for instance, has recently recognized the concept of *reverse veil piercing*, which involves a creditor of the *owner* proving that the owner and the corporation are really one and the same, so that the creditor of the owner can reach the assets of the corporation (as opposed to traditional veil piercing, in which a creditor of the corporation tries to reach a shareholder's assets).[1] This might be a factor in deciding not to form a Virginia entity or to have an entity hold assets in Virginia. On the other hand, Georgia's Supreme Court recently rejected the concept of reverse piercing.[2] The issue clearly is not a settled one among the states. Most state courts have never addressed the issue at all.

Similarly, questions may arise about the proper venue for deciding corporate veil-piercing issues. The owners of the corporation might lack sufficient jurisdictional nexus in their individual capacities sufficient for the courts of the state in which the real estate is located to exercise jurisdiction over them. These owners may thus be able to shift the case from under a hostile judge, who has rendered the underlying ruling on liability, to an indifferent judge in the state of incorporation, who will hear the matter strictly on a technical basis. At best, these issues are difficult to resolve, and, as a result, they may create doubt in the mind of a creditor sufficient to precipitate a favorable settlement.

If possible, financial accounts should be held in a jurisdiction other than one in which the corporation easily can be sued. For example, an Oregon corporation might have its brokerage accounts in New York. If an Oregon court orders the assets of the corporation frozen, the creditor will have to take that order to New York and attempt to have the New York courts enforce the judgment with respect to the New York brokerage accounts. This process can be expensive and time-consuming, with the delay allowing for time to have the brokerage accounts moved elsewhere. If the New York brokerage firm has an office in Oregon, however, the Oregon courts probably could compel the firm to freeze the accounts immediately, without the creditor having to involve the New York courts.

On the other hand, the fact that a corporation owns property in a particular state may subject the corporation to jurisdiction in that state. Accordingly, a corporation should not locate assets in a jurisdiction where the corporation would be at a particular disadvantage in defending a lawsuit.

NEVADA CORPORATIONS

In an attempt to attract new business, some states have adopted new corporation laws that claim to offer certain asset protection benefits. Of these, Nevada corporations have been the most aggressively marketed by far. Indeed, within only a few years, Nevada's corporations industry has grown to rival Delaware's.

Nevada corporations have most of the same advantages as Delaware corporations insofar as no taxes and little fees are imposed upon the entities. However, Nevada touts the fact that it does not have any information-sharing agreement with the U.S. Internal Revenue Service. It also has some other features that may make it more difficult for creditors to discern the ownership of the corporation before they obtain a judgment.

Indeed, some promoters have gone so far as to proclaim that Nevada corporations offer "absolute secrecy" for the true owners of the corporation. This statement conveniently overlooks the fact that, Nevada's state statutes notwithstanding, the courts of other states could compel testimony and disclosures from persons within their jurisdiction about the ownership of the company. Also, federal courts could compel the testimony and disclosures from persons within their jurisdiction, including persons in Nevada, about the ownership of the company. Presumably, the Nevada Secretary of State and other state agencies could also be compelled by a federal subpoena to disclose information relating to a Nevada corporation.

There simply is no absolute secrecy or confidentiality associated with Nevada corporations. True, an additional degree of difficulty is imposed on a creditor that tries to ferret out the ownership of a Nevada corporation on its own, but a determined creditor will be able to do so. Of course, these difficulties may make a difference in a creditor's initial evaluation as to whether or not to go forward with a lawsuit. On the other hand, because of aggressive and often fraudulent marketing by corporate promoters there, Nevada is slowing gaining the same shady reputation that has adversely affected offshore debtor and tax havens. A better strategy may be to blend in with the crowd that uses Delaware corporations.

When used properly and in conjunction with other asset protection techniques, domestic corporations can provide substantial asset protection. In practice, however, the domestic corporation tends to be overshadowed by its foreign counterpart, the offshore corporation as we shall next discuss.

ENDNOTES

1. *C.F. Trust, Inc. v. First Flight L.P.*, 580 S.E.2d 806 (Va.2003).
2. *Acree et al v. McMahan 276 Ga. 880* (2003).

CHAPTER 18

Foreign Corporations and IBCs

Most foreign jurisdictions recognize the concept of the corporation in one form or another. Foreign corporations operate very similarly to their counterparts in the United States, with usually only minor local differences. Unlike, by contrast, a self-settled spendthrift trust, a foreign corporation will typically be respected by U.S. federal and state courts. Indeed, the corporation laws of most U.S. states have specific provisions for recognizing corporations formed outside the United States (which entities are often referred to as *alien corporations*).

Forming a foreign corporation may be desirable for many asset protection reasons. Creditors may have difficulty asserting jurisdiction over a foreign corporation, especially if the foreign corporation does not hold assets in the United States at the time of the lawsuit and has no other U.S. business connections. If the foreign corporation is deemed to be a *necessary party*, the inability of the court to assert jurisdiction over the corporation could terminate the U.S. litigation and force litigation to be conducted where the foreign corporation is domiciled or where it does conduct business. But if even a U.S. court technically has jurisdiction over a foreign corporation, creditors may have difficulty in serving the foreign corporation. And any judgment won in a U.S. court will be of dubious value insofar as the foreign courts typically will often not respect U.S. judgments. Thus, a claimant seeking recovery against a foreign corporation may be required to retain a foreign attorney and litigate the matter in the foreign country—an expensive and time-consuming proposition.

The mere existence of a foreign corporation in a debtor's asset ownership structure can cause problems for creditors. A U.S. judge may not be able to compel the foreign corporation to respond to discovery requests. The foreign corporation may be able to assert the confidentiality laws of its jurisdiction to delay or prevent the disclosure of formation, thus forcing litigation of these issues and delays. Finally, a U.S. judge cannot order a foreign government to involuntarily dissolve and liquidate a foreign corporation. In order to pursue a judicial dissolution, a creditor would have to litigate in the foreign jurisdiction where the corporation was formed. In addition to being very expensive, such litigation may be futile in many cases; a foreign court likely would be inclined to protect entities formed in its jurisdiction when feasible in order to preserve the positive impact of offshore company business on the jurisdiction's economy.

INTERNATIONAL BUSINESS COMPANIES

Offshore havens have succeeded in creating a new variant of the corporation: the *International Business Company*, commonly called an *IBC*. This type of corporation is expressly precluded from conducting most types of business with local persons and companies in its jurisdiction of formation. Thus, its purpose is to conduct business elsewhere. The typical purpose of an ordinary corporation, of course, is to facilitate business within its jurisdiction of formation. The IBC is an anomaly created by the offshore tax and debtor havens for the purpose of attracting company formation and management business to those jurisdictions.

Nonetheless, the typical IBC statute creates an entity that is very useful for many asset protection purposes. In addition to the advantages of all foreign corporations, the IBC has additional significant advantages. The greatest advantage is that the IBC is not taxed in the debtor haven, meaning that there are no tax forms in that jurisdiction that create a paper trail for creditors to follow. (Note, however, that there may be significant IRS reporting requirements for a U.S. taxpayer having interests in a foreign corporation.) Similarly, most IBC acts require minimal filing, so a creditor may have a great deal of difficulty getting pertinent information about an IBC from third-party sources.

Many offshore jurisdictions sanction the use of *nominees* as shareholders, directors, and officers. These are typically local persons whose names appear on the company's records, to the extent they are publicly disclosed, but who act solely at the direction of the true owners. Nominees almost always execute in advance signed but undated resignations from whatever role they are playing, in favor of the true owner or the true owner's designees. Thus, if a nominee does something to displease the true owners, or if the true owners desire to manage the company directly, the resignations are simply dated by the true owners and then placed into the company's books. Theoretically, the resignations may even be backdated so as to throw doubt into whether certain acts were taken on behalf of the corporation. Obviously, the true owners would not want the nominees sued in their individual capacities, as they might then testify to what really happened.

The effect of using nominees is that creditors see a completely foreign company with no shareholders, directors, or officers having any connections to the United States or otherwise doing business in an individual capacity so that they would be subject to U.S. jurisdiction. The idea is to make it difficult for creditors to establish the debtor's ownership and control of the IBC. Any public disclosures relating to the company would reveal these nominees, and not the true owners. A creditor thus must obtain the information by other means, if possible.

Of course, nominees require payment for their services, and these payments can add up, as several nominees are typically required for each company. In some offshore jurisdictions, the nominee business is substantial. For example, a typical resident of the Isle of Sark, in the English Channel (population: 600), might be a nominee director or officer of hundreds of companies worldwide.

Yet the nominee system is not without its perils. The use of nominees may make business transactions difficult, as the signatures of the nominees are not always easy to obtain. Nominees can present problems even if they don't have control over the corporation's assets. For example, a nominee may use the corporation to launder money, which could result in the corporation's assets being frozen. Although the true owners may ultimately be able to convince the courts that the nominee acted outside of her authority, the experience will prove to be time-consuming, costly, and embarrassing.

BEARER SHARES

A few offshore jurisdictions still allow *bearer shares*. These are simply shares of stock that are issued by the company to no particular person. The equity in the corporation represented by these shares is owned by the person who holds, or "bears," the shares at any given moment. The concept of bearer shares is actually an ancient one, going back to the earliest days of corporate entities. Bearer shares allowed corporate stock to be freely and easily traded.

In modern times, most companies issue registered stock with share ownership recorded in a stock ledger. Thus, even if the physical share certificates are lost or stolen, the owner whose name appears in the corporate books as the owner of the shares will be treated as the owner and will have new share certificates reissued to him. Indeed, with registration there is little need to physically issue share certificates to shareholders. A receipt by the new shareholder showing that the shares were purchased will usually suffice to establish share ownership. A modern stock sale is accomplished by the company registering the shares of the new shareholder into the corporate books, without any presentation of the physical share certificates to the company secretary. Thus, bearer shares are an anachronism having almost no legitimate use in modern commerce.

These days, bearer shares are predominantly used by money launderers to disguise the true ownership of a company and to transfer wealth illegally. A simple issuing of the shares of the company in bearer form means that there is no recording of the owners of the shares in the corporate books. Thus, no evidence exists of who owns the shares. Money launderers are thus able to place money into a company and transfer ownership simply by giving the bearer shares to the persons who want the money. Because of this potential for abuse, many jurisdictions have abolished bearer shares.

Nonetheless, any device that has as its result hidden ownership and hidden transfer of wealth is apt to draw attention as an asset protection tool. Indeed, even today many promoters base their planning on the use of bearer shares and disguised ownership of offshore companies. If a creditor appears, the bearer shares are simply handed off to someone else. Bearer shares are used in aggressive offshore tax evasion schemes, usually involving the submission by the offshore company of false or grossly inflated invoices for goods or services to a domestic corporation, to generate artificial deductions for the domestic company and to justify the offshore transfer of funds.

Schemes involving bearer shares should be avoided entirely. First, bearer shares do not avoid the strict tax reporting requirements for owners of foreign entities, and they will not allow the legal avoidance of income tax by a U.S. taxpayer. Second, if bearer shares are truly transferred, the transfer must be either a sale or a gift. If the transfer was a sale and the shares have increased in value in the hands of the transferor, capital gains tax will be owed. If the transfer was a gift, then the gift is likely required to be reported and payment of federal and state gift taxes may be required as well, depending on the value of the stock.

Additionally, because bearer shares are associated in modern times with tax evaders and money launderers, bearer shares carry a heavy stigma. A judge or prosecutor likely will view the existence of bearer shares as a red flag that signals something unseemly. Existing corporate structures using bearer shares should be revised to eliminate bearer shares.

ALTERNATIVE SHARE STRUCTURES

That bearer shares have significant downsides does not mean that all alternative share structures are bad. Many jurisdictions offer alternative forms of share ownership that can be quite advantageous from an asset protection perspective. For instance, some jurisdictions recognize companies limited by *guarantee* or hybrid companies limited by shares and guarantee. A shareholder obtaining shares by guarantee does not contribute assets to the company. Instead, the shareholder agrees to guarantee the debts of the corporation up to a prescribed amount. If the corporation becomes insolvent, the shareholder will be required to pay cash to the company up to the amount of the guarantee. The amount of the shareholder's guarantee is almost always a finite amount. For example, if the amount of the guarantee is $100, the shareholder would be responsible to pay into the company or to pay to the company's receiver or creditors up to $100.

A significant benefit of share ownership by guarantee is that there is no money trail for creditors to follow to discover the shareholder's ownership. If asked questions about corporate ownership under oath, the shareholder would have to disclose ownership of shares in the foreign corporation. Similarly, obtaining equity by guarantee will not relieve the shareholder of IRS reporting requirements and the subsequent paper trail. Yet, especially at the early stages of litigation, the absence of any transfers of money to a company may prevent the shareholder's ownership in the company from being discovered by creditors.

There are also companies that allow the issuance of shares to members who agree to unlimited liability. While at first glance this arrangement might seem extremely undesirable, the unlimited nature of the shareholder's liability may have the effect of tying up the shareholder's assets so that they are not immediately available to the shareholder's creditors.

CONTROLLED FOREIGN CORPORATIONS

The problem with offshore corporations is that IRS reporting requirements force law-abiding shareholders to leave a substantial paper trail for creditors to follow. The failure to file required reporting returns may expose U.S. taxpayers to significant civil and criminal penalties.

Rules concerning *controlled foreign corporations (CFCs)* trip up most U.S. taxpayers who attempt to use foreign companies to achieve tax benefits. A number of promoters claim to have set up *non-CFC* or *decontrolled foreign corporation (DFC)* structures using nominees, multiple entities with interlocking ownership, guarantee companies, hybrid companies, trusts, and other devices. If the company will be controlled by the U.S. taxpayer (or related persons or entities) to whom the DFC pitch is made, and if the bulk of the assets of the DFC come from that person, the DFC in fact will be a CFC or another type of entity the income of which is taxable to its U.S. shareholders under considerably disadvantageous tax regimes, such as the foreign personal holding company (FPHC) rules or the passive foreign investment company (PFIC) rules.

As mentioned in the discussion of bearer shares, offshore companies are often misused in reinvoicing or transfer pricing schemes. These are arrangements whereby artificial or inflated invoices are submitted by an offshore corporation to a domestic company, thus allowing the domestic company to take deductions for the invoices. The money paid pursuant to the invoices goes into the offshore corporation, and is held there, supposedly tax-free, until the true owner (who also owns the domestic company that took the deductions) asserts control over the offshore corporation and takes possession of the money. In both the DFC scheme and the reinvoicing scheme, form will be ignored and the substance of the structure will control the tax treatment. U.S. taxpayers involved in such schemes are likely to suffer harsh civil penalties at best and harsh criminal penalties at worst.

Although these schemes are terrible when used as tax devices, they may be effective as asset protection devices. So long as the U.S. taxpayer does not take deductions for the invoices paid to the foreign corporation, and so long as U.S. tax reporting requirements are met for any owners of the foreign corporation who are U.S. taxpayers (if there are any), these schemes can be effective against all but the most sophisticated creditors.

CHAPTER 19

Charging Order Protected Entities

Charging order protected entities (COPEs) are entities that restrict the remedies of a creditor of an owner to a "charging order" that entitles the creditor to distributions made in respect of that ownership interest, but do not allow—at least initially—the creditor to actually take the ownership interest. From an asset protection standpoint, the advantage is obvious: The creditor has no immediate means of getting at the assets in the entity even though the creditor holds a judgment against one of the owners. In this chapter, we describe the main types of COPEs: partnerships and limited liability companies. In Chapter 20 we will examine domestic COPEs and the Delaware Series LLC, and in Chapter 21 we will examine foreign COPEs.

PARTNERSHIPS

A *partnership* is an association of two or more persons carrying on a business venture as co-owners for profit. Partnerships come in two basic varieties: general and limited.

A *general partnership* consists only of general partners. In a general partnership the owners control the business and there is no statutorily mandated separation of ownership and management as there is in a corporation. Management of a general partnership is vested in all of the general partners. All partners of a general partnership are jointly and severally liable for the debts of the business and for the wrongful acts committed by other partners in the course of the partnership's business. Thus, the personal assets of a general partner are subject to the claims of the partnership's creditors.

A *limited partnership* consists of at least one general partner and at least one limited partner. The management and control of a limited partnership is vested in its general partner(s) and cannot be vested in the limited partners. The liability of a general partner in a limited partnership is the same as in a general partnership. Whereas general partners have unlimited liability for the partnership's debts, limited partners have limited liability for these debts, namely, the amount of their investment. Note, however, that there is no such thing as a "passive-active" limited partner, since a limited partner risks losing her limited liability if she participates in the management of the partnership's business.

Partnerships are afforded *passthrough taxation* by the Internal Revenue Code. The tax items of a partnership's business (for example, income, deductions, and credits) are passed through to the partners, so that only one level of tax is paid on the income of the partnership's business. This can be a big advantage over the double taxation of corporations, which results when profits are taxed at the corporate level, and the dividends that are received by shareholders are taxed as well. Indeed, the advantage of *S corporations* is that they have made an election with the IRS to be taxed similarly to partnerships.

Another advantage is that there is no recognition of gain on the contribution of appreciated assets to a partnership. There are two important exceptions to this general rule. First, if a partner is relieved of liabilities in excess of the basis of the property he contributes to the partnership, he will recognize gain to that extent. Second, if the effect of forming an investment partnership is that the partners diversify their assets, there may be recognition of gain on the contribution of assets to the partnership in exchange for partnership interests.

LIMITED LIABILITY COMPANIES

The *limited liability company (LLC)* is a hybrid type of legal entity that combines certain traits of corporations with certain other traits of partnerships and other noncorporate legal entities. LLCs allow their owners (called *members*) to have the best of all worlds: pass-through tax treatment like a partnership, limited liability like a corporation, unheralded flexibility in ownership and management structure, and charging order protection.

Whereas corporation laws are generally written to accommo-date the needs of businesses with large numbers of passive stock-holders, the LLC acts are generally written with small businesses in mind. Thus, the LLC tends to be a more flexible and more easily understood business entity.

LLCs are managed collectively either by the LLC's members (a *member-managed LLC*) or by one or more appointed or elected managers (a *manager-managed LLC*). While a manager of a manag-er-managed LLC typically is also a member, under the LLC acts of most jurisdictions, a manager need not be a member. Thus, an LLC can be managed with only one level of decision making (and record keeping), as opposed to corporations that are managed both at the executive and board of directors levels.

HISTORY OF THE LLC

Although the LLC is relatively new in the United States, the con-cept has been around for over one hundred years in Europe and Latin America. Have you ever seen the name of a German compa-ny that ends with the abbreviation GmbH or a Latin American company that ends with the abbreviation SRL? GmbH stands for the German phrase *Gesellschaft mit beschränkter Haftung*—literally, "company with limited liability." SRL stands for the Spanish phrase *sociedad de responsibilidad limitada*—literally, "limited liabili-ty company." These are the historical precursors of the modern American LLC.

In the mid-1970s, a company in Wyoming that was dissatis-fied with its available forms of legal entities decided that it would be useful to have a statutory business entity form that would pro-vide all owners with limited liability while allowing the owners to be treated as partners for tax purposes. The result was the passage in 1977 of the Wyoming LLC Act, the first LLC act in the United States.

The limited liability features of the Wyoming LLC were built into the LLC Act. Nevertheless, the IRS determined the tax treatment of this new type of entity on a case-by-case basis. The Wyoming company that started it all applied to the IRS for a private ruling to determine that the LLC would be taxed as a partnership. Eleven years later, the company finally received a favorable ruling. At the same time, the IRS issued Revenue Ruling 88-76, which spelled out the requirements for taxing an LLC as a partnership.

With the issuance of Revenue Ruling 88-76, and the tax certainty it provided, the floodgates opened; an unprecedented torrent of new legislation issued forth. By 1996, every state had an LLC act. Legal and tax advisors scrambled to learn how to use this new entity.

Finally, in December 1996, the IRS issued *check-the-box regulations*,[1] which allow an LLC simply to choose whether to be taxed as a partnership or as a corporation. Now, LLCs don't have to jump through hoops for income tax purposes. Simply check a box, or not. That is all it takes to choose the tax treatment of an LLC. With the advent of the check-the-box regulations, the LLC has rapidly grown in popularity among business, estate, and asset protection planners.

TAX CLASSIFICATION

Under prior law regarding the tax classification of business entities, LLCs were classified as corporations or partnerships for tax purposes based on the individual characteristics of each LLC. If the owners wanted partnership taxation, a minimum number of requirements had to be met. If the owners wanted corporate taxation, different requirements had to be met. The provisions of the particular LLC act under which an LLC was formed were important for tax classification, especially in cases where there was no LLC operating agreement or only a basic LLC operating agreement. All of this changed at the end of 1996, when the check-the-box regulations were enacted.

Under the check-the-box regulations, U.S. corporations are taxed as corporations and cannot elect to be taxed otherwise. However, any other business entity that is not properly classified as a trust or otherwise subject to special treatment under the Internal Revenue Code may elect its tax treatment. A separate business entity with two or more members can generally elect to be classified as either a corporation or a partnership. An entity with only one member does not qualify as a partnership. However, such a single-owner entity may elect to be classified as a corporation or to be disregarded for tax purposes as an entity separate from its owner—and thus to be taxed as a sole proprietorship.

If a new entity fails to elect classification, it is classified under a set of default rules generally providing that domestic entities with two or members are classified as partnerships and domestic single-member entities are disregarded as entities separate from their owners.

Basically, the regulations really are that simple. If you want passthrough partnership or sole proprietorship taxation for a domestic LLC, you do nothing. In that case, it's really a "don't-check-the-box" rule.

If an LLC wants to be taxed as a corporation, it simply files a one-page IRS Form 8832, Entity Classification Election, within seventy-five days after the date the election is to be effective, literally checking a box to elect to be taxed as a corporation. Once an LLC elects to be taxed as a corporation, it is a corporation for all federal tax purposes. So, a domestic LLC that has elected to be taxed as a corporation can elect to be taxed under Subchapter S as an S corporation as well (assuming it otherwise qualifies under the Subchapter S rules). See Figure 19.1 for a simple check-the-box flowchart.

A brief mention of *entity conversions* is in order here. If a general or limited partnership converts to an LLC under local law, the resulting LLC will be taxed as a continuation of the former partnership, unless the resulting LLC chooses to be taxed as a corporation. In the latter case, the conversion will be treated as a dissolution and liquidation of the partnership followed by a contribution by the partners to a new LLC.

If a corporation converts to an LLC under local law, the resulting LLC can elect to be taxed as a corporation. That election causes the conversion to be treated as a continuation of the former corporation, with no tax consequences. If the resulting LLC does not elect to be taxed as a corporation, however, the conversion will be treated as a dissolution and liquidation of the corporation. This treatment can result in a potential resulting tax disaster caused by

FIGURE 19.1

Domestic LLC check-the-box flowchart.

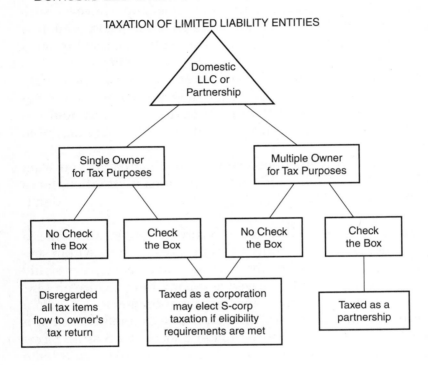

the liquidation distribution of appreciated assets. The conversion will then be treated as a contribution by the former shareholders to a new LLC.

Single-member entities that do not elect to be taxed as corporations are completely disregarded for tax purposes. The simplest example is an LLC with one member, an individual person. In such a case, the tax items of the LLC are the tax items of the individual. The individual simply reports the tax items of the LLC on her own personal income tax return: business activity on Schedule C, capital gains and losses on Schedule D, rental activity on Schedule E, and the like.

Another entity, such as another LLC or a partnership or corporation, can be the single member of an LLC. In that case, the LLC's tax items are reported on the underlying entity's tax return, just as with an individual owner. The tax items of an LLC wholly owned by a corporation, for example, will be reported on the corporation's Form 1120, U.S. Corporation Income Tax Return, along with the corporation's other tax items.

Taking the concept a step further, consider the LLC that is owned by more than one legal owner, all of whom are treated as one for tax purposes (see Figure 19.2). This type of LLC can also be disregarded under the check-the-box regulations.

This concept is best illustrated by example. Say that you decide to do some estate planning and set up a trust for your children. Your estate planning advisor recommends that the trust be a grantor trust for income tax purposes. With this type of trust, the income of the trust would be taxable to you rather than being taxed at the compressed trust income tax rates. Your sister is the trustee. You funded the trust for several years and now the trust principal has grown to about $1 million.

You have $100,000 of your own funds that you would like to invest in a rental property. Your sister, as trustee of the trust, thinks it would be a good investment for the trust as well, and since the trust document gives the trustee wide latitude with trust investments, she decides that the trust will invest $100,000.

You and the trustee decide to form an LLC, with each of you and the trust as a 50 percent member. You choose not to have the LLC taxed as a corporation, so no check-the-box election is filed. The LLC will be taxed as a disregarded entity with respect to you. You are treated as the owner of the assets of the grantor trust and you are, of course, the owner of your LLC interests. So, you are treated as the owner of 100 percent of the LLC interests, even though you do not actually own or even control 100 percent of the interests.

LLCS AND ESTATE PLANNING

LLCs, including offshore LLCs (discussed in Chapter 21), can be used as estate planning tools in the same manner as family limited partnerships. If the LLC is properly structured, LLC interests could be discounted for estate and gift tax purposes for lack of marketability and lack of control. In addition to the discounted transfer possibilities, LLCs are simply a convenient way to transfer assets to younger generations. There is no need to constantly

FIGURE 19.2

Multimember LLC disregarded entity.

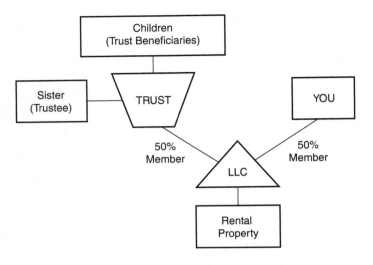

retitle assets to reflect changing ownership, often transfer taxes on real estate and other assets can be avoided, and ancillary (that is, out of state) probate can be avoided for real estate located outside the client's domicile.

Until the end of the 1990s, limited partnerships were preferred over LLCs as estate planning vehicles. They were because most LLC acts lagged behind limited partnership acts with regard to statutory provisions that were favorable for estate and gift tax discounting. However, many states have remedied the problem, with the result that LLCs are now the favored vehicle for estate planning in many states.

To provide limited liability for the general partner of a family limited partnership, many practitioners form a corporation owned by the family matriarch and patriarch to act as general partner. Doing so, of course, essentially converts the general partnership interests to corporate stock, with the adverse asset protection consequences that conversion brings.

An LLC can be used to act as the general partner without the adverse asset protection consequences of corporate stock. However, if an LLC is used as the estate planning vehicle itself, no separate general partner entity is needed, since there is no unlimited liability for LLC managers in the way that there is unlimited liability for general partners. Using an LLC also allows the estate planning vehicle to be formed as a single-member entity with gifts made later. This arrangement can be useful if the children are not contributing assets upon the formation of the entity.

PROTECTING S CORPORATION SHARES

Shares of stock in an S corporation are often difficult to protect. Tax rules prohibit partnerships (that is, entities taxed as partnerships) from owning shares of S corporation stock. So, S corporation shares cannot be owned in an LLC holding company structure if the LLC holding company is taxed as a partnership. However, tax rules permit S corporation shares to be owned in an LLC holding company if the LLC holding company is taxed as a disregarded entity and if the LLC owner is a U.S. individual (or other eligible S corporation shareholder).. So, a dual strategy is often best for S corporation shares. First, convert the corporation to an LLC taxed as an S corporation to obtain the asset protection advantages associated with charging order protection discussed in the next chapter. Then, contribute the membership interests of the LLC taxed as an S corporation to an LLC holding company structured as a disregarded entity.

ENDNOTES

1. Treas. Reg. 301.7701-3.

CHAPTER 20

Domestic COPEs and Series LLCs

One very important difference between being a shareholder of a corporation and a member of an LLC is often overlooked. The shares of a shareholder of a corporation are vulnerable to claims of the shareholder's judgment creditors. In many small businesses, this vulnerability could allow the creditors to take control of the business or even liquidate its assets to satisfy their judgments.

The membership interests of an LLC are more protected. In the United States and in offshore jurisdictions with U.S.-style LLC acts, a creditor of a partner in a partnership or a member of an LLC is entitled only to a *charging order* rather than being entitled to execute directly against partnership assets. A charging order gives a creditor the right to receive any distributions that the owner of the interest would have received. A charging order is simply a court document that directs the managers of the LLC to divert distributions that would otherwise go to the debtor member to the creditor until the judgment is paid.

At first glance, the charging order may not seem like much protection. However, the economic rights to distributions are all that the creditor gets. The creditor does not get the management and voting rights that may go along with the LLC membership interest. The LLC's managers determine if and when distributions are made. In some situations distributions will not be made; in others distributions will be significantly delayed. Some tax professionals believe that the creditor may be taxable on the debtor-member's income, even if the creditor never receives any distributions with respect to the charging order (giving rise to the term *phantom income)*. This belief is suspect, but the uncertainty in this area can make a creditor contemplating a charging order very uneasy about potential exposure to taxes. Indeed, an LLC operating agreement might be drafted in such a way to cause a creditor with a charging order to be taxable.

The charging order is thus not an attractive remedy to most creditors. As a result, the prospect of a charging order may convince a creditor to settle on more reasonable terms than might otherwise be possible. Shareholders of a corporation have little such leverage. Thus, in addition to being a very useful business tool, the LLC can be a valuable asset protection tool.

THE CHARGING ORDER IN ANGLO-AMERICAN LAW

The charging order derives from American partnership law, which derives from English partnership law. Under partnership law as it existed toward the end of the nineteenth century, a creditor of a partner could execute directly against partnership assets to recover the debt of a partner that was unrelated to partnership business. This arrangement proved very disruptive to partnership businesses, and it was perceived as unfair because there was nothing that the debtor's partners could do to prevent the disruption.

Around the end of the nineteenth century, the English Parliament drastically changed English partnership law with the enactment of the Partnership Act 1890. The Parliament decided that it was unfair to disrupt partnership business by having the sheriff seize partnership assets and selling them to satisfy a debt unrelated to the partnership's business. The act provided that, rather than obtaining a writ of execution against partnership assets to satisfy a judgment debt of a partner, a creditor of a partner must satisfy a judgment by obtaining an order from a court charging the partner's economic interest in the partnership. That is, his interest in partnership distributions of profits and capital is charged.

When U.S. partnership law was being codified in the early twentieth century in the Uniform Partnership Act and later in the Uniform Limited Partnership Act, the charging order concept was imported into American partnership statutes. So, the charging order is well established in the American law of partnerships and the concept now has been imported into American LLC law over the last few decades.

SINGLE-MEMBER LLCS AND CHARGING ORDERS

The single-member LLC is something of an anomaly, because LLC law is largely based on the law of partnerships and, of course, there have never been single-member partnerships. Nothing in any LLC act, foreign or domestic, indicates that the charging order remedy is not the preferred or sole remedy available to a creditor of a member of a single-member LLC.

The original policy reason for the charging order, however, does not exist with a single-member LLC. There is no other LLC member who would be unfairly affected by the seizure of LLC assets or of the LLC interest itself in its entirety.

If asset protection via the charging order is a major concern, single-member LLCs should be used with caution. When possible, an additional member should be included to bolster the charging order protection. An additional member often can be added without changing the tax treatment of the LLC—for example, by using a grantor trust or another LLC or IBC.

The issue of the member of a single-member LLC in bankruptcy is yet another potential problem area. In a 2003 Colorado bankruptcy case,[1] the court held that the bankruptcy trustee succeeded to the management rights of the member-manager of a Colorado single-member LLC. That arrangement could cause the LLC to sell its sole asset, certain real estate, and distribute the proceeds to the trustee.

Although perhaps the result is logically correct, from a legal perspective it is subject to criticism. In essence, the court said that by succeeding to the debtor-member's membership interest, the bankruptcy trustee thereby succeeded to the member's control of the LLC. This contravenes the definition of the term *membership interest* in the Colorado LLC Act as meaning only the member's right to receive allocations and distributions. The decision thus rests on a fundamental misapplication (albeit intentional) of statutory LLC law—namely, a failure to distinguish between an LLC member's economic rights and her management rights.

The court also stated that the charging order limitation serves no purpose in a single-member LLC, because there are no other parties' interests affected. Yet, the court entirely failed to address the strongest argument in support of LLC charging order protection, even for single-member LLCs—namely, the plain meaning of the charging order statute.

The court discussed what might happen if the LLC had two-members and the dominant member filed for bankruptcy. In such an event, the court said that if the nondebtor member did not consent to the admission of the bankruptcy trustee as a substituted member, even if that nondebtor member held only an infinitesimal interest, the bankruptcy trustee would not gain management rights. The trustee would only be entitled to a share of distributions and would have no role in the voting or governance of the company.

In short, the decision powerfully supports the asset protection afforded by multimember LLCs. But it is basically incorrect in its stated rationale for denying the charging order protection to members of single-member LLCs.

This outcome does not mean, however, that single-member LLCs are without utility in asset protection planning. As subsidiary LLCs of holding entities, they are still quite useful in segregating liabilities resulting from different sources, such as separate parcels of real estate and separate lines of business. In such cases, it is not the charging order upon which the protection relies but rather the limited liability nature of the LLC. In other words, there is no reason to suspect that the liability shield afforded to "internal" liabilities of the LLC will be any less than that of sole-shareholder corporations.

Where an LLC formed outside of the United States is involved, the members of a multimember LLC should be protected by the charging order in American courts. As noted above, the charging order has a long-established history in the United States. Consider a particular state's law that requires the application of its own LLC charging order law to the interest of a debtor member in an LLC formed under the law of another jurisdiction. That concept is neither alien nor out of line with the state's own public policy regarding the interest of a debtor member of an LLC. A debtor-settlor of a foreign asset protection trust, in contrast, will certainly be forced to wage battle against the long-standing public policy against self-settled spendthrift trusts in all but a few U.S. jurisdictions.

FORECLOSURE

Many asset protection commentators spend a great deal of time worrying about the possibility that a creditor with a charging order can foreclose on the charged LLC interest if the charging order is not quickly moving the creditor toward satisfaction of the judgment. The claim is often made that charging order protection is quickly being "eroded" by the increasing application of foreclosure by courts. That statement implies that some great flood of foreclosure orders is being issued.

In fact, there are only a handful of reported cases of foreclosure. Furthermore, even if a creditor does foreclose on the LLC interest, the creditor simply gets the LLC member's economic interest in perpetuity rather than for the length of time it takes to satisfy the judgment. As a practical matter, in asset protection litigation situations, those time periods can be about the same.

If a creditor were limited to the charging order, he might have to wait a very long time to get satisfaction. A creditor who has foreclosed will also likely have to wait a very long time to satisfy a judgment from LLC distributions, since the creditor is still in no position to force out distributions. A creditor to whom an LLC interest has been transferred in a foreclosure sale is still merely an economic assignee and does not succeed to the management and voting rights of the debtor-assignor.

Another factor weighing heavily against a creditor initiating foreclosure is that while it is uncertain at best whether a creditor with a charging order is taxable on debtor member's share of LLC income, it is a near certainty that a creditor who has foreclosed upon a debtor's LLC interest will be taxable on the debtor member's share of LLC income. Finally, if the LLC manager is in a non-U.S. jurisdiction, the creditor-assignee may be forced to pursue the manager in an inhospitable judicial arena. By the time the creditor-assignee initiates such litigation, the manager may have reorganized the LLC. That situation could leave the creditor with a significant tax bill and no LLC distributions with which to pay it. Or else the manager may have otherwise made the funds practically inaccessible to the creditor.

The concern over the possibility of foreclosure drives the preference for the so-called *charging order exclusivity provisions* of some LLC acts. A few jurisdictions, Nevis included, provide that the charging order is the exclusive remedy by which a creditor of a member may satisfy a judgment from the debtor's interest in an LLC. It is unclear whether this exclusivity is meant to cut off the possibility of foreclosure or instead simply reinforces the idea that no judge should reach back to nineteenth-century partnership law to issue writs of execution to the sheriff to seize LLC assets. The latter interpretation probably is the actual legislative intent in U.S. partnership acts. That intent can be inferred in the many U.S. LLC acts that are derived from U.S. partnership acts. It is also quite clear in Section 18-703 of the recently amended Delaware LLC Act, which refers both to the exclusivity of the charging order remedy and to foreclosure. Nevertheless, the view that exclusivity language precludes foreclosure is so prevalent that it may actually have become the law in some jurisdictions.

FRAUDULENT TRANSFER ISSUES AND LLCS

Another reason to consider the LLC as an asset protection tool is the favorable position of an LLC member from the standpoint of a fraudulent transfer challenge. The fact is that the exchange of property for LLC interests is a transaction for valuable consideration. That can make an asset protection structure based on an LLC preferable to a trust-based structure that requires the gratuitous transfer of a large amount of assets. This fact can also mean, in some circumstances, that LLC-based asset protection structures can be set up at times when asset protection trusts cannot. But very careful badges-of-fraud and solvency analyses must be undertaken first.

Transfers for which valuable consideration is received are difficult to challenge under the fraudulent transfer laws of most jurisdictions. Transfers of property in exchange for pro rata LLC interests will be extremely difficult to challenge as fraudulent in those jurisdictions that require a showing that the transfer be without "equivalent value," regardless of the transferor's intent.

SPECIAL CONSIDERATIONS FOR LLC AND PARTNERSHIP INTERESTS IN BANKRUPTCY

The Bankruptcy Code does not specifically refer to LLCs or LLC members. A few cases have addressed certain issues that arise when an LLC member files for bankruptcy. Recognizing the similarities between LLC members and partners, courts generally have applied partnership-type analysis to LLCs and have arrived at differing results.

As discussed earlier, the charging order can be an effective tool for asset protection planning. It can prevent a creditor of a member of an LLC or a partner in a partnership from directly reaching LLC or partnership assets to satisfy a claim against the member or partner. At the very least, charging order protection can deter many types of creditors, and thus it often facilitates favorable settlements.

Nevertheless, an LLC operating agreement or a partnership agreement may be deemed an *executory contract* under bankruptcy law. As such, a bankruptcy trustee has the power to exercise powers over a debtor's interests in the LLC or partnership agreement. This power can be used to sell or assign the owner's rights under the agreement if the debtor has those rights if a creditor with a charging order would also have those rights. The law of most states would prevent a creditor-assignee from exercising any rights other than the mere economic right to receive distributions.

A well-drafted LLC operating agreement should contain a clause that removes, or gives the LLC the power to remove, a member who is involved in a bankruptcy action. The right to expel might include the requirement that it can only be exercised if the bankruptcy court concluded that the trustee had the power to exercise or transfer the management rights of the owner. In the event of an expulsion, management and voting rights could, under the agreement, be vested in the existing voting or managing owners or, if none exist, in the owners who originally held nonmanaging or nonvoting interests. The expulsion clause may further provide for a diminished payout (for example, equal to book value rather than fair market value) to an owner who is so expelled. The clause also can provide that the bankruptcy action amounts to a material breach of the agreement by the debtor-owner, which entitles the LLC to recover damages from the owner. Furthermore, the clause can provide that this diminished amount be reduced further on account of the damages caused to the LLC by the breach. These provisions reduce any amount that would be paid into the debtor-owner's bankruptcy estate and could persuade the trustee to abandon the executory contract.

A bankruptcy trustee may challenge these types of provisions, but a bankruptcy court should uphold the clause in most jurisdictions. The law of most jurisdictions prevents a creditor of a member of an LLC or a partner in a partnership from assuming rights of a debtor-member or debtor-partner other than mere economic rights to distributions.

THE DELAWARE SERIES LLC

From an asset protection point of view, segregating "dangerous" assets and businesses into separate entities away from other assets, especially "safe" assets, is always a good idea. For example, an individual who owns a gas station and a rental home shouldn't own both within the same entity. Neither should an individual who wants to protect a large amount of her liquid assets (for example, cash and securities) hold the cash in the same entity as a business.

Best practices would dictate that every distinct business or major business asset be segregated into a different limited liability entity. In an ideal situation, someone with twenty-five rental properties would have twenty-five separate LLCs, one for each property. But this setup isn't always practical, because of administrative costs and government fees that must be paid for each LLC. What can such a business owner do to protect his assets from liabilities unrelated to those assets in a cost-effective way?

Enter the Delaware series LLC. The Delaware LLC Act provides for the creation of separate *series* within an LLC, whose debts and other liabilities are enforceable against that series alone (see Figure 20.1). The act also provides that classes or groups of members can be established that have whatever rights the LLC agreement says they have. The combination of the two provisions allows a series to be treated in many ways as a separate LLC. Thus, the series provisions in the Delaware LLC Act allow for the creation of separate protected *cells* within one limited liability *container* without the need to create separate entities. This arrangement avoids the inefficiencies associated with multiple related entities. The concept is similar in function to the segregated portfolio companies and protected cell companies designed for the mutual fund and captive insurance industries in Bermuda, Guernsey, the Cayman Islands, Mauritius, and Belize.

The Delaware LLC Act allows an LLC agreement to designate series of members, managers, or LLC interests that have separate rights and duties with respect to specific LLC property or obligations. So, each series can be tied to specific assets and can also have different members and managers. If the various series within an LLC have different members or different membership rights, each series may be treated as a separate LLC for income tax purposes. This arrangement eliminates some of the administrative advantage of the series LLC.

Each series can have its own separate business purposes. A series can be terminated without the other series of the LLC being

FIGURE 20.1

Delaware series LLC.

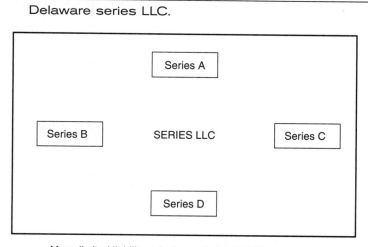

Many limited liability cells in one limited liability container

affected. A series can make distributions to its own members without regard to the financial condition of the other series.

Most importantly, the Delaware LLC Act provides that debts, liabilities, and obligations incurred, contracted for, or otherwise existing with respect to a particular series are enforceable against that series only. They are not enforceable against the assets of the LLC generally or any other series of the LLC. In order to obtain this protection, each series must be treated separately. Books and records must be kept for each series, and the assets of each series must be held and accounted for separately. Finally, in order that the public knows that it is dealing with a series LLC, it must be put on notice by the inclusion of the series limitations in the LLC's Certificate of Formation filed with the Delaware Secretary of State. Having multiple LLCs is usually inefficient and leaves owners vulnerable (see Figure 20.2). Protection is afforded by the use of the series LLC to hold multiple parcels of real property in liability-segregated cells (see Figure 20.3). If the owners of five parcels of real property form and maintain five separate LLCs, the costs would include legal fees and filing fees for five LLCs, partnership tax return preparation fees for five LLCs, annual fees for five LLCs, and possibly registered agent fees or foreign registration fees.

Holding those five properties in five separate series of a single Delaware series LLC could produce significant savings while providing a significant degree of asset protection. In that case, there would be legal fees (albeit likely considerably higher than for a standard LLC) and a filing fee for only one LLC, one tax return preparation fee, one Delaware annual tax of $100, and one Delaware registered agent fee of $100 to $200 per year. Furthermore, if the LLC is required to register to do business in the jurisdiction where the property is located, only one registration fee is required.

One of the problems with domestic limited partnerships and LLCs is that despite legislative acts that are quite favorable to debtors, these entities are well known and creditors are actively thinking up ways to get around their protections. In Chapter 21, we examine forms of these entities that operate very similar to domestic limited partnerships and LLCs but are formed abroad and thus

FIGURE 20.2

Inefficient and vulnerable multiple LLCs.

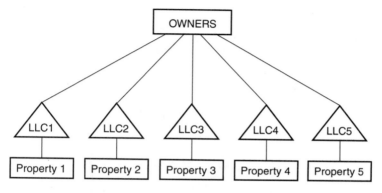

Legal and filing fees for forming 5 LLCs
5 partnership tax return preparation fees each year
5 annual fees paid to jurisdiction of formation each year

FIGURE 20.3

Series LLC applied.

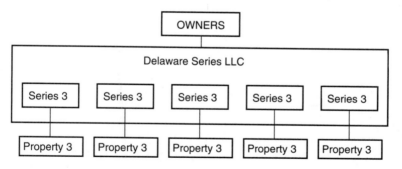

Legal and filing fees for forming one LLC
One partnership tax return preparation fee each year
One annual tax of $200 paid to Delaware each year
If required to register to do business in state where property is located,
    only one registration fee required
One Delaware registered agent fee per year

present peculiar problems to creditors who are looking to exploit their weaknesses.

ENDNOTES

1. *In re Albright* (Bkrpt. Colo. Case No. 01-11367, April 4, 2003).

Foreign COPEs

It is a truism in asset protection that novelty is good. The reasons for this are mostly practical, in that creditors will generally have a tougher time figuring out a strategy that they have never seen before and thereafter devising a means for getting around that strategy. A corollary is that sometimes a strange or unusual structure will give a particular creditor angst because the creditor cannot employ its traditional methods of attacking similar structures.

This does not mean that asset protection planners should implement outlandish plans that utilize entities and transactions that make no sense. Instead, certain types of *exotic entities*, certain sophisticated forms of business organizations available outside the United States, can be introduced into the planning mix to create uncertainty on the part of creditors who are unfamiliar with these types of entities.

EXOTIC ENTITIES

A primary goal of asset protection planners is to subtly integrate into the client's planning an entity that is very similar in its base structure to U.S. entities with which a judge is familiar yet which is structured just differently enough that a creditor cannot pursue the traditional line of attack against the structure.

This is all by way of saying that to successfully utilize exotic entities in asset protection planning, the exotic entity should in

most cases be a hybrid or derivative of a structure that is commonly used in ordinary business planning. For like reasons, the exotic
entity should not be domiciled in a known debtor haven. The fact
that it is might give away its true purpose. Instead, the more successful exotics will be from more traditional foreign countries not
having the reputations as offshore debtor havens such as the
United Kingdom or Canada.

Note that even though a "respectable" jurisdiction like the
United Kingdom is utilized for the formation of the entity, the
debtor still faces one significant hurdle: A U.S. court will be loath
to interfere in the administration of a foreign entity. It is much more
likely to tell the creditor to file an action in the foreign courts and
have those courts give relief. This situation is different than one in
which an offshore debtor haven is involved that the judge may
know or suspect will not give the creditor any relief. That lack of
action in an "unrespectable" jurisdiction might precipitate the
judge to attempt to resolve matters in her own court.

OFFSHORE LLCS

Driven primarily by the desire to market their entities for use by
U.S. clients and planners, several offshore havens have enacted
limited liability company legislation that is very similar to the better U.S. state LLC acts. As of the time of the writing this book, the
three most common offshore LLC acts in use by U.S. persons are
those of Anguilla and Nevis in the Caribbean, and the Isle of Man
in the Irish Sea.

Although many offshore jurisdictions had noncorporate limited
liability entity statutes (like the SRL), none were very familiar to U.S.
legal and tax practitioners. Sensing that the Wyoming-style LLC was
going to be the future business entity of choice for Americans, a few
offshore jurisdictions enacted U.S.-oriented LLC legislation. Anguilla
adopted its LLC Act in 1994 and amended it in 1999. The Anguilla
LLC Act was modeled on the Wyoming LLC act, which in 1994 was
not one of the more modern U.S. LLC acts. As such, the Anguilla LLC
Act has not been updated to provide dissolution and dissociation
provisions favorable for estate and gift tax planning discounts.

Anguilla's LLC act provides for charging orders, but it does
not provide that the charging order is the exclusive remedy of a

debtor of a member. Absent egregious circumstances, however, chances are probably slim that foreclosure would be quickly allowed. And chances are slimmer yet that LLC assets would be reachable directly by the creditor of a member, even in the event of foreclosure.

The Isle of Man adopted its LLC act in 1996. The Isle of Man LLC act is modeled on Manx partnership law, which is, in turn, modeled on English partnership law. As a result, the Manx LLC act looks unlike U.S. LLC acts. In addition to being generally unfamiliar to U.S. persons and practitioners, the Isle of Man LLC act has a number of provisions that many U.S. persons would find objectionable.

Probably the two most important of these objectionable provisions are that Isle of Man LLCs must have two or more members and Isle of Man LLCs must keep certain accounting records in the Isle of Man. Nearly all of the U.S. LLC acts, as well as the LLC acts of Nevis and Anguilla, allow for single-member LLCs (although, as discussed in Chapter 20, single-member LLCs are often undesirable for asset protection planning.). Accounting records, including daily entries of receipts and expenditures, a balance sheet, and annual inventories, must be kept in the Isle of Man. Failure to comply with the statutory accounting requirements subjects every member and manager of the LLC to criminal sanctions, including imprisonment and large fines. Neither U.S. LLC acts nor those of Anguilla and Nevis contain such mandatory accounting provisions.

The Isle of Man's LLC act does not provide for charging orders by statute. Apparently the drafters of the Isle of Man LLC act intended that LLC members would rely on Isle of Man common law to provide charging order protection for LLC membership interests.

The Nevis LLC Ordinance, enacted in 1995, is based on the Delaware LLC Act. In 1995, the Nevis LLC Ordinance was perhaps the most advanced U.S.-style LLC act available to U.S. practitioners. Since then, many U.S. states have taken drastic steps to improve their LLC statutes while the Nevis LLC Ordinance has not been changed. The Nevis LLC Ordinance, however, it is still one of the better LLC acts in existence. The Nevis LLC act was drafted to provide maximum flexibility, maximum estate planning advantages, and maximum asset protection. In the offshore LLC world, the Nevis LLC Ordinance stands head and shoulders above other LLC acts.

The Nevis LLC Ordinance explicitly provides for charging order protection. It also provides that the charging order is the exclusive remedy of a debtor of a member. No mention of foreclosure is made in the Nevis LLC Ordinance. It seems clear that the intent of the Nevis LLC Ordinance is to eliminate the possibility of foreclosure. The Nevis LLC Ordinance also eliminates is the possibility that a creditor of a member could reach LLC assets directly.

Other offshore jurisdictions have European-style LLC acts or hybrid company acts (companies limited by stock and by guarantee), including Barbados, Panama, and the Cayman Islands. Many of these statutes (such as the handful of *limited duration company (LDC)* acts that were enacted) came into place or were amended only a year or two before the check-the-box regulations (discussed in Chapter 19) came into effect. With the advent of check-the-box in the foreign arena, many of these non-U.S.-style LLC acts are basically obsolete for many U.S. purposes. Now, there is a wide range of foreign companies that can provide their owners with limited liability and passthrough taxation, and these are not just U.S.-style LLC acts.

The Marshall Islands enacted U.S.-style LLC legislation in 1996, but like Anguilla's LLC act, it has not been much used because of the popularity of the Nevis LLC Ordinance. The Cook Islands has toyed with U.S.-style LLC legislation for a number of years. It is likely that other jurisdictions will enact U.S.-style LLC legislation, promoting a healthy competitiveness to produce the most advanced cutting-edge LLC act in the offshore world.

USE OF OFFSHORE LLCS AS ASSET PROTECTION TOOLS

The use of offshore LLCs as asset protection tools has only become possible and practical in the last few years because of changes in U.S. tax law and the enactment of U.S.-style LLC legislation in Nevis. In the past, IBCs were popular asset protection tools (although their ultimate value as primary asset protection tools is questionable) to which for-value transfers could be made in exchange for IBC stock. However, the U.S. tax rules relating to gain recognition on contribution of appreciated assets to a CFC and the ongoing adverse income tax treatment made such planning painful from a tax standpoint. Some advisors tried to avoid the gain on contribution issue by first having their clients fund a foreign asset protection trust and then having the trust form and capitalize an IBC. But this arrangement still left the trust vulnerable to fraudulent transfer claims with respect to the initial transfer of assets into it.

Both domestic and foreign LLCs share advantages over trusts with regard to fraudulent transfer claims. Foreign LLCs have some additional advantages over domestic LLCs that help the members of foreign LLCs avoid some of the more common creditor attacks on domestic entities.

A creditor of a member of a U.S. LLC with a U.S. manager may be able to obtain a court order forcing the manager to make distributions which, combined with a charging order, will satisfy the member's judgment debt. The creditor of a member of an offshore LLC with a non-U.S. manager (for example, a British Virgin Islands IBC) may not be able to obtain jurisdiction in the United States over the non-U.S. manager. Even if an order were issued by a U.S. court, the non-U.S. manager could not be forced to comply unless and until a successful action was brought in the non-U.S. manager's jurisdiction. Much uncertainty surrounds the choice of law issues and the potential for success in a foreign jurisdiction. This uncertainty creates additional incentive for a creditor to settle on terms more favorable to the debtor LLC member than would otherwise be likely.

A creditor of a member of a U.S. LLC may also be able to obtain a court order dissolving the LLC. This action would force out liquidation distributions, which would, by virtue of a charging order, be diverted to the creditor to satisfy its judgment. A court in one U.S. state may or may not be able to order the dissolution of an LLC formed under the laws of another U.S. state. If such an order has been entered, uncertainty exists as to whether the courts of the state under whose laws the LLC has been formed must give full faith and credit to the order.

These uncertainties do not exist with an offshore LLC. A U.S. court order purporting to dissolve a foreign LLC, such as a Nevis LLC, is not entitled to full faith and credit in the foreign jurisdiction. If a Nevis court did recognize such an order, absent egregious circumstances, it would be the end of the offshore services industry in Nevis. So, as a practical matter, it is highly unlikely that a Nevis court would enforce a U.S. court order purporting to dissolve a Nevis LLC.

Utilizing an Offshore LLC

Business owners who conduct any type of business that has the potential for liability problems should consider using an offshore LLC, one that has an offshore entity as manager. This entity has an enhanced ability to provide limited liability protection to its owners for debts of the business. It does so to the extent that some assets of the LLC can be held outside the United States in favorable jurisdictions that do not recognize U.S. judgments. Such assets would include working capital and equity stripped out of U.S.-situs property

A judgment creditor of the LLC would be forced to bring an action in each jurisdiction in which the assets were held to attempt to proceed against those assets. Possibly the case would even have to be retried in its entirety. The creditor would be forced to spend the time and money necessary to pursue these additional court actions. Also that creditor would be forced to deal with foreign judicial systems that may preclude punitive damages, forbid contingency fee arrangements for attorneys, and require the losing party to pay the legal fees of the winning party.

An offshore LLC structure might be arranged in any number of ways. One such arrangement is illustrated in Figure 21.1, in which the Nevis LLC is the basic asset-holding entity. The U.S. client holds a 99 percent nonmanaging interest in the LLC, and the other 1 percent interest is a managing interest and is held by an IBC.

In this arrangement, the shares of the IBC are held by a foreign trust settled by the client. That trust is structured as a grantor trust for U.S. income tax purposes, with the client's children (or anyone or anything else, but preferably not the settlor) as beneficiaries. The primary assets of the trust are the IBC shares, and the primary asset held by the IBC is the 1 percent interest in the Nevis LLC. With this setup, there is less of a chance of a fraudulent transfer problem with respect to a transfer to the trust. That is so because the gratu-

FIGURE 21.1

Basic Offshore LLC Structure.

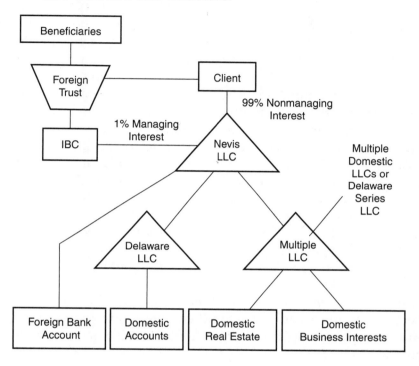

itous transfer of 1 percent of the assets transferred to the asset protection structure would be unlikely to raise questions about insolvency, among other issues.

The trust is a grantor trust and is the sole shareholder of the IBC, which along with the client are the only legal owners of LLC interests. So, the entire structure may be disregarded for U.S. income tax purposes by having the LLC and the IBC elect to be taxed as disregarded entities. Thus, there are no foreign information-reporting requirements. If the client's spouse owns an LLC membership interest, the structure will be taxed as a partnership. The LLC would then be required to comply with foreign partnership information-reporting requirements.

If the client wishes to use the structure to hold U.S. real estate, the LLC might form a single-member Delaware LLC. (This formation is inexpensive and simple, and Delaware LLC law is very good.) The LLC would take title to the property, with the equity being stripped out and the cash invested offshore. The Nevis LLC itself can hold foreign bank and investment accounts. The fact that the LLC is organized under non-U.S. law will make investing in foreign securities and mutual funds easier. However, extreme caution is advised with regard to the U.S. tax implications of foreign mutual fund ownership. Similarly, for U.S. advisors, extreme caution is advised with regard to the U.S. securities law implications of advising clients about unregistered securities.

If the Nevis LLC will be holding foreign stock, the best approach may be for the Nevis LLC to form an IBC and to elect passthrough treatment for the IBC. The foreign securities would then be held by a corporation rather than an LLC, which would make unclear the foreign inheritance tax treatment. This arrangement should enable the client to avoid any inheritance tax problems in the jurisdictions in which the foreign corporations are domiciled whose stock is held by the IBC. If a client wants to use a Nevis LLC to hold and protect U.S. investment accounts, such as an online brokerage account, another Delaware LLC might be formed to hold the account. That undertaking might be necessary because some brokerage firms might not be familiar with or comfortable with an offshore LLC that owns an account, despite best assurances that no tax shenanigans are involved.

If the client is faced with a large judgment, he will eventually have to disclose his ownership interest in the Nevis LLC to the judgment creditor. The creditor then has the option of seeking a charging order against that interest. At the time of disclosure, the client could simply offer to assign LLC interests to the creditor in full or he could offer partial satisfaction of the judgment.

The creditor is now faced with an unenviable choice. He can accept the voluntary transfer of the LLC interest, knowing that he probably will be taxable on the debtor member's share of LLC income. He may no doubt be aware that he will likely face a long court battle in one or more offshore jurisdictions as he attempts to force the IBC, as manager of the LLC, to make distributions to him. Court battles will also likely ensue as he attempts to prevent the IBC from diverting LLC funds elsewhere. Or the creditor can pursue the charging order with two risks: (1) The creditor will have little or no recourse to force the IBC, as manager, to make distributions, and (2) he may be taxable on the debtor member's share of LLC income. Whether the creditor is ultimately taxable or not, the uncertainty may be reason enough for the LLC to send the creditor a Schedule K-1 every year. Doing so would purport to show that the creditor is taxable, and it would make the creditor's position that much more difficult.

An offer by the debtor-member to voluntarily assign LLC interests to the creditor should be looked upon favorably by a U.S. court. If the creditor declines the transfer, the debtor-member honestly can say that she did everything within her legal ability to satisfy the creditor with respect to the LLC interest. If the creditor accepts the transfer, the debtor member can honestly say that she has rid herself of the LLC interest and has no legal ability to do anything else with respect to it. The result of all of this effort should be that the creditor is strongly pressured to settle for a reasonable amount.

Generally, the costs involved in setting up an offshore LLC structure with a Nevis LLC, a IBC, and a foreign trust will be comparable to or sometimes less than the typical costs involved in establishing a foreign asset protection trust structure. Costs will, of course, vary depending on the complexity of the structure (for example, ancillary entities, trusts, investment accounts) and the nature of the assets to be held in the structure. The ongoing administrative costs associated with offshore LLCs—for example, filing fees, registered agent fees, and tax return preparation fees—tend to be slightly higher than comparable costs for domestic LLCs.

In evaluating costs, keep in mind that the protection offered by an offshore LLC structure is dependent, not on the mere existence of the component entities, but rather on the careful drafting of the associated documents. Furthermore, remember that competent planners that practice seriously in this area have invested heavily in due diligence research and travel and take on a considerable amount of risk; they must price their services accordingly.

LLC-based planning does not preclude the use of foreign trusts. There is not an "either/or" choice between LLC-based planning and trust-based planning. For example, one particularly strong structure might include the entities and trust described in Figure 21.1, with the offshore LLC itself settling a traditional foreign asset protection trust. By having the LLC settle the trust, the fraudulent transfer risk is shifted from the client to the LLC.

TAXATION OF OFFSHORE LLCS

Treasury Regulations contain a list of foreign entities which are classified as *per se corporations* and are not eligible to elect passthrough treatment.[1] The per se list includes a few entities occasionally encountered in the offshore world, for example, Costa Rican and Panamanian corporations (in Spanish, *Sociedad Anonima*). However, most offshore entities, including all offshore LLCs and IBCs, are eligible to elect passthrough tax treatment.

A foreign entity that is not classified as a corporation under the Regulations (an "eligible entity" in the parlance of the Regulations) can choose its classification for federal tax purposes by filing Form 8832 within seventy-five days after the date the election is to become effective. A foreign eligible entity with at least two members can elect to be taxed either as a corporation or as a partnership. An eligible entity with a single owner can elect to be taxed as a corporation or to be disregarded as an entity separate from its owner.

Unless the entity elects otherwise, a foreign eligible entity is treated as follows:

- Taxed as a partnership, if it has two or more members and at least one member does not have limited liability
- Taxed as a corporation, if all members have limited liability
- Disregarded as an entity separate from its owner, if it has a single owner that does not have limited liability

Most dealings of U.S. persons with foreign entities will be with entities in which all members have limited liability (for example, an LLC or IBC). Therefore, most foreign entities with U.S. owners must affirmatively elect passthrough tax treatment on Form 8832.

For an idea of how a foreign entity is taxed, see the foreign-entity check-the-box flowchart in Figure 21.2.

Is there any reason why U.S. owners of an offshore entity would want the entity to be taxed as a corporation? What if the U.S.

FIGURE 21.2

Taxation of foreign limited liability entities.

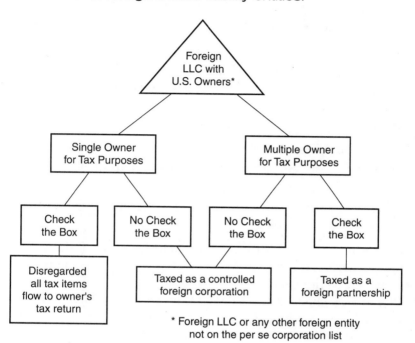

* Foreign LLC or any other foreign entity
not on the per se corporation list

owners of a foreign eligible entity wanted passthrough treatment but forgot to file Form 8832 or filed a defective Form 8832?

Some U.S. owners of foreign entities may want to have an entity taxed as a corporation if the corporation is conducting a business activity for which income tax deferral is allowed under U.S. tax laws or if U.S. ownership is small enough to allow the U.S. owner(s) to defer tax. Generally, for most U.S. persons interested in using offshore LLCs and other offshore entities as asset protection vehicles for cash and passive investments, no tax deferral is available simply by virtue of transferring U.S. assets to offshore entities. Therefore, U.S. owners usually will want to be sure that the entities are taxed as passthrough entities by properly filing Form 8832.

If the typical U.S.-owned foreign LLC or IBC fails to elect passthrough tax treatment, it most likely will be *a controlled foreign corporation (CFC)* for U.S. tax purposes. Certain kinds of undistributed earnings and profits of a CFC (known as *Subpart F income*) are taxed directly to the CFC's U.S. shareholders.

Subpart F income includes the following:

- Passive income
- Net gains from the sale of stock and securities and from property that does not generate active income
- Related party-factoring income
- Certain rents and royalties
- Net commodities gains
- Net gains from certain foreign currency activities
- Net income from notional principal contracts
- Payments in lieu of dividends derived from securities lending transactions

In other words, Subpart F income includes most of the kinds of income on which disreputable offshore promoters tell you U.S. income tax can be deferred.

When a U.S. shareholder sells CFC stock, the gain is taxed as a dividend (that is, as ordinary income) to the extent the CFC has previously untaxed and undistributed earnings and profits. Finally, the transfer of appreciated property by a U.S. person to a foreign corporation in exchange for the stock of the foreign corporation generally causes gain to be recognized even if the gain would not be recognized if the transfer were to a U.S. corporation. Thus, CFC status is usually something to be avoided.

Even if a foreign entity classified as a corporation for U.S. tax purposes is not treated as a CFC, there is a good chance it will be treated as *a foreign personal holding company (FPHC)* or as a *passive foreign investment company (PFIC)*, which will cause tax results similar to those caused by CFC status for the typical U.S. owner of such a company. Foreign corporations also have certain foreign corporation information-reporting requirements that can be burdensome. If these reporting requirements are not met, substantial penalties and fines can result. Failing to elect passthrough tax treatment for a foreign eligible entity can be a disaster.

Generally, the typical U.S.-owned foreign partnership is taxed like a domestic partnership. The former sections of the Internal

Revenue Code that imposed a 35 percent excise tax on the contribution of assets to a foreign partnership[2] have been repealed. Now,
all that is required is to make certain information reporting filings
on Form 8865, *Return of U.S. Persons With Respect to Certain Foreign
Partnerships,* and related schedules. The reporting generally does
not require any more information than the Form 1065, U.S.
Partnership Return of Income, although Form 8865 does ask for
financial information conformed to U.S. *Generally Accepted
Accounting Principles (GAAP),* which may require the partnership
to convert some financial data to conform to GAAP.

Failure to comply with foreign partnership reporting requirements can result in the imposition of significant penalties, including the forced recognition of gain upon the transfer of appreciated
property to a foreign partnership.

Foreign disregarded entities are taxed as if the U.S. owner
owned the assets of the entity directly. Until 2004, there were no
reporting requirements regarding U.S. ownership of foreign disregarded entities. Starting in 2004, U.S. owners of foreign disregarded entities must report certain information about the foreign disregarded entity to the IRS on Form 8858, *Information Return of U.S.
Persons With Respect to Foreign Disregarded Entities.*

THE U.K. LIMITED LIABILITY PARTNERSHIP

The *U.K. Limited Liability Partnership Act 2000* (which became law in
April 2001) created a new form of legal entity in the United
Kingdom, the *limited liability partnership (LLP).* Like a U.S. LLC, the
LLP is a body corporate with separate legal existence. There are no
restrictions on the purposes or powers of an LLP. Like an LLC, the
liability of the members of an LLP is limited to the members' contributions. Unless otherwise provided in a security agreement,
members of an LLP are not liable for LLP debts.

The advantages of a U.K. LLP over a U.K. limited company
are much the same as those of a U.S. LLC over a U.S. corporation:
management flexibility; flexibility in distributing and allocating
profits; and passthrough taxation.

A LLP requires at least two members at all times. The two members may be natural persons, entities, trustees, partnerships, and the
like, and need not be U.K. residents. The business of the LLP is

required to be carried on for profit, but most conceivable LLP purposes, including holding companies, will satisfy that requirement. The LLP must have a registered address and registered agent in the United Kingdom.

Members of an LLP have rights and responsibilities similar to those of members of a U.S. manager-managed LLC. By default, each member has general agency powers and each member may take part in management, but this may be, and usually is, altered by the partnership agreement.

The LLP must have at least two *designated members*. Designated members have certain responsibilities under the act, all of which relate to compliance with disclosure and accounting requirements, discussed briefly below. LLPs are subject to the same annual return and statutory accounting requirements as U.K. limited companies.

However, small and medium-sized LLPs have a number of exemptions from the usual full statutory account requirements of the U.K.'s corporate statutes (the Companies Act 1985). If an LLP used in asset protection planning has less than 2.8 million pounds (£2.8 million) in turnover or less than £1.4 million in net asset value, it will likely qualify as a small LLP. It will then have fairly simple accounting requirements and will file only an abbreviated balance sheet with the Registrar of Companies. An LLP used in asset protection planning with less than £11.2 million in turnover or less than £5.6 million in net asset value will likely qualify as a medium-sized LLP. It will have slightly more stringent, but still fairly relaxed, statutory accounting requirements.

A U.K. LLP is an *eligible foreign entity* for purposes of U.S. tax classification. Therefore, the same rules that apply to most foreign LLCs also apply to U.K. LLPs. A U.K. LLP can choose its classification for U.S. federal tax purposes by filing Form 8832 within seventy-five days after the date the election is to become effective. If no such election is made, the LLP will be treated as a foreign corporation.

The members of a U.K. LLP are taxed as partners in a partnership under U.K. law. There is no entity-level taxation. Tax items flow to the members. U.K. taxation applies only to profits derived from a member if either the profits are derived from a U.K. trade or business or if the profits otherwise are U.K.-sourced. The typical asset protection structure for a U.S. client would not have U.K.-

source income and thus would not subject such a client to U.K. taxation. The position of the U.K.'s tax authority, the Inland Revenue, on the taxation of LLP members relies on the LLP validly carrying on a trade or business. In response to a private-letter inquiry, the Inland Revenue responded that an LLP whose two members are British Virgin Islands (BVI) IBCs managed and controlled from the BVI, and the primary activity of which is to hold shares in a non-U.K. corporation, would be regarded as carrying on a business. Then "only in the most exceptional of circumstances" would it regard the LLP as not carrying on a business.

The U.K. LLP is perhaps most useful for putting a low-profile front-end on an asset protection structure. Often a client may be hesitant to use a foreign entity as a management company because either the client is uncomfortable with the idea of "offshore" companies or the client worries that a stigma will attach because of the use of a typical offshore company. The U.K. LLP allows the use of a tax-transparent foreign entity as the public face of a client's structure as a management company or holding company.

An LLP is a body corporate separate and apart from its members, and the property of an LLP is not the property of the members as such. Furthermore, much of the spirit and letter of LLP law was imported from English partnership law, including the concept that partners should not be forced to take on other partners (for example, creditors of a member). Therefore, it should follow that a creditor of a member may not acquire the member's management rights either by execution or by a charging order. Furthermore, a member may not interfere in the management or administration of the business of the LLP if the member has become bankrupt, granted a trust deed for the benefit of his creditors, or assigned all or part of her interest in the LLP either absolutely or by way of charge or security.

While offshore LLCs offer many benefits, they still suffer from the same problem as any other business entity that is utilized for asset protection, namely: who will control it? In the next chapter, we consider management companies and other forms of corporate ownership.

ENDNOTES

1. Treas. Reg. Sec. 301.7701 2(b)(8)(i).
2. IRC Secs. 1491–1494.

CHAPTER 22

Management Companies, Leasing Companies, and ESOPs

The most difficult issues in asset protection planning involve control, or more precisely, how to have effective absolute control over an asset without having to legally own it and thus expose it to creditors. But even indirect control can lead to implications of ownership. In the context of foreign asset protection trusts, settlors have attempted to maintain distant control through the artifices of making themselves protectors of their trust. These settlors have come to grief when the courts have determined that they had de facto control.

On the other side of the coin, we have also seen how those who run entities can be personally liable for what happens within those entities, including corporate officers and directors, the general partners of partnerships, and the managers of limited liability companies. A primary goal in asset protection planning is to allow a person to benefit from the income and value of assets with maximum flexibility without subjecting that person to personal liability if the management of the asset generates liability.

The determination of these control-decontrol issues shows that asset protection is often less a science than an art. The art comes in navigating around the general rules of law relating to when control becomes de facto ownership and the liability of managers. A uniform resolution of these issues in every case is simply not possible. If it were, the courts or legislatures would eliminate those means in due time.

With rare exceptions, as in the case of a publicly traded corporation, an affluent person should never be a corporate officer or director, as significant liability often arises from such positions. Similarly, an affluent person should never be the general partner of a partnership, or else the liabilities of the partnership will flow directly to him or her. An affluent person also should avoid being the manager of a limited liability company, since negligence in the management of the entity, leading to the entity's liability, could potentially result in her direct liability to creditors.

Direct liability is most worrisome. Although an LLC will protect the manager from personal liability for the debts of the entity, it will not, for example, shield her from personal liability for sexual harassment. In this and similar cases, the plaintiff will sue both the entity and the manager. Thus, the role of manager or decision-maker should be avoided whenever possible.

These restrictions are often difficult for successful businesspersons to abide, especially if they have gained their wealth by an active, hands-on management style. Asset protection planning thus becomes in substantial part an education process for the client, teaching her to transition from being an active manager, who often can be sued, to a passive investor, who usually can't be.

This is not to say that the businessperson must yield all control in investment deals. The deals are simply restructured to give indirect control. Lessons can be learned from the venture capitalists, who instead of managing investments themselves will simply extend debt financing, but will make the debt financing contingent on performance benchmarks. The failure of the company's management to meet the promised benchmarks will result in equity being issued to the investor. Eventually, if the promised performance results are not met, the investor ends up with the entire company and its assets. The performance benchmarks that are tied to equity given to investors if the benchmarks are unmet are known as *ratchets*. Private entities can, and often should, be structured the same way.

MANAGEMENT COMPANY STRUCTURES

Not all clients can be transitioned to purely passive investors. Many clients will have active businesses and will need or desire

FIGURE 22.1

Management company.

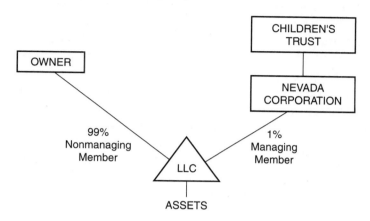

some form of direct management control over the business. If each valuable asset has been placed into its own asset protected entity, the next step is to create one or more management companies to control all the assets (see Figure 22.1).

The owner of a management company should not be the client. The management company might, for instance, be owned by one or more domestic trusts settled for the benefit of the client's heirs, with someone other than the client acting as the settlor of the trusts. This arrangement accomplishes several things.

First, the client is not the legal owner of the management company. If the client suffers a judgment, a creditor will not get control of the asset being managed. The client is, after all, merely the manager and not the owner of the asset. The owner of the management company is the trust, not the client. If the trust is irrevocable, and the trust has formed the management company, the creditor will have great difficulty arguing that the client is the owner of the management company. For more on this topic, refer back to Chapter 12, which discusses spendthrift trusts.

Second, if something happens with the asset that generates liability to the manager, that liability needs to be contained within the management company, which it will be if it is properly formed and operated. To this end, the client should avoid to the greatest degree possible exercising day-to-day control over the assets being managed. He needs to leave the signing of routine documents to others hired for that purpose. The client's personal control should be reserved for occasionally transferring large funds or assets, and not much more.

Third, the management company structure allows the client to take money out of assets that she doesn't own, by way of management fees. So long as these management fees are commercially reasonable and paid in a typical commercial manner according to a management contract, a creditor will have difficulty challenging the payment of fees as some sort of sham. Because the management company is owned by the heirs' trust, any excess management fees will be upstreamed to the trust for the heirs' benefit. This arrangement also allows the client to take only so much salary as she needs to live on, and effectuate a wealth transfer to her heirs with the profits to the management company.

If possible, the trust that forms the management company should not be settled by the client. The reason is very simple: If the client settles the trust, and the original settlement is later set aside as a fraudulent transfer, the potential exists for the entire trust to be set aside and the benefits eliminated. Thus, somebody other than the client should form the trust. Should a client later contribute to the trust by gift, or transfer assets to the trust by way of a private annuity or self-canceling installment note, that activity shouldn't present any problems so long as it is done after the formation of the management company and the transferred property is fairly and contemporaneously valued by an independent appraiser.

OFFSHORE MANAGEMENT COMPANIES

If possible, the management company should be domiciled in a state other than where the managed companies'assets are located. This arrangement may create practical problems for a creditor in getting discovery from the management company, especially if the case is brought in state court as opposed to federal court. Even better, the management company should be formed in an offshore jurisdiction (see Figure 22.2). This can create tremendous difficulties for a creditor.

First, a creditor may have difficulty getting service of process on the management company. If the management company is

FIGURE 22.2

Offshore management company.

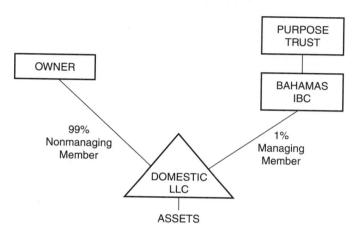

deemed a *necessary party* to the litigation and the creditor is unable to get good service on the management company, the creditor may face serious difficulties in pursuing the case.

Next, a creditor will have great difficulty getting discovery from an offshore management company. Although the persons actually engaged in the management may be in the United States, the company's books and records might be kept outside of the United States. So, the creditor might not be able compel the production of those documents without filing a separate lawsuit in the offshore jurisdiction—and maybe not even then.

Even if the offshore management company is ordered to do something by a U.S. court, it may be able to ignore the order. While the ability of an offshore management company to do this should not be relied upon entirely and certainly should not be flaunted, this ability likely means that a creditor will have to commence a new lawsuit in the offshore jurisdiction to try to make the courts of that jurisdiction issue a similar order and force the offshore management company to comply with it.

For example, say that a creditor was able to get a judgment against a member of a limited partnership and, based on that judgment, get a charging order against that member's limited partnership interest (that is, the creditor would receive any distributions made in respect of that interest). The creditor would not be able to compel in the U.S. courts the making of a distribution to that interest by an offshore management company. Instead, the creditor would have to file a lawsuit in the offshore jurisdiction to attempt to force the offshore management company to make the distribution—a daunting task at best.

LEASING COMPANIES

Leasing companies can play a role in asset protection planning, if they are used correctly. Most often, leasing companies are used to distance the ownership of valuable assets being used by a business from the liabilities of the business itself (see Figure 22.3). For example, if a manufacturing firm owns the real estate the facility sits on, it makes sense to transfer the property to a new company that leases the real estate back to the business. The lease is written so that if the manufacturing firm becomes insolvent, the lease will terminate. A creditor of the manufacturing firm who takes over its other assets is thus left with a firm that does not own the dirt upon which it sits.

Perhaps the best use of asset leasing companies involves *intellectual property (IP)*. Especially with technology firms, the IP constitutes the primary asset of the business. Ideally, the IP should always be placed into a separate asset-protected entity and then licensed back to the primary business. This arrangement protects the IP if the business fails.

In addition to stripping out valuable assets and distancing them from the business, leasing companies can also be used to strip out liability-producing activities and move those activities away from the business. The most common example involves employee leasing companies. By moving the employees to an employee leasing company, various employment-related liabilities, such as age and sex discrimination claims, pension and related claims, and workers' compensation issues can be distanced from the business.

The use of leasing companies is a good illustration of the concept of *unbundling*. This concept recognizes that a business is comprised of distinct parts. The valuable assets of a business should be isolated away and protected from the liability-producing aspects of the business. Likewise, the liability-producing aspects of the busi-

FIGURE 22.3

Leasing company.

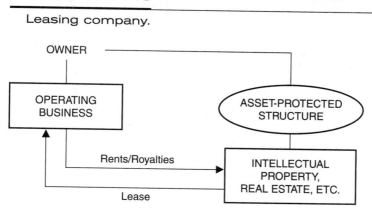

ness should be contained within its own entity and shielded from the other parts of the business. Thus, if a truck owned by a business's distribution network is involved in a bad crash, the liability from the crash may bankrupt the truck leasing company. It might also spill over into the distribution company. But it will be well shielded away from the manufacturing facility and the IP used to make the product.

ESOPs

Employee stock ownership plans (ESOPs) can also play an important role in asset protection planning. The idea behind an ESOP is that the company, or some portion of it, is basically sold to its employees, and the stock is placed into a trust until the employees vest (see Figure 22.4). At some future date, the employees will vest and thus earn a share of the company and benefit by its growth.

A primary benefit of an ESOP is that it effectively dilutes ownership, because each of the employees in the ESOP is deemed to be a beneficiary of the ESOP trust. This dilution of ownership makes it very difficult for a creditor to argue that the entity is just an alter ego of the former owner (before she sold her stock to the ESOP), or that the corporate veil should be pierced.

A common creditor challenge to a corporate structure is that it is the *alter ego* of the owner. In such a case, the creditor claims that the corporation and the owner are one and the same, so that the

FIGURE 22.4

Standard ESOP.

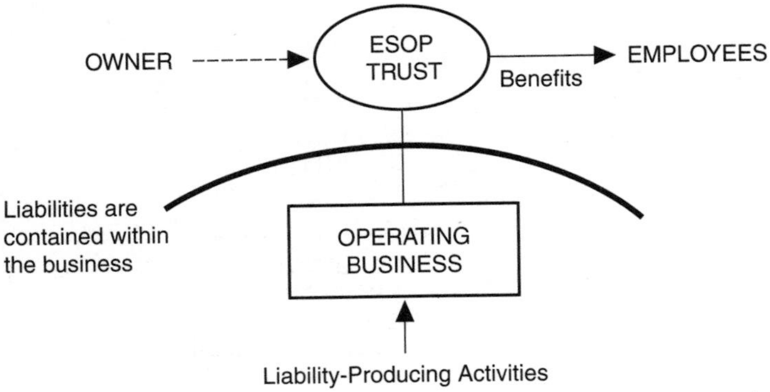

```
OWNER  ------▶  ( ESOP  )  ──────▶  EMPLOYEES
                ( TRUST )  Benefits
```

Liabilities are
contained within
the business

OPERATING
BUSINESS

Liability-Producing Activities

corporation should not be treated as a separate entity and the owner should not be allowed to stand behind the corporate fiction. With an ESOP, it may be possible to dilute corporate ownership after a liability has been generated within the company, and thus avoid the liability passing to the sole owner. The reason is that the law surrounding the assertion of an alter ego theory does not speak to when the test of alter ego should be made: Is it when the bad act occurred, or after the judgment is entered? If the latter, the ESOP should effectively defeat an alter ego claim, because company ownership is now diverse among many employees. At the very least, an argument is created in an area of unsettled law that will concern a creditor and militate toward the creditor's settlement of the case.

But the owner of a successful business probably doesn't want to give up ownership to the employees. There are several solutions to this dilemma. First, no requirement exists that ownership in an ESOP be proportional for all employees. Indeed, a benefits-only ESOP may be created that effectively gives the employees no ownership rights at all but merely allows them to share in the profits of the business. For asset protection purposes, however, the employees need to have some substantial ownership interest in the company, so as to fend off the alter ego and like arguments.

Second, the ESOP could be structured with a preprogrammed buyout provision that will allow the owner to take back the company at some future date at an agreed price that reflects the fair market value of the company. The benefit to the employees in such an arrangement must be real and tangible, but this is usually a small price to pay to protect the owner against possible liabilities of the business. The date of the buyout of the employees need not be specified; instead, there could be various *triggering events* (which the owner could pull the trigger on) that enable the employees to be bought out.

ESOPs can also be used to create management company structures. In a typical arrangement, key management employees will be moved into a management company that is owned by an ESOP; the key management employees are the beneficiaries (see Figure 22.5). The management company then provides management services to the client's businesses. From an asset protection perspective, this arrangement isolates the management function from the assets that may generate liabilities. It also simultaneously consolidates the management function of diverse assets under a single entity.

This structure may also allow the management company to strip income, by way of management fees, from the assets being managed into the management company. Although the IRS has since halted the practice, tax planners have in the past successfully utilized management companies that have elected S corporation treatment, and flowed the paper profits of the management company to the ESOP, while simultaneously funding a nonqualified deferred compensation trust (*NQDCT* or *rabbi trust*) for the owner and key employees. (For more on the asset protective features of deferred compensation arrangements, see Chapter 9). New Treasury Regulations have resulted in the advent of similar structures using nonqualified benefits packages other than deferred compensation.

This structure provides multiple asset protection benefits. First, value is transferred out of the underlying business and away from any potential liabilities of that business. Second, the diversity of ownership given by the ESOP probably prevents the assertion of alter ego claims. Third, the money can be safely protected within the benefits plan, which qualifies for ERISA protection from creditors.

In addition to the incidental, but highly effective, protection given by ERISA to the benefits trust, there is another very important asset protection feature. The assets held in the benefits trust are

FIGURE 22.5

ESOP management structure.

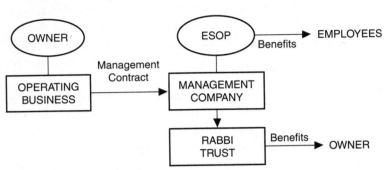

technically not the assets of the beneficiary employee until they vest, which should only occur upon the happening of a triggering event (such as death). The practical implications of this structure are very significant. For example, if an employee is asked to list his assets in a creditor's exam, he might be able to avoid listing these assets on the basis that they have not yet vested (that is, his right to the assets has not matured under the plan). Thus, with an ESOP and a rabbi trust, a business owner possibly could move millions of dollars out of the business and into the rabbi trust without having to place those assets on his own balance sheet. This is a very strong tool indeed—and completely domestic in character.

CHAPTER 23

Advanced Life Insurance and Annuity Strategies

In keeping with the public policy goal of protecting a debtor's spouse and dependents, many states protect life insurance and annuities from the claims of creditors. Statutory exemptions may protect the cash value, annuity payments, death benefits, or some combination of them.

One crucial concern, when assessments are made as to the asset protection afforded to life insurance, is to ascertain to whom these state law exemptions apply. For instance, many states allow for different levels of exemption, depending on whether the debtor is the owner, the insured, or the beneficiary of the policy. Undoubtedly, however, the most important use of life insurance in asset protection planning is in accumulating large amounts of cash value in a protected policy.

Although insurance and annuities are generally afforded some protection in most states, the protections afforded vary greatly from state to state, perhaps for more than any other class of exempt assets. Furthermore, the language of the various state statutes that offer protection to life insurance and annuities is often vague and thus subject to the whims of judicial interpretation.

LIFE INSURANCE

Some states provide little or no protection for the cash value of life insurance policies. Other states provide significant protection. For example, Florida law exempts the entire cash value of a life insurance policy from claims of the policyowner's creditors and the entire death benefit of a life insurance policy from claims of the insured's creditors.

Most states, however, are not so specific. In many states determinations as to what extent the cash surrender value is exempted from the claims of the owner's creditors are difficult, such as where the statute refers vaguely to, for example, the "proceeds and avails" of a life insurance policy. Most state courts that have taken up the issue have determined that such references include the cash value and the death benefit.

Premium payments made with the intent of defrauding creditors will cause the proceeds attributable to those premiums, as well as the cash value attributable to those premiums, to be reachable by creditors. Yet, like other exemption planning techniques involving the exchange of consideration, the purchase of life insurance and annuities is also a potentially useful asset protection technique. It is because the purchase may be difficult for a creditor to characterize as a fraudulent transfer, since such transactions are "for value." Life insurance and annuities are purchased for many legitimate reasons having nothing to do with asset protection. Moreover, even where the ultimate resolution of whether a life insurance policy or annuity contract is protected from creditors remains in doubt, such conversions of cash to life insurance and annuity policies may, in the end, provide a debtor with the additional leverage he or she needs to force a settlement with his or her creditors at something less than the full value of their claims.

Even if premium payments are successfully challenged as fraudulent transfers, a creditor may have to wait until the debtor's death to realize any real value, depending on what state law and the policy itself specify. This result is not likely to be an acceptable one to most creditors. Most would rather settle for a lesser amount. Furthermore, where the protection of life insurance is recognized by the state constitution, as in North Carolina, the constitutional protection arguably would not be affected by fraudulent transfer law in a manner similar to the "bulletproof" protection afforded to the Florida constitutional homestead described in the *Havoco v. Hill* case (see Chapter 9).

Insurance policies are often not owned by individuals. For estate planning purposes, to keep the proceeds out of the estate of the insured, an insurance policy often needs to be owned in an irrevocable trust. Such trusts usually contain spendthrift provisions. So long as transfers to the trust of funds which are used to pay premiums are not fraudulent transfers, the trust assets, including life insurance policies, should be out of the reach of creditors. The settlor of such a trust may have indirect access to the cash value of an insurance policy owned by the trust by naming his spouse as a discretionary beneficiary of the trust. To the extent that the trustee of the trust makes distributions of trust property (for example, cash obtained via policy loans) to the spouse, the settlor can benefit from the cash value during the spouse's lifetime. Such trusts are often referred to as *spousal lifetime access trusts (SLATs)*.

OFFSHORE PRIVATE PLACEMENT VARIABLE UNIVERSAL LIFE INSURANCE (OPPVULI)

Much has been written and discussed about *offshore private placement variable universal life insurance* (abbreviated here as OPPVULI) in the last several years. Understanding its utility begins with understanding what it is. It is "offshore" in the sense that it is issued outside the United States by a non-U.S. insurance company not licensed to issue insurance policies in the United States. It is "privately placed," meaning that the offering of policies is limited to properly accredited wealthy purchasers and not marketed to the general public.

"Variable" refers to the fact that the assets in the policy are allocated by the policyowner to one or more investment strategies overseen by investment managers appointed by the insurance company. The value of the policy's investment account and death benefit varies, therefore, with the investment performance of the investment managers. Most OPPVULI policy issuers allow the owner of particularly large policies (with total premiums in excess of $10 million) to select the investment managers to be appointed by the company.

"Universal," in insurance parlance, refers to a policy for which there are no mandatory annual premiums so long as there are sufficient assets in the policy's investment account to pay current insurance and other policy-related charges. All OPPVULI policies have some minimum premium commitment, usually $2 million or more, to be paid over two to seven years. However, a few insurers offer OPPVULI policies for as little as $100,000 in committed premiums.

Tax Issues

"Life insurance" in the OPPVULI context means that the policy qualifies as life insurance under the law of the jurisdiction where the policy is issued. It also means that the policy qualifies for the favorable tax treatment afforded to life insurance under the Internal Revenue Code. Investment growth in all tax-qualified life insurance policies compounds tax-free to the policyowner. The cash value of certain types of tax-qualified life insurance policies known as *modified endowment contracts (MECs)* cannot be withdrawn or borrowed without taxation to the policyowner if there has been investment growth in the policy. However, the cash value in non-MEC policies can be borrowed tax-free from the policy's cash value, allowing the policy owner tax-free access to potentially significant investment growth. Detailed and difficult IRS regulations spell out which policies will be MECs and which will be non-MECs. Determination is made based on a combination of the amount of the pure insurance component of the policy, the cash value, and the amount and timing of premium payments. Suffice it to say for purposes of this discussion that single-premium policies will almost always be MECs and policies designed to fund with five to seven years of premiums will be non-MECs.

Furthermore, tax qualification requires a certain minimum death benefit for any given amount of cash value. A policy that insures the life of a forty-year old will not be tax-qualified if, for example, it has a cash value of $1,000,000 and a death benefit of $1,000,100. Under the most commonly used IRS test (the *guideline premium and cash value corridor test*), there must be a minimum death benefit of $2,500,000 for that forty-year old insured. IRS regulations will determine the minimum death benefit, which must be calculated by a qualified actuary. Anyone considering the purchase of any private placement life insurance policy must retain competent counsel to make certain that the insurer and the policy are in compliance with IRS regulations so that the policy remains tax-qualified.

Variable insurance policies (and annuities) are subject to certain minimum diversification requirements for tax-qualification. Except for cash, which is always considered to be diversified, each investment portfolio of a variable policy must be diversified among at least five different investments. No more than 55 percent of the total value of account may be invested in any single asset; no more than 70 percent may be in any two investments; no more than 80 percent may be in any three investments; and no more than 90 percent may be in any four investments. Once a portfolio is adequately diversified, then it generally continues to meet the diversification requirements regardless of fluctuations in the values of the investments so long as no new assets are acquired. The diversification test applies separately to each investment advisor's portfolio. Each portfolio in a variable policy subaccount must be adequately diversified in accordance with IRS requirements.

Finally, the assets in the variable policy investment account must be considered to be owned by the insurance company and not by the policyowner. The policyowner must not exercise control over investment decisions. The direct or indirect exercise of control over investment decisions in the policy investment account may result in the policy failing to be an insurance policy for tax purposes. The result would be that all gains and income in the investment account would be taxable to the policy owner.

Offshore insurers must be carefully chosen based on a number of factors. Some of these factors are obvious: solvency, reinsurance capacity, the quality of its reinsurance arrangements, investment flexibility, and jurisdictional protections. However, one important factor is not so obvious: how the insurer itself is taxed under U.S. law. Tax-free flow of income into a tax-qualified variable policy investment account does not necessarily follow simply because an investment is made within that investment account.

Capital gains, interest on publicly traded bonds and U.S. government securities, and bank account interest earned in the investment account of an offshore variable policy generally will not subject the foreign insurance company to U.S. taxation. However, income that is effectively connected with a U.S. trade or business (such as partnership or LLC income from a U.S. business); gains from

U.S. real property interests (including equity interests in entities with significant U.S. real estate holdings); and U.S.-source dividends, rents, and royalties will be taxable to the insurance company even if it is offshore. Those tax costs will be passed on to the policy investment account. As a result, often the most favorable choice is to use an insurer that has elected to be taxed as a U.S. insurance company. The importance of involving competent U.S. tax counsel in an OPPVULI transaction cannot be overemphasized.

Most tax-favored investment-oriented life insurance policies are variable universal policies qualified as life insurance for purposes of the Internal Revenue Code. The special features of OPPVULI policies derive from their foreign and privately placed nature.

Specific Advantages of OPPVULI

OPPVULI policies are negotiated directly with the insurer and are purchased directly from the insurer. This structure has a number of favorable results. Most obviously, it cuts out the middleman insurance agent who is otherwise omnipresent in most life insurance transactions. This arrangement effectively reduces distribution costs to zero, and those savings are passed on to the OPPVULI policyowner. Because an agent is not required to market and sell the policy, no commission cuts into the cash value of the policy. For the typical OPPVULI policy, this results in savings of hundreds of thousands of dollars that would otherwise be paid as commissions.

Privately placed insurance products have considerably more investment options. The typical commercially available variable life insurance policy offers a menu of one to three dozen investment funds that mirror commercially available U.S. mutual funds. A privately placed policy has no investment restrictions. Subject to ever-evolving IRS restrictions, the investment manager of an OPPVULI investment fund can invest in anything anywhere in the world, from mutual funds to individual equities to hedge funds to futures to real estate to private equity partnerships, and so on. However, the shares in the OPPVULI investment fund may only be offered as life insurance portfolio investments and not to the general public. Similarly, a life insurance portfolio cannot invest directly in investments available to the general public. It is restricted to insurance-only funds and cash.

Furthermore, the insurer generally makes its profit from a small percentage-based fee (albeit on a large cash value), so it often does not mark up the actual cost of insurance for the "real" insurance component of the policy represented by the difference between the death benefit and the cash value.

Because domestic insurers have substantial state regulatory burdens, domestic private-placement policies with less than $10 million in committed premium are uncommon. Even if a domestic insurer were willing to accommodate a private-placement arrangement, the insurance company might be prevented from doing so by state-imposed liquidity requirements (typically thirty days) that certain investment managers, such as hedge fund managers, cannot accommodate. An offshore insurance company in a more flexible regulatory environment can allow policyowners to decide which investment managers and investment styles to use without having to worry about meeting arbitrary liquidity requirements.

Furthermore, most offshore insurance jurisdictions have no corporate taxes. The reduced cost of doing business in relation to U.S. insurers is passed along to policyowners in the form of reduced policy fees and charges compared to domestic policies.

Sometimes, a desirable option is to transfer certain assets, such as privately held stock, as in-kind premiums (that is, paid in a form other than cash) to the insurer. This opportunity is not possible with domestic policies. While the transfer of the stock will trigger a tax for which cash must be available to pay, this tax is often offset by the tax benefits of having the asset held in a tax-favored insurance policy.

Finally, because OPPVULI policies are individually negotiated, certain favorable asset protection features may be built in to a policy. Moreover, because of the investment flexibility offered, the assets held in the policy's separate account can be structured to be undesirable (for example, illiquid foreign LLC interests) to a creditor, should a creditor somehow reach policy assets.

Funding the OPPVULI Policy

Funding can be approached in two ways: external funding and internal funding. Where a policyowner has large amounts of cash (or liquid assets that can be converted to cash with minor tax consequences), he should consider putting that after-tax "external" cash to work in a large tax-advantaged OPPVULI policy. This arrangement is in contrast to "traditional" life insurance planning for the financial security of the family of the insured, where the object is to purchase as much death benefit as possible for as little premium as possible. The object of OPPVULI as an investment vehicle is the purchase of as little death benefit as possible while investing as much premium as possible.

A better approach where a policyowner has the opportunity to provide for future "internal funding" is to transfer an asset or opportunity to an OPPVULI policy. That course of action allows the policy to be funded with untaxed dollars. For example, a policyowner may transfer closely held stock as in-kind premium in anticipation of a future initial public offering of the stock. If the IPO is successful, the stock will appreciate inside the policy and later can be sold tax-free; the resulting cash can be invested in a more diversified portfolio. The same concept can be applied to other assets such as patents and copyrights. The assets transferred to the policy at a low cost appreciate rapidly or otherwise produce significant income, thus internally funding the policy.

We must emphasize that these are the rules with respect to OPPVULI policies at the time of this writing. The IRS is aware of aggressive tax strategies involving these policies and can be expected to release further guidance that will restrict the utility and tax efficiency of these insurance products.

Asset Protection Features

In addition to the general asset protection features discussed earlier in this chapter, life insurance policies, including OPPVULI policies, usually have special asset protection features.

Because the OPPVULI policies are individually negotiated, certain favorable asset protection features may be built in to a policy, including, for example, *level surrender value provisions*. These provisions effectively freeze the cash value available to the policyowner at the amount of premiums paid in, less the cost of insurance and other administrative costs. Where the policy is structured for internal funding after the policy has been externally funded with low-value in-kind assets, only a small portion of the account value will be available to the policyowner—and thus to the policy-owner's creditors.

In some situations, the policy can be drafted or renegotiated to completely eliminate cash value. Although the policyowner will not be able to access the cash value, because there technically is none, the policyholder may be able to indirectly access the separate account by means of secured loans from the separate account or from third-party lenders funded by separate account assets. The policy can have cash value when there are no creditors, it can be renegotiated to eliminate cash value while creditors are lurking, and after creditor issues are resolved, the policy can be renegotiated again to give the owner the ability to borrow against cash value again.

Moreover, the assets held in the policy's separate account can be structured to be undesirable to a creditor (for example, illiquid foreign LLC interests). Should a creditor somehow reach policy assets, the policy can allow payment of policy distributions in kind so that a creditor gets only undesirable illiquid assets. These may be structured further to cause unfavorable tax consequences to the creditor in the form of phantom partnership income or phantom interest income (that is, income taxable to the creditor but which the creditor never actually receives).

OPPVULI policies offer an added advantage of stealth. The only information readily visible to a creditor is the investment in the policy and not the underlying assets. Since the creditor has no claim against the insurance company that issued the policy, the creditor cannot easily determine what assets are held in the separate account. A secure structure is for the OPPVULI policy to be combined with a protected holding entity such as a third-party foreign trust (for example, a trust funded with seed money by the client's parents and then utilized in an installment sale transaction) or a foreign LLC. Under such circumstances, an OPPVULI policy can be an ideal asset protection plan component.

For example, assets held in the separate account might be used to back secured loans made to the policyholder's personal residence, vacation homes, and commercial properties, effectively stripping the equity from those assets. Assets held in the separate account might also be used to fund equipment-leasing companies that provide vehicles, aircraft, manufacturing equipment, and other types of equipment and supplies for a business owner's operating companies. Finally, assets held in the separate account might be used to finance trade receivables and purchase intellectual property rights, which can then be licensed to an operating entity or another party, thus removing those assets from the reach of creditors.

The effect of all of these arrangements will be to remove assets from the reach of creditors of the policyowner and the operating business. While the potential exists for tax benefits as well, extreme caution should be exercised in determining the tax consequences of such transactions. Most arrangements of this type probably cross the line drawn by the IRS for abusive transactions. Only the most well-conceived and conservative of such arrangements can be expected to pass IRS muster.

In addition to asset protection considerations with regard to availability of the policyowner's interest in the OPPVULI policy to his creditors, asset protection considerations should be given to the insurance company itself. In addition to normal due diligence inquiries into the solvency and reputation of the company and its principals, inquiry should be made into the insurance legislation of the jurisdiction. An insurance company located in a jurisdiction that has *separate-account legislation* provides significant legal protection for investments. Such legislation provides that the investment assets of a variable policy are maintained in a separate segregated account and those assets can be used only to satisfy obligations under the policy. The separate-account assets cannot be used to satisfy any other obligations of the insurer, even in the event of the company's insolvency or bankruptcy. Furthermore, note also that, in most cases, the investment manager or another financial institution, not the insurance company, would have custody of the separate-account assets, thus providing another layer of protection.

Separate-account legislation does not, however, provide the policyowner any protection for the amount of death benefit in excess of the value of the policy's segregated investment account. This amount, known as the *net amount at risk*, is a general liability of the insurance company. Most offshore insurers companies mitigate this risk by reinsuring nearly all of it with large multinational insurance companies.

INSTALLMENT SALES AND ANNUITIES

As with exemptions for life insurance, state law exemptions for annuities, both the cash value and the right to annuity payments, vary widely. Florida, Texas, and Michigan, for example, exempt the entire value and proceeds of annuity contracts. Georgia, Missouri, and Utah, on the other hand, protect proceeds of an annuity contract only to the extent reasonably necessary for the support of the debtor and the debtor's dependents. Other states place dollar limitations on the protections, while still others do not protect annuities at all.

As may be expected, where unlimited protection is afforded to annuities, postjudgment litigation focuses on whether the property interest of the debtor is in fact an annuity. As is generally the case, the debtor can use uncertainty to her advantage. Consideration should be given to structuring or reformulating as an annuity any assets that cannot be better protected. For example, a note receivable might be renegotiated and restructured as an annuity. A judgment owed to the debtor for personal injury or wrongful death might take the form of a structured settlement. A lump sum of cash or other valuable assets otherwise unprotected might be transferred to a trust settled by a related party in exchange for an annuity from the trust. Courts in all of these situations have held these annuities valid and effective at defeating creditors' claims. Converting nonexempt assets into exempt assets is not fraudulent per se, but structuring such annuities with nonasset protection goals to avoid characterization as fraudulent is key to obtaining asset protection.

Although generally regarded as tax planning tools, private annuities and installment sale transactions can be valuable asset protection planning devices as well. All private annuity and installment sale techniques can effect a "freeze" on the value and appreciation rate of an asset for estate and gift tax purposes, and they can allow long-term deferral of gain on the sale of an asset.

The basic concept for both private annuities and installment sales, discussed below, is the same. A valuable asset is sold (usually to a family member or to a trust or entity controlled by or for the benefit of family members) in exchange for the buyer's promise to pay the seller a fixed amount of money on a periodic basis (usually annually) for the seller's lifetime or for a fixed term. The price of the asset must be its fair market value. However, the minimum interest rate that must be used to calculate the periodic payments is set by the IRS. It is usually lower than commercial interest rates, and it is always considerably lower than the expected appreciation rate of the asset sold. The tax to the seller on the gain is deferred over the period of the payments. The potential appreciation on the asset sold is shifted to the benefit of family members.

The principal differences between installment sales and private annuities lie in the payment period, the ability to secure the buyer's obligation to pay the seller, tax treatment to the buyer, the types of assets that can be sold, and the estate tax treatment of the asset upon the death of the seller.

Installment Sale

In a simple *installment sale*, the seller transfers an asset to the buyer in exchange for a note in which the buyer promises to pay the seller a fixed amount plus interest over a fixed period of time. The note is almost always secured by the asset sold; if the buyer defaults on the note payments, the seller has the right to take back the asset to recover unpaid payments. Upon the death of the seller, the unpaid balance of the note is included in his or her taxable estate for estate tax purposes, but the asset that was sold is out of the estate, including its appreciated value.

Self-Canceling Installment Note (SCIN)

A *self-canceling installment note (SCIN)* is a twist on the traditional installment sale technique. It involves a sale of property in exchange for an installment note with a fixed payment period. But it is canceled upon the seller's death if the seller dies before the end of the payment period. Because the note may expire before the payee receives payments equal to the note's face amount, an additional premium (either additional principal or a higher interest rate) must be paid for the self-canceling feature so that the value of the note equals the value of the property. As in a traditional installment sale, a sale for a SCIN is almost always secured by the asset sold. Because the note is canceled upon the death of the seller, there is no unpaid balance to be included in the seller's estate.

Because the SCIN is calculated with a premium based on the possible death of the seller, it is a for-value transfer (and not a gift). So, it will typically be very difficult for a creditor to set aside as a fraudulent transfer. Thus, the creditor's only remedy may be to garnish each periodic payment as it comes due and hope that the seller doesn't die very quickly, since upon that contingency the payments will automatically cease. The creditor's delay in receiving payments and risk that the payments could terminate are factors that will play upon the creditor's mind in making a decision to settle for less than the full amount of the payments due.

Private Annuity

An alternative to a SCIN is a *private annuity*. While a SCIN has a fixed maturity date, payments under a private annuity agreement continue until the death of the seller, regardless of when the seller dies. As such, the private annuity is a useful tool if the seller is not expected to live out his otherwise normal life expectancy.

Keep in mind that the assets transferred in a private annuity will be owned by the transferee and thus within the reach of the transferee's creditors. Even in this situation, however, the assets can be protected if the transfer is made to a spendthrift discretionary trust for the benefit of the intended transferee. The transaction also can be made more comfortable for the seller if nonvoting or nonmanaging interests are transferred in exchange for the private annuity.

Private annuities are sometimes used in conjunction with offshore private-placement variable universal life insurance policies as a means of funding the insurance policy's investment account. Instead of effecting an asset freeze that shifts value to a child or trust, the private annuity transaction is structured to shift value to the insurance policy's investment account where it can grow taxfree.

This transactions takes place in several phases. First, an income-producing asset is transferred to an offshore entity (which has elected passthrough tax treatment) owned by a trust established for the benefit of the seller's children in exchange for a private annuity. This gets the income-producing asset into the LLC. The LLC is obligated to the seller for the annuity.

Next, the annuitant establishes an irrevocable life insurance trust (ILIT) for the benefit of his spouse and children, funded with a relatively small amount of cash, perhaps $100,000. The ILIT purchases an OPPVULI policy on the life of someone other than the annuitant. Then, the investment manager of the insurance policy's investment account purchases the ownership interest in the off-shore entity from the children's trust for notional value. He does so because the offshore entity, while having the valuable income-pro-ducing asset, also has an entirely offsetting liability in the obliga-tion to pay the annuity for the life of the annuitant.

Once the offshore entity is owned by the separate account, the income produced by the asset flows to the insurance policy's investment account, increasing the cash value of the insurance policy. The trustee of the ILIT can borrow funds tax-free against the cash value of the policy. The trustee can also distribute those proceeds to the beneficiaries of the trust, which include the annu-itant's spouse, thus giving the annuitant indirect access to the funds.

This transaction has been heavily marketed in recent years. However, some planners and the IRS have expressed concern with it. The IRS outlined its potential attack in a series of international tax conferences. In order to withstand a potential IRS attack, such a transaction must meet at least the following criteria:

- The annuitant in the private annuity and the insured in the life insurance policy cannot be the same person.
- The annuity obligor must be a valid independent entity that is validly taxable as a passthrough entity, and the annuity arrangement must not be a sham.
- The sale of the ownership interests of the annuity obligor to the investment account of the life insurance policy must not be prearranged.
- All foreign entity reporting and foreign trust reporting requirements must be satisfied.

Asset Protection Planning with Installment Sales and Private Annuities

Creditors usually have a singular motivation: cash. Creditors want the debtor's cash, and they want it now. If the debtor has assets other than cash, then the creditor's goal is to liquidate those assets into cash as quickly as possible (even if at sheriff's sale liquidation prices) and apply the cash proceeds from the sale toward the judgment. What creditors do not want is an illiquid asset, or an asset that requires repetitive work to get at the cash.

Annuity payments give creditors indigestion. Instead of getting a lump of cash all at once, annuity payments trickle out monthly. This means that every month the creditor must serve a new garnishment on the obligor so that the obligor sends the annuity check to the creditor and not the debtor. If the debtor lives in a number of states that either protect the annuity payments (such as Florida) or do not allow for garnishment (such as Texas), the creditor may be left without a means of getting at the payments.

Even worse for the creditor, the annuity payments could cease at any time because the annuitant-debtor (increasing in age) could die, and the death of the annuitant-debtor would terminate the annuity payments. A paranoid creditor might even suspect that the annuitant-debtor will die early just to spite the creditor. At any rate, what the creditor is left with is an asset that is difficult and costly to get at, which may in the end have little value to the creditor. All of this facilitates settlement on terms favorable to the annuitant-debtor.

Additionally, if the private annuity is deferred (a complex drafting task for the planner, but feasible) the creditor will typically have to wait until the annuitant-debtor elects to annuitize before the creditor even has a chance of getting at the payments. The annuitant-debtor may also elect to defer until she has moved to a state that either protects annuity payments or does not allow garnishment. And if these problems were not enough, the creditor also risks the insolvency of the obligor.

For all of these reasons, creditors typically view annuity payments as nearly uncollectible assets. Thus, if the creditor cannot attack the annuity arrangement collaterally, such as claiming that the initial transfer of assets amounted to a fraudulent transfer, the creditor might just leave the annuity payments alone. At any rate, all of these factors help to facilitate settlement on terms favorable to the debtor.

If asset protection is a primary consideration, installment sales and private annuities can be structured with poison pills. Such poison pills may include deferral of payments, increases in interest rates coupled with deferral of payments, and provision for in-kind payments (for example, in-kind payments of illiquid LLC interests). All of these poison pills are effective for two reasons. First, while the creditor gets nominal value on paper, he gets no cash. Second, in the case of deferred payments, the creditor will be taxable on interest deemed to accrue during the deferral period. In the case of in-kind illiquid payments, the creditor will receive taxable income but will not receive cash to pay the associated income tax.

Competent estate planning and tax counsel should be consulted when installment notes and private annuities are being structured outside normal forms. However, sometimes asset protection concerns will outweigh estate tax and income tax concerns.

Because a private annuity must be unsecured to qualify as a private annuity for tax purposes, the seller is given the opportunity to convert a valuable asset into an unsecured annuity stream with perfect reasoning: The IRS made me do it. Finally in states such as Florida where annuities are protected by exemption laws, private annuities are very valuable tools for converting vulnerable assets to safe, exempt assets.

An unsecured installment note may be more difficult to justify from a fraudulent transfer perspective without an increased interest rate to reflect the increased repayment risk. However, even a secured installment sale can be an effective asset protection planning tool, particularly where the note allows payment in kind and is a SCIN which will terminate at the seller's death. This structure increases the creditor's uncertainty of payment, which is an important element in negotiating a favorable settlement for the debtor.

Offshore Private Placement Deferred Variable Annuities

An *offshore private placement deferred variable annuity* (abbreviated here as *OPPDVA*) is another tax-deferral vehicle that is offered by some international insurance companies in addition to OPPVULI. As with OPPVULI, the attractive features of an OPPDVA are tax deferral, investment flexibility, and asset protection.

Because an OPPDVA has no life insurance component and therefore no associated costs for life insurance, it is usually a more efficient way to accumulate cash value. However, unlike life insurance, all of the gains in a DVA will be taxed at ordinary income tax rates, if they are distributed in the form of outright distributions or loans. Furthermore, the gains could be subject to an additional 10 percent penalty tax, if they are distributed prior to the annuitant reaching age 59½.

Despite the potentially unfavorable tax consequences, an OPPDVA can be a useful planning tool, for many of the same reasons that an OPPVULI is so useful, particularly where the annuitant is not insurable and unable to obtain a life insurance policy.

Captive Insurance Companies

Insurance typically involves transferring risks to insurance companies that underwrite the risks for the agreed-upon price of the premium. The rationale of the insurance companies in accepting these risks is twofold. First, they can spread their risk over a number of insureds, not all of which will have claims. Second, the insurance companies can charge a sufficiently high enough premium that they have a chance profiting from their underwriting.

At some point, however, a business owner may begin to wonder whether or not he would be better off just keeping the premiums and essentially self-insuring against his own claims. This rationale presents several problems. First, the business owner does not have the ability to spread risks over many policies, as do insurance companies. Second, and much more importantly, his business is not allowed to take a current-year tax deduction for setting aside reserves to pay claims as tax laws allow insurance companies to do.

The business owner, nevertheless, may decide that it is best to self-insure. He may have a variety of insurance needs for which he cannot find an insurance company to accept the risk for a reasonable premium, or he may own a sufficient number of related business that he can spread his risk among them. At some point the business owner will wonder whether he would be better off just owning his own insurance company, underwriting the risks of his various businesses, and keeping the underwriting profits for himself instead of allowing those profits to go to elsewhere. The business owner may consider that he understands his risks better than any-body. Thus, the business owner may consider what is known as a *captive insurance company*, which is loosely defined as an insurance company that is mostly restricted to underwriting the insurance needs of the owner's other businesses.

Indeed, captive insurance is the risk management tool of choice of most large corporations. Nearly all large corporations have captive insurance companies that underwrite substantial parts of their insurance needs. Some of these captive insurance companies have even grown to be some of the largest insurance companies in the world. Their owners have spun them off, making sizeable profits in the process, as independent, standalone insurance companies.

The formation of a captive insurance company is relatively simple, and many jurisdictions, foreign and domestic, cater to the captive insurance marketplace. An application is filed with the insurance commissioner of the jurisdiction chosen as the captive domicile, who issues the company a license. The company must have underwriters, actuaries, and an insurance manager who is resident in the jurisdiction of formation. The captive will keep reserves, underwrite risks, and be subjected to an annual audit. The insurance company will, in all respects, be a fully operating insurance company, although most of its underwriting business will be to other companies owned by its owners.

INSURANCE COMPANY ECONOMICS

An insurance company operates much like a bank. The insurance company's policyholders effectively loan the insurance company money through premium payments. The insurance company repays the money at some time in the future to policyholders who have claims. The insurance company primarily makes its profits by investing these monies (the *reserves*) and its own capital (the *surplus*) at a higher rate of return than underwriting losses.

The insurance company will also attempt to generate profits from underwriting activity. But the insurance company can be profitable even if its underwriting results in a loss. For example, let's say that an insurance company takes in $1 in profit and three years later pays out $1.06 in claims. Bad underwriting, you might say? Hardly, for the insurance company has "borrowed" money for $0.06 over three years, or at an effective rate of 2 percent per year. If the insurance company is able to successfully invest the money over three years with an average annual return of, say, 8 percent, it will have $1.24 before paying claims, leaving 18 cents for administrative costs and profit.

So, insurance companies can be, and routinely are, profitable even when they have underwriting losses. During bull markets, insurance companies often sell insurance cheaper than its true cost because they anticipate investment returns will exceed their calculated underwriting losses. What is important to the insurance company is making investment profits on its reserves and surplus. If the insurance company must suffer underwriting losses to attract this investment capital, it is simply part of the cost of capital, and it can still allow for profitable business so long as investment returns exceed underwriting losses.

These economics mean that in bull markets the cost of insurance becomes artificially cheap as insurance companies compete for investment capital. During bull markets, insurance companies may elect to price premiums well below the true underwriting risk of the insurance company. By contrast, during bear markets, when insurance companies are not capable of generating investment capital, the insurance companies are loath to underwrite risks at a loss and, thus, increase their premiums, which makes insurance more expensive.

Insurance companies have a significant advantage over ordinary businesses: Amounts added to reserves against future losses are deductible for corporate income tax purposes. If an ordinary business, for instance, anticipates $3 million in losses over the next five years and attempted to reserve against those losses, those reserves would not be deductible. In contrast, an insurance company deducts those reserves from income, meaning that an insurance company is legally allowed to shelter income within the reasonable and actuarially determined limits of its reserves. This is the reason why insurance companies never seem to turn a (taxable) profit but have enormous assets and seem to own everything in sight.

Of course, a captive must be a bona fide insurance company with a commercially reasonable business plan. All transactions involving the insurance company, from capitalization to under-writing, must make economic sense. This means that the insurance company must have underwriters, insurance managers, and actu-aries, and they must actually be in the business of insurance. It is not enough for the company to call itself an insurance company or to have an insurance license. The real question is whether the insurance company is actually engaging in the business of insur-ance, such as underwriting and issuing policies, administering reserves, settling claims, and the like.

Because of the tax benefits of captive insurance companies and closely held insurance companies, or CHICs (discussed later in this chapter), there has been a steady growth in the number of cap-tives and CHICs formed. There has also been a corresponding growth in the number of people who believe they have the exper-tise to create and manage insurance companies. Many offshore ser-vice providers are now pushing costly captives and CHICs with the pitch that they can get a company licensed—a claim that is nearly irrelevant for U.S. tax purposes. Although a license is one factor in the determination as to whether an insurance company is an insurance company for tax purposes, it is far from the disposi-tive factor. The key inquiry is whether the company is primarily in the business of insurance and not whether the company has an insurance license hanging on the wall.

For tax purposes, an insurance company must at a minimum conduct real insurance underwriting for third parties, spread and share risks, employ or contract actuaries and underwriters, be ade-quately reserved and capitalized, have a long-term insurance busi-ness plan, and have as its primary purpose the business of insur-ance. Substance (all of the foregoing) again trumps form (the incor-poration certificate and the insurance license).

A major advantage of an insurance company over other types of companies is that an insurance company is allowed to underwrite insurance policies, accept premium payments, and deduct reserves for tax purposes. Of course, risk is transferred from policyholders to the insurance company on a calculated basis. But wealth is also transferred from the insureds to the insurance company to the extent the insurance company has profits. So in addition to being excellent risk management vehicles, insurance companies are excellent wealth accumulation and preservation vehicles.

CAPTIVE INSURANCE COMPANY STRUCTURE

A captive insurance company is one that shares common ownership with another business and typically underwrites some or all of the other business's insurance (see Figure 24.1). The legitimacy of the "captive" relationship, and the deductibility of premiums between parent and captive, is well grounded in existing case law and further bolstered by the recent landmark opinion known as *United Parcel Service v. Commissioner.*[1] In that case, the appeals court reversed the Tax Court and held that premiums paid by the United Parcel Service (UPS) to its Bermuda captive were deductible by the UPS and the arrangement was not a sham. It determined that arrangements had demonstrable economic substance, even though the premiums were quite clearly excessive in commercial terms. The business that is purchasing insurance from the insurance company should, if the insurance is real and the premiums are reasonable, get a current-year deduction for the amount of premiums paid.

For the premiums to be deductible to the other business, the insurance company must also underwrite certain risks for, and receive premiums from, persons or entities unrelated to the owners of the insurance company. Moreover, the premiums charged must also be reasonable, which is usually proven by way of actuarial assessments. If the premiums are not reasonable, the arrangement is subject to challenge.

FIGURE 24.1

Captive insurance.

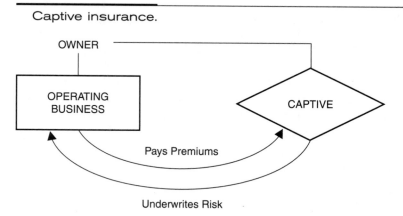

Although domestic captives are becoming more popular because of aggressive marketing by Delaware, Hawaii, South Carolina, and a few other states, most captive insurance companies are formed offshore. They are formed there not so much for tax reasons as for avoiding the bureaucracy of state insurance regulators. A not uncommon situation is for captive insurance companies to actually elect U.S. taxation[2] so as to take advantage of the very favorable U.S. tax treatment of insurance companies.

Keep in mind that although the insurance company is formed offshore, there is no requirement that assets be moved offshore or placed in control of an offshore person. Indeed, assets are typically invested in the United States. One of the benefits of captives is that both the insurance company and the insurance company's assets are controlled by the client as the insurance company owner.[3] There is no reason or need to obfuscate ownership or control or to trust some other person with ownership or control.

The fact that the insurance company is formed and licensed in an offshore jurisdiction does not mean that it is wholly without regulation. The Insurance Commissioners and Financial Services departments of the major offshore jurisdictions strictly regulate the insurance companies they have licensed so as to protect their jurisdictions' reputations. Annual audits are almost always required by these regulators. A mandatory requirement is for the insurance company to have a local manager available to personally meet with the insurance commissioner to resolve any issues that arise.

CAPTIVES AND RISK MANAGEMENT

Insurance involves the management of legal risks by transferring those risks to an insurance company in exchange for actuarially calculated premium payments. However, insureds often encounter pricing inefficiencies in the insurance marketplace. These inefficiencies may occur for many reasons, including a poor understanding by the insurance company underwriters of the particular business sector, lack of competition among insurance companies in particular markets, and poor investment decisions by the insurance company in investing reserves and surplus or in hedging against downturns in the economy.

For example, a business owner may own a widget factory and have never been sued, yet she may pay the same or similar premium amounts for insurance as her business competitor across the street who has been subjected to numerous lawsuits and paid many settlements. This situation occurs because the underwriters of the insurance company have declared the business owner to be basically in the same risk category as her sloppy competitor across the street, and her premiums are basically subsidizing her competitor's true cost of insurance.

Another example is that when the stock market fizzles, rates are likely to go up for reasons totally unrelated to how well risks have been managed and claims avoided. Very simply, the insurance company's investment activity can no longer subsidize underwriting losses. To the contrary, the insurance company will attempt to raise its premiums to cover investment losses. Thus, in a bear market, insurance premium rates will skyrocket, even when no increase in claims occurs.

For any risks for which insurance is unavailable or unaffordable, business owners have self-insured those risks, whether they realize it or not. In other words, if claims materialize, the business owners will have to dig into their own pocket to pay the costs of resolving the claims. Unfortunately, current tax law does not allow a regular business company a deduction for reserving against unrealized potential future claims. An insurance company, however, is allowed to do precisely that.

When a business is large enough, or a person is wealthy enough (a good rule of thumb is at least $3 million in net assets), that business or person should consider owning their own insurance company to manage their own legal risks. As mentioned, nearly all of the largest corporations worldwide own as subsidiaries their own insurance companies precisely for this purpose. These insurance companies are know as "captives" because their business is often (but not required to be) limited to underwriting the risks of other subsidiaries within that business structure.

Business owners have substantial motivation to form captive insurance companies. First, a captive allows the business owner to know exactly the amount and quality of the insurance company's reserves. It should never be an open question as to whether the insurance company has the financial ability to pay claims. The business owner also knows that the insurance company will not wrongly dispute claims, pay slowly, or otherwise act in bad faith toward the business.

Next, the business is often able to obtain certain types of insurance that are not commonly available, since the captive can underwrite any risk of the business. Equally as important, the policies can be tailored for the specific needs of the business instead of the business being forced to accept a generic form filed with the state insurance commissioner, which a third-party insurance company may not desire to alter. The benefits of the business owner being able to draft specific policy language cannot be overstated. Policies can be written, for instance, to only provide litigation expenses and indemnification to the business. They can expressly prohibit the assertion of rights directly against the policy by claimants and creditors.

A captive insurance company also allows the business owner to price the policies based upon the business's specific claims experience. The price does not have to be based upon industry experience rates that may, for whatever reason, not be indicative of that particular business's specific risks. The captive arrangement may also allow the business owner to underwrite certain favorable layers of coverage. The owner can then use the captive as a vehicle to procure third-party insurance more cheaply, by way of reinsurance contracts.

ASSET PROTECTION AND CAPTIVES

An active business has the potential to create liability for itself and its owners. If the business generates profits that are left in the business, those profits are available to creditors. By like token, if the profits are upstreamed to the owners, they are then available to the creditors of the owners and must be separately asset protected.

By paying premiums to the insurance company, the business exchanges cash for an asset (the policy) that may be valueless to creditors (see Figure 24.2). Cash is thus moved out of harm's way and into the insurance company, which itself is separately asset protected from creditors. If the insurance provided and the premiums paid are reasonable and backed by actuarial studies, and if they are also made in the normal course of business, the payment

FIGURE 24.2

Asset protective component of captives.

The asset protection effect of a captive is to take cash out of the
Operating Business where it would otherwise
be exposed to the business's creditors.

of the premiums will likely not be set aside as fraudulent transfers.
They won't because the premium payments should be deemed to
be "for value," if they are reasonable and supported by an actuarial study of the risk.

Another advantage is that premium payments are not one-
time transfers but occur monthly or quarterly. Thus, once the captive arrangement has been implemented, a mechanism thereafter
exists for quietly moving wealth from the underlying business on
a regular basis. That arrangement can continue so long as the
underlying business can support the insurance payments.

Captive insurance companies are tremendous risk-manage-
ment tools. They allow a business owner to protect himself against
risks that he otherwise has no insurance against (known as *naked
risks*). The typical business owner will typically have some of the
following exposures, which the closely held insurance company
can be used to insure against:

- Payment of other policy deductibles
- Excess exposure (claims over the limits of existing insur-
  ance)
- Regulatory or administrative actions (suspension or revo-
  cation of license)
- Variations in the economy, including interest rate fluctua-
  tions and currency risks
- Environmental and hazardous materials
- Suits involving sexual harassment, age or sexual discrimi-
  nation, violations of the Americans with Disability Act

- Many other risks for which the business owner is uninsured

These risks are exemplary; there are literally hundreds of types of risks against which the business owner may insure. In 1999, many businesses insured against "Y2K" software defects. Since 2001, business owners often insure against terrorism risks, including financial losses caused by swings of the economy due to terrorism.

This does not mean that the business owner has just created a large pool of available assets for creditors who will be paid by way of the policies. The captive can draft policies as so-called *litigation expense policies*. These policies do not make moneys available to third-party claimants or creditors for claims. Instead, they only pay the out-of-pocket costs to administer the claims, such as to pay attorney fees and court costs. The idea with this type of policy is that the creditor sees a policy that exists only to provide the business with a "war chest" to fight the claim but does not pay money to the creditor if the creditor wins.

The policies can also be written on claims that only the owner will assert, such as to compensate the underlying business for the loss of a key customer or for business losses caused by an unforeseen change in interest rates. For example, an architect might purchase insurance from her own captive to protect against the expenses of litigating an attempted revocation of her license. Or a real estate developer might underwrite his own risks of not being granted developmental licenses for certain lands that he owns. In both examples, real risks would be borne by the architect and real estate developer, but payment of the policies would not be made to any creditor.

CLOSELY HELD INSURANCE COMPANIES

Captive insurance companies are most often used by very large companies and are meant to benefit all shareholders. The primary goal of such captives is to reduce the company's insurance costs to increase shareholder value. No one but the company's shareholders will benefit directly from the company's use of a captive. Indeed, it would be a violation of officers' and directors' fiduciary duties at least—and perhaps a violation of state and federal securities laws, at worst—for a captive to be used to divert profits from a captive to persons other than shareholders.

In contrast, what we term a *closely held insurance company (CHIC)* is a captive insurance company meant for use only with privately held businesses. In addition to a reduction in insurance costs and a consolidation of risk management functions, a CHIC has as a significant goal the distancing of the wealth in the CHIC from the business owner, and consequently, the distancing of the wealth in the CHIC from the business owner's creditors. In a CHIC structure, any underwriting income (premiums paid less reinsurance costs, administrative costs, and net claims paid) essentially represents a transfer of wealth from the operating business to the CHIC. As a result, the CHIC can shift value away from the operating business and its creditors.

Although many CHICs are owned by the business owner, an even better arrangement is for a CHIC to be owned by the business owner's intended heirs and beneficiaries. Just as a CHIC serves to transfer wealth away from the liability-producing business, so may a CHIC transfer wealth away from the business owner who may be personally exposed to lawsuits. These are benefits that are ancillary to the primary purposes of CHICs, which are to lower insurance costs and to consolidate risk management functions, but they are important benefits nonetheless.

When properly structured as part of an overall succession plan, a CHIC is an excellent vehicle for intergenerational wealth transfer and wealth accumulation (see Figure 24.3). For instance, if a CHIC is formed for the business owner's children, grandchildren, or both, and if it provides insurance to the owner's business, there is a transfer of the net underwriting income from the reach of the creditors of the business and its owner to the owner's heirs. So long as the insurance arrangements and the premiums paid are on arm's-length terms, no fraudulent transfer risks should be incurred. The insurance company might also issue a life insurance policy on the life of the business owner, allowing the family's insurance company to earn the fees and investment income rather than a commercial insurance company. The possibilities are limited only by the extent that insurance policies and reinsurance treaties are otherwise utilized within the insurance marketplace, the economic reasonableness of the transaction, and complex insurance tax law considerations.

FIGURE 24.3

Wealth transfer with CHIC.

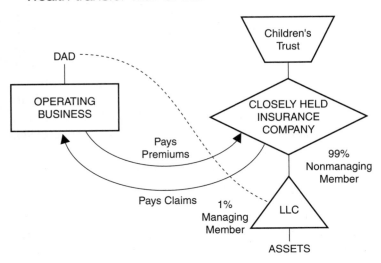

Another advantage of a CHIC is that it can explore niche insurance market opportunities that larger insurance companies may overlook. Indeed, many of the major publicly traded insurance companies started as small insurance companies that fulfilled otherwise neglected insurance needs. True, a CHIC is usually formed offshore and generally is not permitted to solicit or underwrite insurance in the United States. (It can, however, still write many policies for U.S. insureds, particularly for related parties.) But at some future time a CHIC may be admitted in one or more U.S. states to serve select insurance needs in those states. The ultimate goal of a CHIC, as with any company, is to build a separate business with substantial value. With appropriate reserves and careful underwriting, a CHIC can qualify for insurance company ratings from one of the insurer rating firms. That may cause it to have significant value beyond its simple net asset value, which may one day be realized in a sale to a larger insurer.

CHICs represent the culmination of advances in risk management, asset protection, and insurance. However, a CHIC is a real insurance company, and its owners must take on the associated economic risks, including relatively expensive maintenance costs.

If a client is willing to accept the responsibility and the risks along with the rewards, a CHIC is an ideal planning solution. However, if a client wants the tax rewards without the associated risks, then other tools should be considered.

ENDNOTES

1. *United Parcel Service v. Commissioner*, 254 F.3rd 1014 (11th Cir. 2001).
2. Internal Revenue Code Section 953(d).
3. A more typical occurrence is for the client to act as the manager of a limited liability company that holds the insurance company's stock.

CHAPTER 25

Other Advanced
Methodologies

We live in an increasingly sophisticated financial world, where sharp minds in New York, London, Tokyo, Hong Kong, and elsewhere develop new and unique financial products and strategies for their clients on a regular basis. Many of these products and strategies have unrealized potential to serve asset protection purposes. These methodologies are considered advanced, primarily because they are little known, and also because the implementation of these strategies requires legal and financial planning far beyond traditional financial, transactional, and estate planning.

Recall that asset protection rarely should be done for its own sake and in its own name. Instead, it should be undertaken to further broader economic and risk management purposes, with proper attention paid to ancillary asset protection benefits. Thus, the most clever asset protection planning will take advantage of as many strategies as possible that are used in ordinary business and finance.

As we discussed in Chapter 8 relating to challenge analysis, in asset protection planning the general rule is that novelty is good. Novel strategies are less likely to be identified by creditors or courts as having an asset protection intent. Strategies and structures that are heavily marketed for asset protection purposes will alert creditors and courts to the fact that a debtor's motivation in planning was asset protection. A creditor may be comfortable attacking known asset protection strategies or might even desire to make an example out of a debtor who has engaged in them. Novel strategies, on the other hand, can unnerve a creditor, because the creditor and his attorneys are likely not to have seen the strategy before, and may not have much familiarity in the particular area of business or finance upon which it is based. All of these factors make settlement on terms favorable to the debtor more likely.

Advanced strategies also attempt to alter the fundamental character of the debate regarding the debtor's actions. For example, instead of the debtor focusing entirely on the statute of limitations for fraudulent transfers, the debtor might instead focus on persuading the court of the low value or the high value, as the case requires, of a particular asset in dispute, such as with a complex financial instrument like a convertible bond. If there is a dispute, it will be the debtor's financial expert's word against the creditor's financial expert's, if the creditor can find one. The issues will likely be so esoteric that it will be difficult for a court to determine that the debtor had any intent to lessen the rights of creditors, even if that was precisely the result.

CORPORATE STRATEGIES

Some advanced strategies exist to foil creditors once they have started their attempts to pierce entities to assert liability directly against the owners. These strategies can also be implemented before creditors appear, in order to reinforce the asset protection structures already in place. Most of these strategies take advantage of ordinary corporate law, but with some unique twists.

One such method involves recapitalizing a company by having the owners contribute illiquid long-term debt instruments (such as a promissory note from another entity they control) to the company to increase the company's value temporarily (see Figure 25.1). This strategy, known as *recapitalization*, allows the shareholders then to extract valuable, vulnerable assets from the company by liquidating or redeeming shares. What has happened is simply that the extracted vulnerable, attractive, and liquid assets of the corporation have been replaced by less vulnerable, unattractive, and illiquid assets. The benefit of recapitalization is that the balance sheet of the corporation is relatively unchanged, even though the liquid assets have been stripped out. A creditor must wait for these

FIGURE 25.1

Recapitalization.

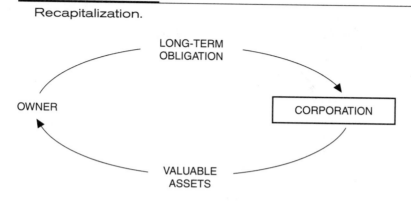

long-term obligations to come due, instead of immediately collecting against the assets. Few creditors will wait a few decades to be
paid. More importantly, few creditors' attorneys will wait even a
few months, much less a few years, to be paid. So, such a recapitalization can help achieve a more favorable settlement for a
debtor.

Recapitalization can also be utilized to increase the company's
capital so that the company is less susceptible to claims that it was
merely an undercapitalized shell. By adding capital to the company and otherwise ensuring that the company is maintaining its separate identity, the owner will risk a much smaller portion of his
personal assets than he would risk if the corporate entity were disregarded.

Of course, for the recapitalization to be more than a mere
sham, the obligor on the debt instrument contributed to the corporation must have a realistic ability to pay the debt to the corporation when it comes due. This ability to pay is measured as of the
time the creditor seeks to challenge the recapitalization. However,
after the crisis has passed, the obligor can attempt to restructure or
discharge the obligation. To facilitate this later planning, the oblig-
or should not be an individual. Instead, the obligor should be an
entity established for this specific purpose.

A *dilution* strategy involves the subsequent issue of additional shares from that corporation to another entity (see Figure 25.2).
This has the effect of reducing the value of the stock for the original holder, with a corresponding accretion of wealth to the holder

FIGURE 25.2

Dilution.

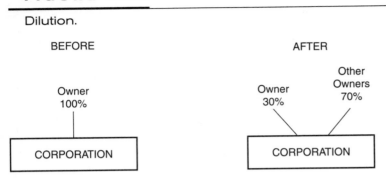

of the newly issued stock. Thus, if the stock of the original holder is later attached by a creditor, the creditor will receive less value than before the dilution.

So long as there is a reasonable economic justification for the dilution, and it is not close in time to the appearance of a creditor of the shareholder being diluted, a creditor will have difficulty asserting that a fraudulent transfer has occurred. Instead, a creditor taking the shares will probably be compelled to bring a shareholder's derivative action against the issuing corporation. This will be a difficult action at best, particularly if the original shareholder consented to the dilution. A not uncommon occurrence in many companies is for preferred stock, in particular, to be at risk of a dilution. If a significant amount of time passes between the date of the dilution and the time that the creditor seeks relief, the creditor's likelihood of recovery will be very low.

Dilution can be very difficult for a creditor to detect. The creditor must trace the debtor's original investment in the company and compare that with what the creditor received from the liquidation of the stock. Even if the creditor finds that the original shareholder was diluted, the creditor may not suspect that the dilution was intended to reduce the value of what the creditor received.

MIGRATION STRATEGIES

The process of creating multiple layers of entities, and then transferring assets through those layers until they are distanced from entities carrying potential liability, is termed *migration* (see Figure

25.3). Migration strategies are sometimes employed in the sale of an asset from a vulnerable entity, for example, in the transfer of patent rights away from a company that has product liability concerns.

Successful migration strategies typically are planned well in advance, using several layers, and are implemented over a relatively long period of time. After the assets have been transferred through one layer, the resulting shell entities are sold to a foreign partner not subject to the jurisdiction of U.S. courts. The shell entities are liquidated, or kept in place, but dormant, for future use after a predetermined period of time has passed, such as the statute of limitations period for a fraudulent transfer. The sale of an intermediary entity to a foreign partner likely will create difficulties for a creditor in determining the specifics of the transfers and the subsequent ownership structure of the entities. It will because the foreign partner and the corporate documents of the entities used are outside the jurisdiction of the court. They are not susceptible to discovery without extreme and unlikely intervention on the part of foreign courts.

FIGURE 25.3

Migration.

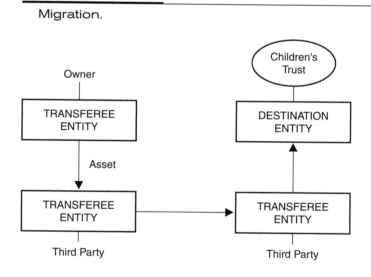

Creditors can chase assets only to the extent that they can trace title from entity to entity. The interposition of an offshore entity may severely impair a creditors' ability to trace title. Or, at least, it will impair the creditor's ability to prove that an entity receiving title down the line was anything but an innocent purchaser for value. The first transfer puts some immediate distance between the asset and potential creditors. Succeeding transfers and the passage of time create additional assurance that the asset will not be attacked.

The keys to migration are patience and subtlety. The transfers should not be made on the same or successive days; instead, they should be spread out over a long period of time, preferably years. With each year, the entity is more distanced from the original owner who has the creditor concerns. The transfers should appear as arm's-length transfers between unrelated purchasers and, to the extent possible, they should *be* arm's-length transfers. It is unlikely that the transfers will be to unrelated purchasers, but if the creditor tracing the asset thinks that the purchasers are unrelated, so much the better.

REDEMPTION

Redemption methodology is similar to migration. Redemption seeks to eliminate unknown potential past liability in an entity by selling the entity to a liability-insulated third party (often offshore). Then the core business assets are purchased back, or *redeemed*, in a new, liability-free entity. (See Figure 25.4.) At least a year should pass between the time of the original sale and the time of the redemption sale. Ideally, the later redemption transaction would not occur until the fraudulent transfer statute of limitations for the original transfer has run.

This strategy avoids a direct transfer in the traditional sense from the client's old company to the client's new company. The assets themselves are not transferred; rather the *redemption rights* to the assets are transferred. These rights may be difficult to value, which will cause a creditor trouble in a fraudulent transfer claim. Even if a creditor successfully invalidates the transfer of the redemption rights, the creditor may have difficulty in forcing the original owner to exercise those rights, particularly if the payment

FIGURE 25.4

Redemption.

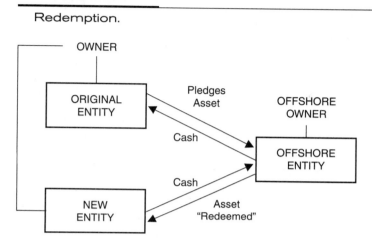

of cash to the foreign party is required, and because of other contingencies written into the contract.

For example, assume that the owner of an asset held in Company A, which may be in a high-risk business, desires to move the asset into Company B. If the asset were simply sold from Company A to Company B, a later creditor might contend that the transaction was fraudulent in nature since, because of the overlapping ownership, Company B might be considered an "insider." Instead, Company A sells the asset to a Bahamas IBC owned by a citizen of the Bahamas. After some passage of time, the Bahamas IBC sells the asset to Company B (or, otherwise stated, Company B "redeems" the asset). Under this scenario, there is no direct connection between Company A and Company B, and the passage of time may present difficulties to a creditor who wants to argue that the two transactions amounted to a single fraudulent transfer.

As with the migration strategy, the principal benefit of a redemption strategy is that a third party has been substituted within the chain of potential transferees. These methods are immediately effective to a substantial degree upon the initial sale, and are probably unchallengeable after several years have passed. Also, there has been an immediate for-value transfer of the asset to the third party, thus giving the asset some substantial and immediate protection upon the initial transfer and even before the redemption takes place. The primary disadvantages to the redemption strategy are lingering secondary liability, typical high expense involved in the structuring and transfers, and difficulty in planning and implementing these arrangements.

DEVALUATION METHODOLOGY

Devaluation methodology seeks to take an asset through several sales, and in each step the asset is devalued in some way. Eventually, the devalued asset is sold to a third-party purchaser "for value" (at the devalued price). Subsequently, the third party sells the asset at the depreciated price to a controlled entity, which may then either hold the asset or sell it at the true market value.

Subtle changes to the asset are made that have the effect of devaluing it, such as temporarily canceling a business's right to use certain patents. These changes can later be fixed when the asset is repurchased from the third party, which makes the lost value reappear. Another way to devalue an asset is to break it up into component parts, which separately are worth less than the whole. The devalued parts are sold in successive transactions over a period of time. After the statute of limitations for fraudulent transfers has run, the parts of the asset are repurchased by a new entity owned by the client. The parts are then reconstituted into the whole asset within this new entity.

The effect is to take value off the owner's balance sheet, with the value then reappearing in the new entity. This maneuver decidedly is not a tax strategy, and it should not be exploited as such. But it may have significant asset protection benefits.

BACKWARDIZATION

In the financial context, *backwardization* refers to the market situation in which prices are progressively lower in future periods than at present, a situation that is usually the result of a shortage in the supply of a commodity or currency. In other words, "if you wait, you'll get it cheaper." In the asset protection context, backwardization refers to an arrangement in which a contract for an asset purchase is arranged at a price that is relatively high, if it is completed immediately, but which is set at a lower and lower price as time progresses. The effect of this arrangement is to provide a high asset sale value (that is, higher value as consideration) at the onset, when creditors may not yet be identified, but to finally lower the cost after a defined period. By that time any creditors have been identified and claims resolved.

If a creditor does appear, the high initial sale price will mitigate the possibility of the transfer being deemed a fraudulent transfer. Over time, as the threat of any fraudulent transfer claim wanes, the sale price drops more and more, so that by the time the sale closes, at a value well below current market value, considerable value is shifted away from the potential target of litigation. Of course, the sale contracts are identifiable by a "relation back" feature, which is finally negotiated away (if conditions permit) at the last minute before the sale is finally consummated. In other words, once it is determined that no creditor has appeared, the contract is effectively rewritten at the lower price desired by the parties.

STRUCTURED FINANCIAL PRODUCTS

The cutting edge of asset protection involves complex financial arrangements known as *structured financial products (SFPs)*. These are arrangements commonly used in the financial markets to hedge a financial position or to exploit arbitrage opportunities arising from market inefficiencies or simply for specific complex speculative investments. SFPs have tremendous, albeit unintended, wealth-transfer potential in ways that most creditors cannot imagine. SFPs simply are among the most powerful asset protection tools available. On the other hand, the use of SFPs is rather limited, because of their complexity, the heavy regulation of the securities and commodities markets, and the general unfamiliarity of planners with financial transactions that are so sophisticated that they are handled only by a relatively few financial professionals.

Replication methodology involves the use of structured financial derivative products (and so-called *exotic derivatives*). These derivatives remove value from a debtor's investment portfolio, with the value being reconstituted elsewhere in a protected vehicle, either immediately or after the passage of a fixed amount of time (see Figure 25.5). Value simply disappears in one place, because of bad financial decisions, and then materializes elsewhere, as a result of good financial decisions. The bad and good financial decisions involved are, of course, the opposite sides of the same transaction, but creditors find it nearly impossible to recognize this transaction unless they are specifically looking for it, and even then it still may be difficult to uncover.

Replication strategies involve the use of complex options strategies such as collars, involving multiple, staggered call and put options. An asset protected entity or related party, such as heirs or a spouse takes an opposite market position, acting as the counterparty in the transaction.

The strategy is implemented so that the client seeking to transfer value from himself to a protected party is a loser in the transactions most of the time—for example, 80 percent of the time. So the client will lose 8 times out of 10, meaning that the counterparty will win 8 times out of 10. Because the 2 times out of 10 that the counterparty wins in this example offsets 2 of the counterparty's wins, the client makes a successful transfer to the counterparty 6 out of 10 times.

In this example, the client will show a trading loss 60 percent of the time, and the counterparty will show a trading profit 60 percent of the time. This arrangement allows the two parties to effectuate a continuing wealth transfer until the client's assets have been totally depleted. Over time, the person seeking to transfer can point to a complete loss of his assets, fairly attributing the loss to

FIGURE 25.5

Replication.

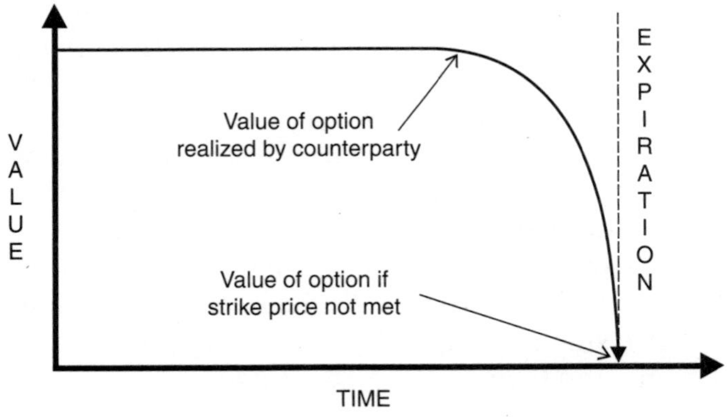

speculative derivatives trading. This explanation will be supported by the client's brokerage statements. Few, if any, creditors are likely to investigate further.

The advantage of replication methodology is that it is immediately effective with each trade that goes as intended. Also, valuation issues involved with complex derivatives positions are difficult to sort out, making it very difficult for a creditor to contend that the transfer was not for value or that it was made for any reason other than for the legitimate pursuit of financial gain.

The primary disadvantages of replication methods are, first, that they require the cooperation of a securities broker-dealer (or sometimes several broker-dealers engaged in the trading of derivative instruments) and, second, that they can be expensive to design and carry significant trading costs.

Another example of a structured financial product is the creation of a standard debt instrument to facilitate the transfer of an asset, with the subsequent sale of only the interest component of the instrument to an unrelated party. The debtor will be left holding what is known as *a zero-coupon instrument*, meaning that the creditor that attaches and seizes the debt instrument will not receive any interest payments but must wait for the instrument to mature before seeing cash. Chances are that the creditor will have to pay income tax on deemed interest income while waiting for the instrument to mature while never receiving cash with which to pay the income tax. Thus, such an instrument will not be a desirable asset for a creditor to attach.

The key, as with nearly all asset protection strategies, is subtlety in the design of the instrument and the subsequent stripping and sale of the interest component to a third party. The instrument may be drafted to include hidden anticreditor provisions that will make the instrument very undesirable should a creditor attach it. For example, the interest rate may be significantly increased, consequently significantly increasing the creditor's income tax liability while not providing the cash flow to make the income tax payments. All the while the creditor will be left unsure if she will ever be paid by the obligor. These instruments can be very useful for facilitating other asset protection strategies such as recapitalizations and even for seemingly ordinary transactions. They can wear down and discourage a creditor, thus promoting a settlement.

CHAPTER 26

Specific Situations

As a means of tying together some of this book's strategies in a practical manner, in this final chapter, we will examine a few particular types of clients, their needs, and some potential solutions.

REAL ESTATE DEVELOPERS

Some of the best candidates for comprehensive asset protection plans are real estate developers. Because of the nature of their business, real estate developers are subject to construction-defect liabilities, which last a decade or longer in some states. Real estate developers are subject to environmental liabilities. They may be liable for the acts of subcontractors working on their behalf. Plaintiffs' attorneys are now giddy due to the prospects for bringing large class action lawsuits for health problems due to toxic mold. Furthermore, the projects of real estate developers are usually heavily leveraged and their buyers also rely on borrowing, meaning that a sudden spike in interest rates or dramatic unemployment could reverse their fortunes very quickly.

Real estate developers thus have significant risk management needs, but they also need access to their cash for new projects. Because of lenders' requirements, developers often cannot encumber themselves with personal debt or they risk being denied access to the borrowed capital they need. Many of the developer's concerns can be alleviated through insurance policies to cover general liability, constructions defects, and environmental liability, but these policies typically have significant exclusions and large deductibles.

First, each significant project should be developed within its own entity. An option here might be to use a series LLC to hold individual properties. Thus, the property at 101 Maple Street could be placed in Developer LLC, 101 Maple Series, and the property at 103 Maple Street could be placed in Developer LLC, 103 Maple Series, and so on. Although the issue of the liability separation of the individual series of a series LLC has yet to be resolved in most states, the series LLC structure might cause enough consternation to a plaintiff's attorney to precipitate a favorable settlement.

Second, a common problem with real estate developers is for them to be personally involved in each project and entity, either as an owner of the entity (or worse, owner of the real estate directly), or as an officer, partner, or manager. Where possible (that is, if allowed by lenders), the real estate developer should use a management company to administer all projects, distancing himself from direct relationships with development projects. Note that the real estate developer can still be a purely passive investor in his own name by extending credit to the entities in which the projects are developed.

Real estate developers are often ideal candidates for captive or closely held insurance companies. With a captive insurance company, a developer can cover deductibles and excluded risks. And after they accrue sufficient reserves, economic market risks, such as interest rate risks, can be insured. Furthermore, if capitalized and reserved well enough, the surplus and reserves of the company may be suitable for investment into the developer's own projects. Thus, to an extent, the captive or CHIC can operate as the developer's private bank, providing financing as necessary while also insuring against risks for which the developer has no coverage.

CORPORATE DIRECTORS

The risk analysis for a director of a publicly held corporation would be very different. Liability is most likely to arise from one direction: a shareholder's derivative lawsuit, against which the director will probably have some measure of protection from the corporation's directors' and officers' (D&O) liability policy.

However, what most directors fear, unfortunately all too realistically, is that because the damages in a derivatives action may be measured by a drop in stock prices for millions of shares of stock, the limits of the D&O policy will be exceeded by far, and the director will be financially ruined.

On the other hand, corporate officers and directors must be careful to avoid extensive asset protection planning and offshore planning. Such planning could give rise to the inference, justly founded or not, that the corporate director or officer knew that she was acting improperly and was attempting to protect her assets before her improprieties were discovered. Asset protection planning for an officer or director of a publicly traded company must be extremely subtle and should avoid schemes that are known to have an asset protection purpose.

The director should set aside assets and income by using subtle strategies that have a practical asset protection effect but that are not commonly utilized for asset protection. Because of the nature of a derivative action, and relatively long limitations periods—lengthened by discovery provisions that operate to suspend limitations periods—the director should avoid making gifts, since the gifts may be susceptible to being set aside as fraudulent transfers. Private annuities and private placement life insurance are often a good fit for a director, especially if, in the event of a catastrophic claim, she is willing to reside in Florida or another state that has substantial protections for annuities and life insurance.

BUSINESS OWNERS

Entrepreneurial business owners face more risks than anyone. First, they have substantial economic risk in that the business may fail, resulting in an immediate loss of income, and the probable loss of assets to lenders to which the business owner has provided personal guarantees. Second, an infinite number of potential liabilities arise from business operations. If a truck driver is involved in a wreck, the company and the owner probably will be sued. If an elderly employee is terminated, the company and the owner probably will be sued. If a neighbor of the manufacturing facility develops a mysterious illness, the company and the owner probably will be sued.

As with real estate developers, the first step with asset protection for business owner is to distance the owner from the operations of the business through use of holding companies. Next, the business should be unbundled, with each significant valuable component segregated into its own entity. It should then be leased or licensed back to the operating business on terms that provide that if the operating business fails, the leases or licenses will terminate. The assets will then be freed up for future use by the owner. Employees should be segregated into companies based on their functions in relation to the operating business and the component leasing entities in order to contain employment liability to the fullest extent possible. Key management personnel should be segregated into one or more management companies.

The owner may participate in the management company, perhaps best by acting as a consultant to the management company. This arrangement allows the owner to advise the management company on running the business, while putting distance between the owner and potential liability resulting from that advice. As for ultimate control, if the officers of the management company do not follow the owner's nonbinding advice, the owner of the management company (probably a trustee friendly to the business owner) may decide that it is necessary to terminate the management company's officers. Part of the business owner's compensation arrangement as a consultant might include a deferred compensation plan that allows the owner to put away business profits in a subtle, protected manner.

Closely held insurance companies usually make a great deal of economic sense for business owners, because they have substantial uncovered liability exposure. A CHIC can provide insurance for employment claims, environmental liability, and even business umbrella coverage against all types of claims. The policies can be drafted as *litigation expense policies* that do not make funds available to third-party claimants but rather are strictly limited to paying for defense costs.

If a business owner intends for his wealth to be passed to his heirs effectively and efficiently, he must consider estate and succession planning, and he should integrate that planning with his asset protection planning as soon as possible, for two principal reasons. First, by transferring the business (or at least a part of it) to heirs early, the value of the business will grow outside the owner's estate for federal gift, estate, and generation-skipping tax purposes. Second, the substantial estate planning benefits will justify some of the planning that has asset protective benefits. Again, private annuities and private placement life insurance arrangements are ideal. They are difficult for creditors to set aside, and they can accomplish significant wealth transfer with a minimum of taxes. They are also relatively easy to administer, once they are established.

PHYSICIANS

Because physicians face newsmaking medical malpractice lawsuits with regularity, a popular notion has arisen that physicians are ideal candidates for asset protection planning. In some ways, this conception is true, and in some ways it is not. Physicians can be difficult clients, with good reason. They are aggressively bombarded with overmarketed asset protection schemes by attorneys, financial planners, accountants, life insurance agents, and offshore promoters. This predicament leads to justifiable distrust of advisors on the one hand and, on the other, it leads to substantial misconceptions by physicians about what asset protection is and what it can do for them.

Many promoters use scare tactics to convince physicians to implement the latest crackpot scheme. True, large medical malpractice verdicts are reached every year, and, indeed, most doctors know a colleague who has been hit with a substantial medical malpractice verdict. However, relatively few physicians are hit with verdicts in excess of their medical malpractice coverage limits. Even fewer medical malpractice judgment creditors ever see more than the defendant physician's coverage limits. So, the number is a relative few, but for many physicians a few is a few too many. So what goes wrong in these high-verdict cases? A defendant physician is susceptible to being lured into a gamble by his insurance company. Unfortunately it is a gamble with a limited downside for the insurance company—the coverage limits—but an unlimited downside for the physician.

Even in most serious cases, the plaintiff will settle for policy limits, assuming the policy limits are reasonably high. If the insurance company agrees, with the physician's consent, a sum equal to the policy limits is paid to the plaintiff and the case is over. Often, however, the insurance company would prefer to gamble by taking the case to trial. For the insurance company it is a no-lose proposition. If it settles, it will lose the policy limits. If it loses at trial, it likely will lose the policy limits. However, if it wins at trial, it is out only its attorney fees.

Of course, the physician has no reason to enter into this gamble. If he settles, he loses no money out of pocket. But if he goes to trial, he faces nearly unlimited liability over and above his policy limits. The best move that a physician can make when he finds himself the defendant of a lawsuit is to hire his own attorney. (Remember, the attorney defending the case for the insurance company has been hired by the insurance company.) That attorney can review the case and, if necessary, demand that the insurance company settle the case within the policy limits. This puts the insurance company on notice that, if it fails to settle and the physician is liable for a sum beyond the policy limits, the physician may bring a bad-faith claim against the insurance company. The insurance company and the attorney hired by it may try to persuade the physician that a settlement is certain to besmirch his professional reputation and that the physician should proceed to trial, where a win is the only way to save his reputation. Many excess verdicts occur as the result of an attempt to save a reputation that in many cases would not have suffered significantly if the case had settled.

The bottom line is that a reasonable amount of medical malpractice coverage from a financially strong insurer will make all but the most extreme of cases go away. The choice of insurer—where the physician *has* a choice—can be crucial. Physicians face substantial risks from financially unstable insurers, perhaps greater risks than those posed by patients. Some physicians in some states have little choice but to purchase coverage from a less-than-ideal insurer, or they may find themselves without coverage after the failure of an insurer. Asset protection planning can and should be done for these situations, and for extreme excess verdict cases. But to the extent that a physician can afford a reasonable amount of medical malpractice coverage from a quality insurer, the physician should rely on that for protection. Asset protection planners who encourage their physician clients to get rid of their medical malpractice coverage are giving their clients very poor advice.

For the foregoing reasons, a physician-owed *risk retention group* (RRG)—insured-owned insurance companies that are similar to captive insurance companies—is often a good alternative to either a traditional medical malpractice insurance carrier or the physician's "going naked" against negligence claims. Typically, RRGs will stabilize premium rates and be more attuned to the specific needs of their physician-owners than most insurers. Unfortunately, RRGs tend to admit only physicians with low claims histories, and often will not underwrite physicians who have had significant claims.

In our experience, physicians who have come to us for planning tend to have lost more wealth due to divorce and bad financial decisions rather than due to malpractice claims. Asset protection planning for divorce is very case specific, and ideally is dealt with prior to marriage in a prenuptial agreement. Because they are targets of every kind of financial planner, schemer, and salesperson, some physicians inevitably will become involved in bad investment schemes or tax shelters.

A number of physicians faced bankruptcy in the late 1980s not having understood the implications of being general partners in risky oil and gas investment partnerships. During this same period, many physicians were burned in real estate limited partnership tax shelters and had to cough up back taxes, penalties, and interest. Some are still having problems with negative tax consequences coming home to roost twenty years later. In the technology stock boom of the late 1990s, many physicians bought into tax shelter schemes again, some aggressive but plausible, and others downright evasive. As we progress through the first decade of the twenty-first century, more and more physicians are getting the dreaded call from an IRS agent. Physicians, like other business owners, should educate themselves to conduct their investment business as purely passive investors through holding company structures.

The unfortunate reality of the last decade is that reduced fees for services and increased insurance premiums make it difficult for the average physician to afford top-shelf asset protection solutions. For example, at first blush, a closely held insurance company sounds like an ideal solution for a physician to insure excess medical malpractice exposure and related risks. Unfortunately, the economics simply do not pan out for someone who cannot capitalize a company with several million dollars in assets. There are excellent asset protection solutions, however, such as advanced retirement planning solutions that do make economic sense. A by-product of retirement planning solutions is that they impose a forced financial discipline and can be used by the physician as an excuse to prevent colleagues and financial advisors from luring them into questionable investment schemes.

Finally, physicians often carry substantial accounts receivables. Factoring and receivable financing vehicles are now available that can both free up operating cash immediately and leverage the receivables against a possible future creditor attack. Some of these programs are cookie-cutter deals implemented by large banks, which offer only superficial creditor protection. But if properly arranged, these methods can have substantial asset protection advantages.

HOLISTIC PLANNING

The relationship between asset protection and financial planning is poorly understood, yet is critically important. As we repeatedly assert, asset protection fundamentally is risk management. Any given client is considerably more likely to lose wealth due to poor asset allocation, self-interested financial advisors, and plain bad investments than to the predator plaintiffs that are talked about at such great length in asset protection seminars. At the same time, asset protection often involves tying up assets in such a way that they are not available to creditors, but at the same time they will be less available than might be desired by clients. Naturally, clients have present and future cash flow requirements and other financial needs. These financial needs have to be taken into account when protection strategies are being implemented.

Financial planning often provides the economic justification for the client to rearrange his or her affairs, during which asset protection planning can be subtly implemented. A client may decide that in order to provide her heirs with the best financial benefits, she will sell the mutual funds she owns and use the funds to invest in cash-value life insurance. Of course, this has an ancillary asset protection effect. Mutual fund shares are very exposed to creditors, but the cash value of life insurance is protected from creditors in many states. Even in a worst-case scenario, if the client does not live in a state that protects life insurance, the client can move to a state that does offer protection, achieving a significant asset protection benefit.

The financial planning required for successful asset protection planning often must encompass more than simply converting nonexempt assets into exempt assets. Most asset protection structures will have a definable effective life, after which the client will either want the assets available to him personally or transferred to heirs. It makes little financial sense for an entity that is designed to protect assets for ten years to engage in risky short-term trading with potential loss of principal. Instead, that structure ideally should hold an investment that is designed to return the greatest amount of money at the end of the ten-year period, with a level of financial risk acceptable to the client.

Several times, the authors have implemented very effective asset protection strategies only to see, against our advice, the assets frittered away by bad investment decisions. A planner who does not deal with the potential loss of principal, which is every bit as real as money lost to the mythical predator plaintiff, is doing the client no favors. If the client is not willing to invest the assets sensibly within the asset protection structure that is created, perhaps the client should be advised that the asset protection planning may not be cost-beneficial. After all, assets that are likely to be lost to bad financial decisions do not require a great deal of asset protection planning. Indeed, some asset protection planning maneuvers may interfere with the client's ability to use investment losses to reduce his income tax burden. The bottom line is that the holistic approach to asset protection planning that we have advocated throughout this book should apply with no less fervor to financial planning.

REMEDIATION AND THE PLANNING PROCESS

A considerable portion of the authors' work involves remediation— that is, fixing defective asset protection structures and working clients out of bad tax or financial situations. Why is this so? Part of the answer is that asset protection has become an industry, and it is one that is very heavily marketed. Some of the marketing is simply bait and switch, where the asset protection planning is the bait to lure the client in at which time the advisor switches the focus to financial and insurance products that generate large commissions. This often results in the client's asset protection needs being largely unmet, abandoned in the pursuit of the big commission.

Perhaps a bigger problem is that most asset protection planners offer only one or two cookie-cutter strategies to their clients, regardless of the client's situation. For example, if a planner's cookie-cutter structure is an offshore trust, then every client who walks into that planner's office will walk out with an offshore trust. If the client needs a will, she gets an offshore trust. If she needs a business entity for an investment venture, she gets an offshore trust. No matter what their clients really need, they get an offshore trust. Remarkably, many of these promoters do their planning in states, such as Florida, with liberal creditor exemptions, which would be much better planning tools than offshore trusts. But offshore trusts command big fees, and homestead protection doesn't, even if homestead is proven to be effective and an offshore trust may land you in jail. This is product-pushing and not asset protection planning at all. Certainly, it bears no resemblance to the holistic risk management form of asset protection advocated throughout this book.

We probably spend more time gathering information about clients and analyzing that information than doing anything else. A new client who comes to us will be requested to provide numerous documents, including financial statements, litigation history, company documents, wills, trusts, business and personal tax returns, business and personal insurance policies, and many other documents. When available, we review these documents prior to the first meeting. We review these documents to learn as much as we can about the client so that we can provide the best planning services. But we also do so to assure ourselves that the client is not involved in illegal activities. We often discuss the client's situation with the client's other advisors to ascertain what planning has been implemented already and how the client conducts business. Then we begin to assemble a menu of planning alternatives to be discussed directly with the client.

We prefer to meet clients in person, although because our clients are all over the world, sometimes this meeting is not practical. However, by meeting a client, we can get a feel for his personality and how he conducts his business and personal finances. We can discuss alternatives and determine where the client wants to go, personally and with the business. We can also get an idea how the client would appear before a judge or jury if called to the witness stand in a trial, which may dictate subtle aspects of the planning we recommend. Also, we can gather information that is not reflected in financial statements or tax returns, such as the stability of a marriage or the trustworthiness and reliability of business partners and family members.

We then develop an understanding with the client as to the planning to be implemented, a timeline for the implementation and the costs involved, including legal and consulting costs and third-party costs, such as formation fees, trustee fees, and appraisal fees. Sometimes, implementation first will require remediation of prior bad planning or client neglect. The corporate books and records of the client's existing entities may need to be updated. Defective structures may be reorganized or restructured, and the client may be advised to relinquish certain positions as officer, director, general partner, manager, trustee, or protector, and if possible, the education process begins to transition the client from an active investor to a passive investor.

If we determine that the client may have engaged in tax fraud, tax evasion, or particularly aggressive tax planning, we typically will not accept the representation of the client unless and until the client has retained a criminal tax attorney and has begun taking affirmative steps to come into full tax law compliance. By engaging in asset protection planning for a client who has engaged in tax fraud, or who may owe a significant tax liability to the IRS, the planner himself may be caught up in tax fraud or money laundering claims.

Too many planners implement cookie-cutter strategies for clients, after which their relationships with clients effectively end. By contrast, we endeavor to continue our advisory relationship with our clients well after the initial engagement, as an ongoing matter. We assist our clients with management issues, help keep documents current, and generally act as a sounding board for new issues. By assisting our clients on an ongoing basis, we can often keep them out of trouble, which of course is the best asset protection planning of all.

Asset protection must be efficient. If the asset protection planning is not efficient, it will not be maintained by the client. Thus, the financial circumstances of the client are critically important. What makes sense for a client with a $250 million net worth will make no sense at all for a client with a $2 million net worth. We do not turn away clients who do not have a large net worth. We merely advise them that they are best served not by exotic, complex planning structures but by a combination of exemption planning, financial and retirement products, and basic entity structuring, onshore and offshore. The complex structures can be implemented as the clients accumulate wealth.

We present our clients with up-front cost estimates for the initial planning and the annual maintenance costs. Depending on the strategies utilized, we sometimes will provide the solution on a turnkey basis so that the client can base his or her decisions on a single annual number for each strategy suggested. If a strategy will be too costly, that determination is better made before implementation than after.

An asset protection strategy that requires the signing of a confidentiality agreement is one that should not be implemented. A strategy that cannot be reviewed by equivalent professionals is unlikely to work when it sees the light of day in a courtroom. As often as not, there is no real need for the confidentiality agreement. The strategy is often yet another cookie-cutter strategy dressed up with a confidentiality agreement as a marketing ploy to make clients think they are getting something special. That implies fundamental dishonesty on the part of the planner from the very outset, and a dishonest planner is one to avoid at all costs.

A recent trend is for some promoters to claim that their product or strategy is "patented." This is pure marketing hype, since the fact that a strategy is patented is of no benefit to the person buying it. To the contrary, the fact that a strategy is proprietary often has a negative connotation that implies that it is abusive. It also means that the strategy itself is what is important, rather than how the strategy fits a person's needs. In other words, "patented" is just another word for "cookie-cutter." These strategies, and the promoters who sell them, should be avoided.

It is important for a client's other advisors to be aware of our asset protection planning, the reasons for implementing it, and how it must be maintained. The client's other advisors may have concerns about the client's situation that the client may have neglected to mention. We encourage clients to bring their existing advisors into the planning and to meetings, and thereafter to be closely involved in the implementation and maintenance. This gives us the luxury of another set of eyes to keep tabs on what the client is doing so that the planning continues to work well with the client's other planning.

SOME FINAL WORDS

Many people need asset protection planning. It is perfectly legitimate if implemented correctly and conservatively, without the intent to defraud or harm anyone. As the sector continues to move into the mainstream of legal and financial planning, it is important that the development of new strategies be founded on fundamental legal principles. It is also important that moral and ethical issues be considered in developing asset protection planning strategies, lest the legislatures implement their own solutions.

The authors have created a Web site at *www.assetprotection-book.com* to support this book. The Web site has supplementary materials, additional information, updates, and an active discussion forum on various asset protection issues.

The Web site has an online form for contacting the authors. Also, readers who would like to contact the authors about using their professional services may call, toll-free, 1-888-359-8851.

INDEX

ABOUT THE AUTHORS

Jay D. Adkisson is one of today's foremost authorities on contemporary asset protection. Founder of the internationally popular asset protection website quatloos.com, which receives tens of thousands of hits each day, Adkisson has appeared as an expert witness before the United States Senate Finance Committee and has been quioted in the *Wall Street Journal, Forbes,* and other influential publications.

Christopher M. Riser is a U.S. tax attorney specializing in asset protection and business/estate planning for high net worth individuals. Vice Chair of the American Bar Association's Asset Protection Planning Committee, Riser has traveled widely to visit and research offshore service providers. He is a popular speaker on asset protection issues, and is regularly quoted in major legal and financial publications.